Reluctant Interveners

Genocide, Political Violence, Human Rights Series

 EDITED BY ALEXANDER LABAN HINTON, STEPHEN ERIC BRONNER, AND NELA NAVARRO

Reluctant Interveners

AMERICA'S FAILED RESPONSES TO GENOCIDE FROM BOSNIA TO DARFUR

EYAL MAYROZ

RUTGERS UNIVERSITY PRESS
New Brunswick, Camden, and Newark, New Jersey, and London

Library of Congress Cataloging-in-Publication Data

Names: Mayroz, Eyal, 1964– author.
Title: Reluctant interveners: America's failed responses to genocide from
    Bosnia to Darfur / Eyal Mayroz.
Description: New Brunswick : Rutgers University Press, [2019] | Series: Genocide,
    political violence, human rights series | Includes bibliographical references and
    index.
Identifiers: LCCN 2019006129 | ISBN 9781978807037 (pbk.: alk. paper) |
    ISBN 9781978807044 (hc-plc)
Subjects: LCSH: Genocide intervention—Government policy—United States. |
    Humanitarian intervention—United States. | United States—Foreign
    relations—1989-
Classification: LCC JZ6369 .M378 2019 | DDC 364.15/1—dc23
LC record available at https://catalog.loc.gov/vwebv/search?searchCode=LCCN
&searchArg=2019006129&searchType=1&permalink=y

A British Cataloging-in-Publication record for this book is available
from the British Library.

www.rutgersuniversitypress.org

Manufactured in the United States of America

To my wife Ruth and my two boys Yotam and Gitai

Contents

Preface

The genesis of this study can be traced back to one of my first classes as a graduate student at the Centre for Peace and Conflict Studies, University of Sydney. Instructed by my lecturer to articulate a key question I was troubled by and wished to pursue, I hesitated only a little: "Why has the international community been sitting on its hands while countless children, women, and men were being massacred, often by their own governments?" I asked. "And why do states continue to stand by in the face of mass atrocities even today?" I carried this question with me throughout my studies, into my PhD research and thereafter. But each time I thought I had figured out the answers, I found myself faced with new uncertainties.

Some of the dynamics in the international failure to act became clear almost immediately: governments would nearly always prioritize subjective pragmatic considerations over moral concerns, especially beyond the water's edge. Cost-benefit calculations and narrow conceptualizations of the "national interest" have long trumped humanitarian imperatives, particularly when believed to be in competition with one another. Such a claim was clear, logical, and easy to support by evidence. But if this had been so, why have we, the citizens of democratic states, allowed our elected officials to ignore victims' cries for help? This I could not understand.

Gradually my focus crystalized around the foreign policymaking of the United States, the most powerful actor on the global stage. Earlier I had researched my way through the international arena where prevention and intervention decisions were negotiated, or not. I saw collective responses being strongly influenced by domestic processes in powerful countries such as the United States, whose policy positions could help make and at times break international action. I observed the academic field of genocide studies expand its scope, from the history, causes, and consequences of genocide to international and domestic legislation, justice in its various forms, memory and commemoration, colonization and indigenousness, culture and the arts, gender, education, and more. I witnessed positive developments taking shape in such areas as early warning, risk analysis, conflict prevention, international law, and peacebuilding in target states. Yet on many of these fronts, one key stakeholder was frequently missing or relegated to the sidelines: The citizenry! Us!

Described as a vehicle for advancing moral imperatives for action, public opinion has been flagged also as an absent actor in national policy debates in third states. Samantha Power's theory of society-wide silence during times of American bystanderism helped to substantiate this "missing participant" hypothesis in relation to the United States. Add the traditional realist view of the American public as "disinterested, ill-informed, emotional, capricious, and unable to see the long-term requirements of the national interest in foreign policy," and the campaign to stop genocide may well have been deprived of its strongest asset: the voices and consciences of the citizenry. To expand our understanding of this underdeveloped subject, this study makes a case for a more systematic research agenda for exploring the role of domestic politics in shaping dominant states' responses to mass atrocities.[1]

While the book's main focus is on the US public-media-policymaking nexus during historical foreign events, it foreshadows also questions about the effects of a rising domestic populism on critical power relations, particularly between mass and elite opinion. Would the current nationalist trend lead more Americans to adopt xenophobic isolationist positions toward much of the rest of the world? Or would emergent counterforces help bring forth a more cosmopolitan but respectful and humane America? The longer-term objective is to construct and implement a research agenda, informed by insights and findings from this book and other studies like it. It is high time to dig deeper into the promises and challenges associated with the most significant and undertapped resource in the fight against apathy—*we the people*. The better we understand public silence during genocide, the greater will be our capacity to support the development of innovative strategies for addressing the perennial gap between words and action in responses to mass atrocities.

Reluctant Interveners

Introduction

During a televised debate held in October 2000 in Salem, North Carolina, presidential nominees Governor George W. Bush and Vice President Al Gore were asked by the moderator if the United States should have intervened in 1994 to stop the Rwandan genocide. Remarkably, both contenders professed support for President Clinton's noninterventionist policy at the time, which effectively had allowed the killings to continue. Bush's answer was, "I think the [Clinton] administration did the right thing. . . . It was a horrible situation . . . they made the right decision not to send U.S. troops into Rwanda."[1] Gore had initially argued that intervening to stop genocide was a fundamental American strategic interest, supported by American values. But in relation to Rwanda, his position was essentially the same as Bush's: "Because we had no allies and because it was very unclear that we could actually accomplish what we would want to accomplish by putting military forces there, I think it was the right thing not to jump in, as heartbreaking as it was."[2]

In hindsight, their responses were somewhat unexpected. According to several accounts, majorities of Americans at the time of the debate believed the US inaction over Rwanda had been a grave error.[3] President Clinton himself later described his policy as one of the biggest regrets of his time in office.[4] Why then did both candidates choose to endorse such an ethically problematic position? Were they so out of touch with the public? Or were their views so robust as to risk unpopular responses in such an important forum? Or perhaps they had other reasons, such as doubts about the US citizenry's real commitment to protecting "faraway others" against genocide?

This book sets out to achieve two objectives: to increase our knowledge about domestic attitudes in the United States toward situations of "genocide"—threatened or ongoing, alleged or confirmed—and to explore the impact these attitudes had on the making of US policies. Anecdotal evidence to the underdeveloped state of these areas of scholarship appeared in Kenneth Campbell's 2001 book *Genocide and the Global Village*, which focused mainly on American responses to the crime. While Campbell devoted a whole chapter to the relationship between opinion and policy

(Chapter 4, "Misreading the Public"), the entire chapter ran less than five pages.[5] More than a decade and a half have passed since, and attention to this fascinating topic has increased a little, but our understanding is still lacking.

The role of the American public was discussed in greater detail in Samantha Power's 2002 Pulitzer Prize–winning book, *"A Problem from Hell": America and the Age of Genocide*. Over the course of the twentieth century, argued Power in her conclusion, the battle to stop genocide was "repeatedly lost in the realm of [US] domestic politics." Notwithstanding isolated voices, she wrote, a society-wide silence during most genocides caused US officials at all levels of government to conclude that the political costs of getting involved far exceeded the costs of remaining uninvolved.[6] Yet Power's findings of a society-wide silence appeared to be at odds with results from national opinion polls, which over decades have shown majority citizenry support for robust US responses to genocide. Therefore, an important question is provoked: If Americans did support strong action, what factors were responsible for their acquiescence to repeated *inaction* by their leaders?

In response to these knowledge gaps, I explore in this book three interrelated themes: (1) the domestic and external factors that have shaped, enabled, or constrained American responses to mass atrocities, particularly the crime of genocide; (2) how opinions and behaviors of the American public have affected official policy decisions about whether and how to react to alleged manifestations of a faraway genocide, and what efforts were made by administrations to "manage" the attitudes of the citizenry; and (3) the political consequences of labeling a crisis genocide and the insights that can be gained about administrations' policy objectives based on their invocation or circumvention of the term during real-time events. In my analysis I compare the use or avoidance of the label "genocide" in relation to US policies on Bosnia, Rwanda, and Kosovo during the 1990s with its significance to the making of the US Darfur policy in 2004.

Few efforts have been made thus far to empirically explore these dynamics, allowing their implications to remain largely hypothetical. Recently, the impetus to understand the role of the label reappeared. In March 2016, the Obama administration and the US House of Representatives issued two genocide determinations on the targeting of ethnic and religious minority groups in Iraq and Syria by the so-called Islamic State.[7] Since then many have asked whether and how these determinations should have affected the management of the war against the group by the US. In August 2018, a genocide determination was issued by a UN fact-finding mission over the brutal treatment of the Rohingya minority in Myanmar, triggering calls for the US State Department to follow suit.[8] Understanding the consequences of applying the label to violent conflicts is important owing to the purported contradictions between a high moral standing of the term "genocide" in American dominant culture and undesirable effects its invocation is said to have had on US political will for action.

As a final point, the US presidential election of 2016 raised a number of questions pertinent to the theme of this book concerning power relations between America's elites, mass opinion, the media, and the political establishment. The same dynamics manifested in the 2018 midterm elections, suggesting that national populist influences in US politics are likely to persist, at least for a while. Will these trends include the decline we are seeing in the prominence of elite opinion as setters and forecasters of public opinion? If so, in what ways and to what extent will these transformations, currently manifesting in domestic politics, apply also to foreign policy? In the past, faraway atrocities had rarely exacted a notable influence on everyday life in America. But with terrorism scares and stories about refugees routinely leading national news these days, there is arguably a much broader constituency to make the case to about the importance of addressing distant conflicts *before* they disintegrate into mass violence, destabilize regions, generate refugee flows, and facilitate the creation of safe havens for terrorist groups.

THE SIGNIFICANCE OF THE GENOCIDE LABEL

In today's world, and especially in the West, the word "genocide" carries different meanings for different people. It was originally coined in 1943 by Raphael Lemkin, a jurist and Polish-Jewish refugee who had escaped the Holocaust and sought to describe "the destruction of a nation or of an ethnic group."[9] In 1948, the term was enshrined as a legal concept in the UN Convention on the Prevention and Punishment of the Crime of Genocide (hereafter the Genocide Convention), where it was defined as the intent to "destroy, in whole or in part, a national, ethnical, racial or religious group, as such."[10] However, significant variations developed soon after between legal, political, literary, journalistic, and other scholarly or popular interpretations of the word, reflected among other things in the diverse situations to which it was applied. In the period between 1948 and 1999, up to fifty instances of genocides and politicides were perpetrated around the world, but the international community's efforts to confront them had often been insufficient or came too late.[11] Worse still, some atrocities had been carried out with the acquiescence or complicity of major powers, including France, China, the Soviet Union, and the United States, or by their own hands.[12]

For many around the world genocide is the crime of crimes. Right or wrong, such perceptions have led survivors of legally recognized, contested, or even mistaken instances of genocide to the belief that nothing short of the "G" label could capture and bestow public recognition on their personal tragedies. This book's focus on the significance of the term was driven partly by these perceptions and their potential effects on anyone in a position to influence responses to mass atrocities: from high-level policymakers to ordinary citizens. In the heart of the enquiry is the question of how critical the success or failure of affirming an ongoing violent conflict as a case of genocide—morally, legally, or politically—may be to the fates of those whose lives are threatened. Would the labeling of a crisis as genocide, rather than, say, a crime against humanity, increase, decrease, or not affect the prospects of outside help?

Discussing the question in relation to the crisis in Darfur, French academic and historian Gerard Prunier wrote,

> At the immediate existential level this [determining whether or not genocide has occurred in Darfur] makes no difference; the horror experienced by the targeted group remains the same, no matter which word we use. But this does not absolve us from trying to understand the nature of what is happening. Unfortunately, whether the "big G-word" is used or not *seems to make such a difference*. It is in fact a measure of the jaded cynicism of our times that we seem to think that the killing of 250,000 people in a genocide is more serious, a greater tragedy and more deserving of our attention than that of 250,000 people in non-genocidal massacres.[13]

The belief in the power of "genocide" to influence people's choices—purportedly a key lesson from Rwanda—had informed efforts by many advocates to hitch the label to their causes.[14] However, an official US genocide determination on Darfur in September 2004 did little to strengthen the American response to the crisis beyond referring the situation to the UN Security Council.[15] Secretary of State Colin Powell, who had announced the decision, argued that the determination did not necessitate any change in America's response since the Bush administration was already doing everything in its power to manage the crisis.[16] But as the book's findings demonstrate, after failing to mobilize sufficient international political will to address the crisis, the Bush administration ended up leaving the security of the African Sudanese people of Darfur in the hands of their government, the same government that the United States itself had concluded was behind the genocide. Consequently, faith in the legal and moral potencies of the term was quashed for many.

For some years now the political significance of the label has been debated in the field of genocide studies. A 2008 report by the Cohen-Albright US

Genocide Prevention Task Force articulated clearly the practical aspects of the challenge: "The dilemma is how to harness the power of the word [genocide] to motivate and mobilize while not allowing debates about its definition or application to constrain or distract policymakers from addressing the core problems it describes."[17]

Leading the debate was David Scheffer, former US ambassador-at-large for war crimes issues in the Clinton administration (1997–2001) and later a professor at Northwestern University School of Law. Scheffer's proposal was to separate the public and political uses of the word "genocide" from its legal definition, to allow governments and international organizations to apply the term more freely in political contexts.[18] This would permit them, in Scheffer's words, "to publicly describe precursors of genocide and react rapidly either to prevent or to stop mass killings or other seeming acts of genocide. They [governments] should not be constrained from acting by the necessity of a prior legal finding that the crime of genocide in fact has occurred or is occurring and, once that legal finding has been made, that governments are somehow obligated to use military force in response."[19] Instead of labeling a crisis as genocide, Scheffer proposed a new broader term, "atrocity crimes," which would amalgamate four types of international crimes: genocide, crimes against humanity, war crimes, and the emerging crime of ethnic cleansing.[20] In his opinion, the "unification" of crimes would lead also to greater clarity in public discussions, news coverage, and decision making.[21]

To further this discussion, I analyze in the book elements of the distinctiveness of genocide related to both imperatives and hindrances to action. Better understanding of this distinctiveness—its nature, scope, and characteristics—will add valuable insights to our understanding of the role and significance of the term.

A Global Challenge, American Focus

Have genocide victims in war-torn societies been abandoned because of insurmountable challenges faced by otherwise willing interveners? Or have policymakers and publics in powerful countries like the United States been recycling expressions of concern and condemnations or at best sent humanitarian aid, to hide deliberate failings by the former and ease the consciences of the latter? The most disconcerting aspect of this question relates arguably to the implied dynamics between policymakers and their constituents. If states had chosen inaction rather than failed to act, then their own citizens were either oblivious to the events, were led to believe that their political leaders were faultless, or, the worst case scenario, elected to close their eyes when their government took up the role of "bystanders to genocide" in their name. Regardless of which of these accounts best matches the historical record, the importance and value of learning more about the opinion-policy relationship in this context are clear.

As the leading superpower since the end of World War II, the United States has played pivotal roles in international responses and nonresponses to genocide and other mass atrocity situations. When in their perceived interests, US governments were able to influence international political will—or at least invested considerable resources in trying to do so—not only for strong policies and actions but at least as often against them.[22] In their discourses on genocide, American presidents have repeatedly reaffirmed the nation's principled commitment to the pledge of "never again."[23] But when faced with actual genocidal situations, they have chosen time and again not to acknowledge that the unfolding atrocities had amounted to genocide. Presidents Ford and Carter refused to apply the term to the actions of the Khmer Rouge in Cambodia (1975–1979); Ronald Reagan avoided using it in relation to the 1988 Anfal campaign in northern Iraq, as did George H. W. Bush and Bill Clinton over Bosnia from 1992 to 1995.[24] In 1994 the Clinton administration went to extreme lengths to avoid labeling the horrific events in Rwanda as genocide. To be sure, the hesitation to commit to action was not confined to the executive branch. Despite the dominant role played by American officials in the development and signing of the Genocide Convention of 1948, it had taken the US Senate a staggering forty years to consent to the ratification of the treaty, and even then with significant reservations.[25]

The "Opinion Policy" Nexus

Research has tended to focus on transnational institutions as the space where responses to mass atrocities are negotiated and adopted. Yet, the policy positions of dominant states, which have often shaped these responses, are formulated not internationally but domestically. Governments therefore play dual roles as lead actors in the making of foreign policy at home and as unitary representatives of their countries in multilateral processes. In limiting our attention to the international sphere, we risk ignoring the challenges and competing interests that underlie, complicate, and often determine the formulation of national policies prior to the negotiation of a multilateral response.[26]

As implied already, a key question explored in this book concerns the part played by the US citizenry in allowing American administrations to escape political costs for their failures to act on genocide. According to polls, Americans have placed broad concerns for the well-being and safety of faraway "others" well below their own self-interests.[27] Such prioritizations are not surprising however, nor unique to the US public. Economic and security concerns occupy citizenries the most, not the successes or failures of their governments' policies on low salience and often little understood, man-made humanitarian tragedies. Knowing this, US policymakers have learned to manage the political risks of inaction through a combination of moralizing rhetoric, half-measure actions, and deliberate framing of the information they release to the public. As described and discussed in this book, the relative ease with which administrations were able to contain potential fallouts increased the probability that in many situations the US public was, by and large, at least *okay* with being managed. The findings suggest that Americans did want their leaders to help stop genocides; but when presented with the purported risks, costs, and other hindrances to strong action, many considered them a high price to pay to save non-Americans. Domestic concerns about faraway others were thus outweighed, and questions about the efficacy of the policies meant to help protect these others were muffled. If these interactions were indeed at play, then the efforts by administrations to manage the public toward such outcomes had been more consequential than appreciated until now.

Managing the Public

The desire and need to legitimate official policies to the American public constitute important dynamics in US foreign policymaking. Former chairman of the Senate's Foreign Relations Committee Jesse Helms once stated that "there is only one source of legitimacy of the US government's [foreign] policies—and that is the consent of the American people."[28] Notwithstanding the cliché, in real life politicians tend to invest more efforts in marketing their preferred policies to the citizenry than in incorporating the preferences of the latter into these policies. To study the relationships between Americans' attitudes and administrations' conduct in the context of genocidal events, I use an adapted *framing* analysis to explore how officials gauged public opinions and behaviors, how they interpreted incongruities between the two, how they acted on these interpretations, and to what effects.

Political actors frame information to try to influence how other actors—in our context media outlets, the general public, and political and cultural elites—understand and react to policy issues or events.[29] Analyzing the frames employed by American presidents to legitimate and later justify preferred policies allows us to learn about their objectives, including how they might have assessed the utility of invoking or circumventing the genocide label in specific situations. The data examined for this study show that presidents and other high-ranking administration officials indeed sought to legitimate their policies by framing facts and other information in purposeful ways. Deliberate frames were employed to set public agendas (e.g., emphasize or de-emphasize a crisis), push particular interpretations of events (crisis, con-flict, civil war, tragedy, disaster, genocide, ethnic cleansing, etc.), highlight desirable policy options and ignore unwanted ones, and assign responsibility for action, or blame for inaction, to other actors. There would have been nothing wrong in these efforts, except that many of the policies proved indifferent, acquiescent, or at times actively complicit in the commission of mass atrocities.

American Exceptionalism?

As the main superpower and, at least rhetorically, a self-appointed cham-pion of human rights in the world, how far did America's moral and legal responsibilities to protect faraway strangers go? How far should they have gone? And as a primary power, arguably capable of applying pressure on other members of the international community to meet the pledge of "never again," how much "hard" or "soft" power was it willing to invest to these ends?

In many of the situations mentioned so far, US policies and actions stood in sharp contrast to the country's benevolent image held by most Americans. This cultural ethos of virtue and righteousness took shape early in the nation's history and over time became embedded in the identity of its people.[30] At its core was a firm belief in America's unique place in the world in terms of values, political institutions, and in setting an example for other nations.[31] However, fears of "foreign entanglements" at different times led to disagreements over what this setting of example had meant in practice.[32]

In recent decades the "exceptionalist" narrative was forced to weather some difficult situations, particularly the trauma of Vietnam and more recently the consequences of the war in Iraq.[33] Each jolt prompted scholars to grapple with the empirical manifestations of the contradiction, which could be described—borrowing a phrase from political scientist Samuel Huntington—as the gap between political ideals and political reality or between ideals and "institutional practices."[34] By exploring normative aspects of America's policies on genocide, this study increases our under-standing of the nature of the relationship—gaps or otherwise—between American exceptionalism and US responses to the "crime of crimes."

ORGANIZATION OF THE BOOK

Analysis of genocide studies and other relevant literature has pointed to an array of recurring factors, internal and external, that have shaped, enabled, or constrained US responses to genocide and other atrocity crimes. Mostly deterrents to action, they have manifested either in domestic policymaking processes or in multilateral negotiations at the UN and regional bodies.

Rather than aim for an exhaustive list, the schema in figure I.1 is intended to help guide the book's enquiry by focusing on factors relevant to

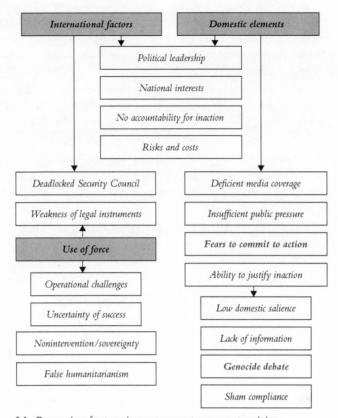

I.1. Recurring factors in responses to mass atrocities.

America's relationship with genocide. Much of this focus is on the domestic elements in the schema: dynamics, interactions, and processes in US foreign policymaking on genocide. Notably, I have found most of these factors to be as relevant to non-genocidal atrocity situations as to genocidal ones. This finding is discussed in later chapters.

Chapter 1 explores dominant patterns in US responses to genocide and begins the analysis of associations between and across domestic imperatives and obstacles to action. Chapter 2 continues exploring the domestic elements in the schema and develops a framework for studying the relationships between US opinion and policy on genocide.

The ensuing chapters present results and findings from the empirical study of America's relationship with genocide. Chapter 3 examines gaps between US official rhetoric and official policies from the Cold War to the crises of the 1990s in Rwanda, Bosnia, and Kosovo. The findings challenge the widely popularized notion that some American presidents had committed the United States to taking strong action on genocide. Extending the examination, Chapter 4 focuses on the relationship between expressed opinions and actual behaviors of the American public and other domestic actors and their influences on official US policies.

Moving to the case study of Darfur, Chapter 5 explores the policymaking processes that shaped US policy on the crisis during 2004. For this, a narrative is constructed of reactions to the events by President Bush and other high-ranking administration officials—before and after the official genocide determination. Their discourses are examined to learn how imperatives to action or obstacles to it were framed and integrated into or omitted from the discussion of America's moral, legal, and political obligations to act on Darfur. Chapter 6 discusses constraints to strong US action, analyzes different effects of the genocide label on the making of the US Darfur policy, and reconstructs an image of how administration officials might have read and interpreted the attitudes of the public in relation to the crisis. The conclusion ties together the findings of the book and offers ideas for improving our responses to mass atrocities.

Much of this book is about the relationship between morality, legality, and politics in the context of genocide, between "ought" and "is" in the foreign policymaking of the United States. It is also an attempt to move a primarily theoretical debate into the realm of empirically observed political actuality. Applying interpretivist lenses to the tension between the ideal of "never again" and the reality of "ever again," the book captures and describes multifaceted relationships among key actors and factors. We would have been far off the mark had our exploration of the genocide label not been conducted in the context of the opinion–policy association. At the same time, exploring public attitudes without a firm grasp of the political processes involved would have likely been as deficient. Rather than focus on one or the other, the framework is expanded to integrate both public opinion and government policies within the normative scope delineated by a number of alleged cases of genocide.

A similar reasoning has informed the selection of the case studies—Rwanda, Bosnia, Kosovo, and Darfur—which were all visible to the American public in real time. Driven as it was by opinion–policy interactions and the framing of information, this visibility was essential to the empirical research. It is regrettable therefore that less well-known but, in many cases, no less tragic situations of genocide did not receive the attention they deserve in this study.

It is the confounding nature of persistent gaps between words and deeds in the failures to prevent or halt genocide that motivated the research for this book. Admittedly, in referring to "failures" I am professing a normative bias in favor of "doing something" about the crime. But as recounted in the following pages, few public objections to the moral imperative to do just that: "something," have ever been professed by the United States or by other states. It is rather the decisions about *what* to do, *when*, and by *whom* that have been at the heart of the challenge to stop or, better still, prevent the perpetration of the crime. Building on the findings of the book, a case is made for a new direction of inquiry in genocide studies research, one that focuses more systematically on better understanding the role of public opinion and other domestic actors in foreign policymaking on mass atrocity prevention.

America's Relationship
with Genocide

IN 1993, Michael Scharf—attorney-advisor for United Nations affairs at the US State Department—helped draft an internal memorandum to the heads of the department. Cleared throughout the office of the State Department Legal Advisor, the memo argued that the United States had enough information to conclude that "a one-sided, well organized campaign of genocide was taking place in Bosnia."[1] Disregarding the legal advice, Secretary of State Warren Christopher continued to deny publicly that genocide was taking place and to depict instead the civil war as "an ethnic feud."[2] According to Scharf, this rhetoric was meant to allow the Clinton administration to argue that there was no moral imperative for US military intervention in Bosnia, out of the concern that American casualties would derail its ambitious domestic agenda for health care reform, crime prevention, and education.[3]

Years later, the State Department's legal adviser of the time, Conrad Harper, recalled the genocide debates that had taken place in relation to Bosnia and Rwanda: "In my view they [Bosnia and Rwanda] were genocides. But there were a lot of policy concerns about being that blunt, including what obligation we had under the Genocide Convention to act—so it was a tap dance. But I never had any doubt in my own mind, and I made it clear that was my view. But the Legal Adviser doesn't make the ultimate decisions, *even about characterizing something as an international crime.*"[4] The insipid role of legal opinion in US foreign policy decision making was acknowledged by other former State Department legal advisers during roundtable conversations held in 2004.[5] Summarizing the discussions, Scharf outlined the functions of international law under four categories: legitimating political actions, rallying support for policies, imposing restraints, and persuading policymakers to choose a particular course of action in order to achieve desired goals.[6] As important as some of these functions may appear to be, the legal advice on the applicability of the "genocide" label to the cases of Bosnia and Rwanda had been just that: advice.

One approach to theorizing "foreign policy" is to consider the objectives or *goals* that state officials seek to attain abroad, the *values* that give rise to these goals, and the *means* used to pursue them.[7] The process itself may be broken into three broad activities: formulation and adoption of orientations and strategies,[8] making decisions, and taking actions (i.e., state behavior).[9] This chapter explores relationships between and among these elements, with a focus on the domestic processes that influenced US support for or obstructions of international action on genocide. Its purpose is to review the current literature on America's relationship with genocide to provide background and context for the empirical study presented in later chapters. Discussed first are patterns in official responses to genocidal or alleged genocidal events since World War II. Next examined are central elements from the *recurring factors* schema presented in the previous chapter. Finally, the chapter pits political calculations against normative imperatives for action in the context of the relationship between opinion and policy.

OMISSIONS, COMMISSION, AND SELECTIVE INTERVENTIONS

During the twentieth century, wrote Samantha Power in *"A Problem from Hell,"* US administrations had repeatedly and knowingly avoided investing the resources required to lead effective responses to impending or ongoing genocides.[10] In her conclusions, she suggested that "modest improvements" in US policies were more than offset by policymakers' repeated refusal to risk strong action.[11] Not only did they refuse to deploy ground forces, but more "shockingly," as Power put it, they "did almost nothing to deter the crime."[12] She attributed the failures to meaningfully intervene in major genocides to a lack of political will, owing mainly to the absence of significant national interests and other risk-benefit calculations.[13] After weighing costs and gains, American leaders were not willing to invest the military, financial, diplomatic, and/or domestic political capital needed to stop the genocides.[14] Instead, they succeeded in achieving— with passive backing from Congress—two seemingly contradictory goals: minimizing engagement with conflicts that posed little threat to narrowly defined American interests and at the same time containing the political costs and avoiding the moral stigma associated with allowing genocide to occur.[15]

Power had amassed remarkable amounts of data about the seven case studies that formed the backbone of her work: the Armenian Genocide, the Holocaust, Cambodia, Kurdish Iraq, Bosnia, Rwanda, and Kosovo. Most of them were visible man-made tragedies, in relation to which the United States was expected to play the rescuer but did not or toward which it had acted weakly, belatedly, or otherwise inaptly. Put more sharply, in many cases US responses had amounted to "failures of omission." Little attention was given by Power in her book to the scores of less well-known genocides and atrocities, some which the United States had been accused of acquiescence to or even complicity in their perpetration.[16] Intentionally or not, one significant consequence of Power's choices and narrative was the popularization of a narrow prism through which Western audiences have since learned to think about and debate America's relationship with genocide.[17]

The crises in Cambodia, Bosnia, and Rwanda were at the center of two other US-focused studies, by Peter Ronayne and Kenneth Campbell, published in 2001. Integrating rationalist and constructivist theories, in *Never Again? The United States and the Prevention and Punishment of Genocide since the Holocaust* Ronayne analyzed the influences of power, self-interest, fears of taking risks, ideas, and norms relevant to US responses to genocide.[18] Similarly to Power, Ronayne's contention was that the United States had lost many leadership opportunities to act against genocide.[19] Instead of taking resolute actions, he wrote, the United States had opted mostly for "nonresponses," settling on everything from "determined non-intervention to willingness to ignore or look away."[20] US choices hindered the evolution of an international norm for the prohibition and prevention of genocide, which could have saved hundreds of thousands of lives.[21] Therefore America's responses to genocide contrasted sharply with the nation's "sense of self": the "exceptionalist" belief in a unique mission and obligation to a suffering humankind.[22] In his conclusions, Ronayne constructed a list of factors that he described as "a paralyzing combination of domestic political concerns and geopolitical imperatives that have distracted the United States and stunted its policies on genocide."[23]

Some American policies were seen by Ronayne as successful, including the US leadership (even if belated) in NATO's aerial bombings of the Bosnian Serbs after Srebrenica in 1995 and in Kosovo in 1999 and US support for international post facto efforts to punish genocide.[24] This support included assistance to the international criminal ad hoc tribunals of Rwanda and the former Yugoslavia, provision of support for the arrest of wanted war criminals in the Balkans, creation of a position of US ambassador-at-large for war crimes issues, and establishment of an interagency Genocide Early Warning mechanism to support prevention efforts.[25]

In his book *Genocide and the Global Village*, Kenneth Campbell assigned "the most powerful nation in the post–Cold War era" with much of the blame for the international failure to stop genocide.[26] These shortcomings, he wrote, had much to do with US policymakers' misunderstanding of the "strategic nature of genocide" and their failures to treat its prevention or "suppression" as a vital national interest.[27] Consequently, military force was employed inappropriately or not at all.[28]

According to Campbell, officials had misread domestic public opinion, assuming that ordinary Americans would fear American interveners' casualties and refuse to support a decisive use of force to stop genocide.[29] Whereas Power had stopped short of accusing the executive branch of deliberately misleading the public about the potential costs of interventions,[30] Campbell pointed to (in his view) intentionally deceptive framing of crises as non-genocidal as key causes for lack of support for action on the part of the public.[31] The motivations of US governments, he wrote, were to minimize political risks by avoiding the legal obligation to intervene under the Genocide Convention.[32]

To support his argument, Campbell presented a poll-based analysis that pointed to a marked increase in the willingness of Americans to support military interventions when survey questions used the word "genocide."[33] In his conclusions he identified three main conditions for progress in the efforts to stop genocide: political will, international capacity to carry out interventions, and the existence of a normative public consensus on action.[34]

America's Selective Interventions

For many observers, primarily outside the United States, the failures of omission studied by Power, Ronayne, and Campbell conveyed only part of the story of America's relationship with genocide. Critics have pointed to two centuries of US military interventions;[35] to questionable humanitarian pretexts, employed by administrations to justify breaches of other nations' sovereignty;[36] and to the contentious considerations that had guided decision makers' choices about *where*, *when*, and *how* to carry out these interventions.[37] Echoing such sentiments, international relations scholar Mohammed Ayoob wrote about the 2003 US-led invasion of Iraq: "Third world concerns have become more acute as a result of the process through which decisions have been made since 1990 to identify targets for intervention and the way in which such decisions have been implemented. The arrogation by the Permanent Five (P-5)—some would argue the P-3 or the P-1 [i.e., the United States]—of the right to determine cases that are ripe for intervention and the subcontracting of interventionist ventures to coalitions of the 'willing and the able' have made such interventions gravely suspect."[38] For some, the US (and British) behavior in Iraq attested to the necessity to reinforce, rather than reduce, the safeguards of state sovereignty and nonintervention, even if at the price of adverse effects on responses to genuine emergencies.[39] Misuse of humanitarian imperatives and the resultant fear of neocolonialism thus continued to undermine "good global citizenship," decades after the colonial era had officially ended.[40]

From the opposite side of the debate, the case for selective interventions was supported by two key arguments. First, it was claimed, mobilizing political will for costly and potentially risky policies cannot be done on the basis of humanitarian concerns alone.[41] The second argument, articulated by President Clinton in a 1999 speech, was that while American power could not and should not do everything or be everywhere, this fact ought not proscribe all humanitarian interventions.[42] On this latter point, strong disagreements existed and would continue to exist over which interventions *should* be counted as humanitarian or even partially humanitarian.

The evidence examined suggests a pattern of US omissions in the face of genocide. With some variations, Power, Ronayne, and Campbell emphasized three key challenges to US action: the absence of sufficiently strong political interests, policymakers' ability to get away with inaction, and missed opportunities by US leaders to mobilize domestic support for robust measures. The latter had much to do with misconceptions about their ability to rally the citizenry and fears of being penalized in the case of US casualties or mission failures.[43] These calculations were said to outweigh for US officials the perceived advantages that could be gained by strong action and to undermine the moral imperative for action generated by the "genocide" label and by other normative considerations.

VALUES, INTERESTS, AND RISKS AS DETERMINANTS OF POLICIES

So far, we have identified a substantial number of factors that played a role in shaping America's relationship with genocide. Some of them were recurring, others were unique and case specific; some provided imperatives for action, others, obstacles to it. We move now to explore some of the most commonly recurring among them, beginning with the significance of ethical imperatives and moralizing rhetoric in the making of US foreign policies.

American Exceptionalism and American Values

In his book *American Foreign Policy* (1974), former secretary of state Henry Kissinger wrote, "It is part of the American folklore that, while other nations have interests, we have responsibilities; while other nations are concerned with equilibrium, we are concerned with the legal requirements of peace."[44] Coming from one of America's foremost champions of realpolitik, this remark underscored the perceived significance of a set of convictions and cultural norms, celebrated since early in the history of the United States under the banner of "American exceptionalism." Political scientist Trevor McCrisken portrayed American exceptionalism as a belief that provided and continues to provide the cultural and intellectual framework "within which US domestic and foreign policy is framed, conducted and presented to the American public."[45] Short of determining policies, he wrote, exceptionalist beliefs provided the underlying assumptions and terms of reference for foreign policy debates and conduct.[46] International relations scholar John Kane described American exceptionalism as a mythical tradition "grounded in British history and Enlightenment hope, affirmed by the nation's founding elites, carefully elaborated by its historians, instilled in its schoolchildren over succeeding generations, attractively portrayed in its popular culture, embraced by its citizens, promulgated to and eagerly accepted by masses well beyond its shores."[47] It was, he wrote, an eighteenth-century optimism about human progress, transformed into a national epic that gave America and Americans a transcendent purpose, an "inspiring narrative of a people selected by Providence from the Old World to found a New World of liberty and hope, not just for themselves but for the entire human race."[48]

Indeed, since early in the history of the United States, majorities of Americans have conceived of their nation as defender and promoter of the values that underpinned American exceptionalism.[49] Domestic in character but universal in scope, the terms associated with this tradition included liberty, equality, democratic rule, individualism, and an expansive interpretation of the notion of freedom. Because America's mission had been associated with the betterment of mankind, Americans grew accustomed to the (often misguided) notion that what was good for them and for their country was necessarily also good for the rest of the world.[50]

America's righteous self-image held firm despite repeated flouting of American values by its own institutions and citizens. At home, liberal ideals cohabited with dispossession and genocide of Native Americans, the enslavement of Africans, and discriminatory policies and other transgressions against these and other minorities. Overseas, repeated violations of the sovereignty of other nations were carried out in support of aggressive national security objectives or in the service of economic interests, at times on behalf of "special interest" lobby groups.[51] Some of these campaigns involved direct mass killings of civilians;[52] in others American officials propped up dictatorships and colluded in the oppression and murder of their citizenries.

For many non-Americans these acts have become emblematic of US foreign policy and have overshadowed whatever good America was doing across the world. Yet even after the horrors of Vietnam and the mishandling of the 2003 Iraq War weakened their trust in their elected officials, most Americans have continued to believe in the righteousness of the nation itself.[53]

Cosmopolitan Concerns within the American National Interest

For centuries theorists and statesmen of the Old World belittled the significance of ethics in the making of foreign policies of states.[54] Discussing national responses to distant genocides, social scientist Jacques Semélin wrote (dejectedly) in 2009: "It took me a long time to admit that states are not really interested in preventing genocide as long as their own populations are not targeted. In other words, they are not really concerned about rescuing foreign people. It is simply not their priority."[55] In the United States, even though concerns for "faraway others" were never explicitly excluded from public deliberations of foreign policy, they were hardly factored in the calculus of administrations—Republican and Democrat alike.[56] Defending these practices, Hans Morgenthau wrote in 1945 that since elected officials were obliged to look after the interests of their constituents, it would have been morally wrong for them to take risks or bear costs that could not be justified based on these interests.[57] Since cosmopolitan values were regarded generally as incompatible with dominant parochial conceptions of the US national interest, they were seen to be much less attractive.[58]

The same notions dominated the organizational culture of America's foreign policy bureaucracy. According to former USAID administrator Andrew Natsios, foreign service and US military officers "get trained, advance their careers, and make decisions each day based on the central presumption that national interests are defined exclusively on a geopolitical or geostrategic basis."[59] Brent Scowcroft, national security adviser to George H. W. Bush, commented in relation to the Bosnian conflict, "We were heavily national interest oriented, and Bosnia was of national interest concern only if the war broke out into Kosovo. . . . If it stayed contained in Bosnia, it might have been horrible, but it did not affect us."[60] This line of thinking, which ended up governing the attitudes of the Clinton administration as well, contributed to the passive role played by the United States in Bosnia and even more so over Rwanda.

Still, in the final decades of the twentieth century, these norms became contested. Part of the debate centered on the question of how much room for moral choices decision makers had in a world that according to the realist view was beset by intense competition among nations.[61] Major points of contention in this regard related to the nature and sources of the American national interest.[62] According to theorist Joseph Nye, values in democratic societies may be integrated into the national interest of the state if considered important enough by the citizenry.[63] If the public is informed by its leaders and by experts of the costs involved in indulging certain values and is still willing to incur them, then in Nye's view the public has the legitimacy to affect such decisions.[64] A democratic definition of the national interest, he argued, does not accept the distinction between moral-based and interest-based foreign policy, since moral values are little more than intangible interests.[65]

Nowadays the "realist" label comprises a plurality of views about the role of ethics in foreign policy, and although the more traditional attitudes can still be heard, they are not as prevalent. According to Joel Rosenthal, president of the Carnegie Council for Ethics in International Affairs and a self-proclaimed realist, realists have learned to accept the moral imperative in foreign affairs as an integral part of America's self-conception of national interest. A realist who fails to recognize this, he wrote, will ultimately fail politically in the American system.[66]

Fear of Casualties

After Vietnam and Somalia, the fear of losing US soldiers without a clear national interest had dampening effects on policymakers' keenness to launch military operations overseas. This "body bag" or Vietnam syndrome offered important checks on risky misadventures, but at other times it thwarted crucial responses to humanitarian tragedies. Among other things, it discouraged US involvement in Rwanda, delayed the aerial intervention in Bosnia, and, right or wrong, precluded deployments of ground troops to Bosnia and Kosovo. More than a moral dilemma, the challenge to reconcile the imperative to protect "strangers" with administrations' responsibility for the safety of their own soldiers became inextricably intertwined with political and electoral considerations. Nicholas Wheeler called this catch the main counter-imperative to the ethical argument behind humanitarian interventions.[67] Samantha Power pointed to it as the most common justification for administrations' unwillingness to intervene militarily in genocide.[68] According to Andrew Natsios, "Losing soldiers for vague purpose in distant countries with names most Americans cannot pronounce is unlikely to tempt most American political figures unless they have a humanitarian commitment or are robust internationalists."[69] A president, wrote John Shattuck, former assistant secretary of state for democracy, human rights, and labor, "is not likely to take the politically risky step of intervening in a humanitarian crisis—especially if loss of life of US forces is possible—unless there is strong public support for intervention."[70]

What were the views of the citizenry on this contested issue? According to public opinion scholar John Mueller, the American public indeed "does not have—and never has had—much stomach for losing American lives in ventures and arenas that are of little concern to it."[71] In the short term, the data seem to confirm Mueller's claim. For instance, in October 1993, immediately after the botched "Black Hawk down" firefight in Mogadishu,

Somalia, that led to the deaths of eighteen US Army Rangers, Clinton's approval rating dropped by 6 percent and by another 3 percent the following week.[72] Yet as noted by Mueller himself, in the long term the political costs of failures in low-salience missions, such as in Somalia, may have been exaggerated:

> There is little or no long-term political loss from international failures when the perceived stakes are low—unless the failure becomes massively expensive. This means the U.S. can abruptly pull out of many failed missions without having to worry too much about loss of face or effective political back-biting. . . . If a venture is seen to be of little importance, a President can, precisely because of that, cut and run without fear of inordinate electoral costs. As the experiences with Lebanon [1983] and Somalia suggest, by the time the next election rolls around, people will have substantially forgotten the whole thing. Thus, the situation does not have to become a quagmire.[73]

In a rare commentary on the effects of the term "genocide," public opinion researcher Steven Kull argued that in cases where Americans were reminded of the moral imperative generated by the label, they were willing to incur casualties to halt the crime:

> Over the past decade there have been three cases that arguably fall into the category of genocide and in which the U.S. has considered intervention: Bosnia, Rwanda and Kosovo. At every decision point it was claimed the American government was significantly constrained by the American public—by its *unwillingness to put U.S. troops at risk in a military operation to address these problems . . . this was an incorrect perception of the public.* Policy makers were not in fact constrained by the public from taking that action. At every point, the public was actually highly receptive to arguments that genocidal behavior created a moral imperative to act.[74]

According to Kull then, it was the misreading of the public and not its actual preferences that constrained action in situations of genocide. He cited opinion polls that should have allayed official concerns about public objections to humanitarian interventions, based on the risk of casualties, but had not.[75] These polls are examined in Chapter 4.

LITTLE CONCERN FOR "FARAWAY OTHERS" IN THE US DEPARTMENT OF STATE

In a seminal study published in 1998, political scientist, historian and demographer Rudolph Rummel estimated that during the twentieth century US governments were responsible for the *"democide"* (murder by a government) of between 583,000 and as many as 1,641,000 foreign nationals, mostly during foreign wars.[76] Even if grossly exaggerated (which it may not have been), this staggering number suggested an unsettling indifference by US foreign policy officials to the lives of non-American "others." It also raised by extension questions about omission situations (as distinct from commission) that had not been included in Rummel's statistics. Put differently, if American officials were willing to take active part in mass killings, how much easier would it have been for them to look the other way when atrocities were being perpetrated by others? The following section contrasts two such instances—one of commission, and the other of omission.

Sidelining Human Costs in Vietnam and Bosnia

In 1971, two former officials from the State Department and the National Security Council (respectively), Anthony Lake and Roger Morris, published a candid, soul-searching, inside commentary about the State Department's management of America's war in Vietnam.[77] The significance of the commentary, groundbreaking at the time of its publishing, would later grow, as Anthony Lake became national security advisor for the Clinton administration during the crises in Somalia, Haiti, Bosnia, and Rwanda (1993–1997).

The policymaking process in relation to Vietnam was not unique, argued the authors, but reflected a common view of international affairs within the bureaucracy and political establishment.[78] Based on this mind-set, human costs—both to Americans and for populations overseas—were rarely factored into major foreign policy decisions but instead were looked at almost invariably in terms of their effects on US public opinion and on tactical decisions:[79] "Whether in the State Department, the Defense Department or the White House, whether in Democratic or Republican administrations, this same dehumanized pattern of decision-making on all foreign policy issues has been evident. It is the way nations traditionally carry on their business in the world."[80] The motives behind these practices, argued Lake and Morris, originated from an understanding of foreign policy as a lifeless set of abstractions. "A liberalism attempting to deal with intensely human problems at home abruptly but naturally shifts to abstract concepts when making decisions about events beyond the water's edge. 'Nations,' 'interests,' 'influence,' 'prestige'—all are disembodied and dehumanized terms which encourage easy inattention to the real people whose lives our decisions affect or even end. This conceptual approach is shared in our school classrooms no less than in our bureaucrats' offices."[81] The two then portrayed a sinister yet compelling account of a structural repression of agency:

Policy—good, steady policy—is made by the "tough-minded." To talk of suffering is to lose "effectiveness," almost to lose one's grip. It is seen as a sign that one's "rational" arguments are weak. . . . The implied choice is posed between "people" and the "effectiveness" of a policy. The imagined consequences in those abstract terms—prestige, interests, credibility—are unfailingly greater than the potential price people must pay. This does not touch on the myriad of other influences that quarantine a decision from contact with the human consequences: the obsessive quality of bureaucratic infighting, the immersion in technical details, or the personal hesitations of men caught up in a career system.[82]

A more humanistic foreign policy would not be more interventionist, isolationist, or pacifist, suggested the authors; however, it *would* require "weighing human costs and benefits as one of the principal and unashamedly legitimate considerations in any decision."[83] This does not necessarily mean the avoidance of human costs: "No policy-maker could freeze himself into automatic inaction whenever faced by a decision which would involve suffering or death. But we must face the magnitude of the human costs involved in some exchange of short-run sacrifice for long-run advantage."[84] Lake and Morris's commentary provided insights into the norms that influenced policymaking in the State Department during Vietnam, policymaking characterized by low concerns for the lives of faraway "others" and to an extent (at the time) of US soldiers as well. However, Vietnam was not a humanitarian intervention, and the worst violence had been perpetrated by the United States itself.

Fast-forward twenty-one years to 1992. In August of that year, George Kenny, acting Yugoslav desk officer in the State Department of the George H. W. Bush administration, resigned in protest of the US policy over Bosnia. In his resignation letter (published in the press on 25 August 1992), Kenny wrote that he was leaving his job to help develop a stronger public consensus over the idea that the United States must act immediately to stop what he called "genocide."[85] Kenny's story and that of other State Department dissenters to the US Bosnia policy was recounted by Samantha Power in "A Problem from Hell." According to Power, there were three different groups inside the State Department: "the dissenters who favored U.S. intervention (mainly in the form of airstrikes); the senior policymakers who actively opposed it; and most numerous, Department officials who supported bombing but had assumed it would not happen, so did nothing."[86] Interviews conducted by Power portrayed a departmental climate that had prohibited even mentioning a humanitarian intervention option in relation to Bosnia. Coupled with a fear of being seen to "rock the boat," this proscription was said to have shaped the thinking of staff and undermined dissenters' efforts to enlist active support among their colleagues. The use of moral arguments to support intervention was seen as "necessarily suspect in a Department steeped in the realist tradition." One dissenter commented later that talking about "the right thing to do" guaranteed one a reputation of a moralist and exclusion from the next policy meeting. To talk about human suffering remained something that was "not done," "Those who complained about the human consequences of American decisions (or here, nondecisions) were still branded emotional, soft, and irrational. The language of national interest was Washington's lingua franca, and so it would remain."[87] Internal opposition at the State Department was managed by embracing the rebels as "official dissenters." They were "heard," and then discounted or dismissed.[88] Consequently, exactly a year after George Kenny's resignation, three other State Department officials followed his example.[89] Two of them used the term "genocide" in relation to Bosnia in their resignation letters.

Between Commission and Omissions

Social scientist Daniel Feierstein has made the argument that the study of America's relationship with genocide should have been expanded to cover the active role played by US governments in the perpetration of mass violence around the world. A focus on failures of omission, he wrote, obscures the fact that much of the violence, which over the years has triggered calls for humanitarian interventions, was the direct or indirect outcome of unscrupulous US foreign policies, mainly but not only during the Cold War.[90] According to Feierstein, some important conclusions about the consequences of actions taken by the United States and other Western nations, including their effects on the story of genocide, would have been revised and even reversed had academic research advanced beyond the case studies of omission discussed by Samantha Power in her influential book.[91]

While it is may be incorrect to equate America's commission of mass killings in Vietnam with its inaction over Bosnia years later, some of the parallels cited above are still hard to ignore. Both accounts portrayed the consequences of indifference inside the American foreign policy bureaucracy, in the late 1960s and mid-1990s, to the lives of "faraway strangers." In both cases humanitarian concerns had been neglected. It was certainly more difficult to make decisions that would result in mass killings in Vietnam than to assume a bystander's role to the massacres committed by others in Bosnia and elsewhere. However, this does not reduce the value of the lessons from Vietnam for this analysis—analysis of continuity and change in the tension between narrowly perceived interests and humanitarian considerations within the US foreign policy establishment. Extending our understanding of these tensions to more recent years, the chapters dealing with the US Darfur policy offer new insights in relation to these questions.

SUMMARY

This chapter explored patterns in America's responses to genocidal or alleged genocidal crises and relationships between imperatives and constraints to US action. Examined were competing conceptions of the American national interest, direct and indirect effects of concerns about risks, and influences (or lack thereof) of moral imperatives on the American foreign policy bureaucracy. Better understanding of these factors and their effects would provide useful background and context for the upcoming exploration of domestic political processes and the significance of the "genocide" label—key objectives of the study.

The violence in Darfur erupted a year or two *after* the publications by Power, Ronayne, and Campbell had gone to print. Consequently, new openings for evaluating some of the key claims made by them became available only later. Of particular importance was the opportunity to explore the opinion-policy nexus in the context of an officially declared genocide. To help facilitate this exploration, undertaken in Chapters 3 to 6, the next chapter covers relationships and communications among the public, media, and policymakers in the context of US foreign policy on genocide and other mass atrocities.

CHAPTER 2

A Policy-Opinion Nexus

LEGITIMATING INACTION ON GENOCIDE?

THIS CHAPTER CONTINUES THE SURVEY of elements from the *recurring factors* schema that influenced the deliberation, formulation, or enactment of US policies on genocide.[1] The enquiry covers three central themes: the role of domestic legitimation efforts in managing public attitudes and behaviors; relationships between presidential leadership, public opinion, and the media; and the effects of domestic salience on political accountability. Described are the characteristics of mutual influences between US policymakers and their constituents, as reflected in and affected by the transmission of bidirectional information up and down the political edifice. A framework is developed for studying the impacts of these exchanges on the formulation and enactment of official policies. This framework is employed in the empirical part of the book to explore opinion-policy associations and their influences on the US interventions and noninterventions in Bosnia, Rwanda, Kosovo, and Darfur. However. we commence with the increasingly salient role of legitimation in foreign policy.

STUDYING POLICY LEGITIMATION

For some years now, the functions and significance of legitimacy in international politics have been attracting growing scholarly attention.[2] Ian Clark described legitimacy as a "key concept in the study of international relations and . . . a distinct feature of its practice."[3] He pointed to two main sources of legitimacy: states' commitments to international consensus and internal appeals by governments for domestic credentials.[4] The first view conceptualizes legitimacy as a property of international society, bestowed by international approval and a minimum level of international consensus based on international norms. In the second view, the proper source for legitimacy is the domestic democratic sanctioning of the people themselves.[5]

Political scientist Philip Powlick pointed out that legitimacy in a democratic society requires popular consent, referring to the desirability of a "significant degree of harmony between public opinion and government policy—or at the very least, public acquiescence in policy."[6] During the days of George W. Bush's second administration, this view was espoused by high-ranking officials, including Secretary of State Condoleezza Rice, Republican senator Jesse Helms, and former ambassador to the UN John Bolton.[7] As noted by Helms (cited earlier), "There is only one source of legitimacy of the US government's [foreign] policies—and that is the consent of the American people."[8]

Political scientist Thomas Trout defined national level legitimation practices as "the continuing effort to provide the necessary 'quality of "oughtness"' to a society's presiding political institutions and to their actions."[9] The process of legitimating specific acts of a regime was in Trout's view mainly interpretive, that is, to translate "narrow political interests into concrete representations of the guiding norms of the society": "Political action is equated with societal purpose, and, as a result, short-term and substantive matters of policy are given broad teleological meaning. A more immediate and direct requirement of the legitimative process is thereby fulfilled, that is, to provide the regime with supporting social conditions for effective policy."[10] Rather than to adapt policies to reality, suggested Trout, the purpose of legitimation is to ensure the normative soundness of the pragmatic actions that policies dictate, by constructing an image of reality that is compatible with these actions.[11] This may be accomplished by invoking rhetorical symbols grounded in societal norms.[12] Once a legitimation structure is established for a policy, subsequent defense, or justification, of actions would be based on this structure.[13]

A similar theme featured prominently in Richard Melanson's research of US foreign policy.[14] Building on Trout, Melanson argued, "Presidents and their foreign policy advisors try to provide interpretive images of the international situation that are compatible with domestic experience to justify the necessity, urgency, and character of their action. Legitimation establishes the broad purposes of policy by translating its objectives into an understandable and compelling reflection of the domestic society's dominant norms. As such it represents a political act within the context of national politics and characteristically relies on politically potent symbols to link foreign policy and these internal norms."[15] According to Melanson, a US president can achieve foreign policy legitimacy only by convincing enough members of the executive, Congress, and the electorate that his policy objectives are desirable and feasible.[16] Whereas feasibility reflects the president's success (or failure) to convince others of his (or her) ability to achieve these goals, desirability is determined by the degree to which the policy appears to embody and enhance core national values and national interests.[17] Thus, by examining the discourses employed by American presidents to legitimate or justify their foreign policies, we can learn which imperatives or constraints they considered useful to highlight or hide, to advance their objectives.

Exceptionalist Language in American Presidents' Rhetoric

In a study of Vietnam's effects on US official discourse, McCrisken explored the use of exceptionalist language by American presidents.[18] Based on his findings, exceptionalist frames were employed to legitimate policies not only to the public and Congress but also in private discussions: "Presidents and their foreign policy advisers frequently use arguments couched in exceptionalist language during private meetings and in personal memoranda. They do so even when perfectly good practical arguments for policy options exist and they often phrase even strategic, economic or political justifications in exceptionalist terms. The belief in American exceptionalism, therefore, provides the framework for discourse in US foreign policy making even if it is rarely the main determining factor of policy itself."[19] Greater skepticism of exceptionalist narratives was expressed in a 2003 critique, penned by Daniel Whelan:

> From time to time, and depending on the audience, the current administration [of George W. Bush] will rely on important values—such as democracy and freedom—to provide the moral foundations upon which America's new-found engagement with international politics ultimately rest. And it will claim those values as uniquely American. Some surely will maintain that American presidents are allowed—and even expected—to lay it on thick when it comes to "rallying the troops" and garnering public support for military intervention. Otherwise, we should not take such talk seriously. We should treat such appeals to "American" values, morality, and patriotism as so many "little white lies" similar to what parents tell their children.[20]

It is widely recognized that American presidents, regardless of the sincerity of their intentions, were consistent in prioritizing strategic, political, security, and economic interests over the values and moral concerns embedded in the exceptionalist story.[21] To appreciate the significance of these narratives for our study, we first need to establish the importance of presidential leadership in the making of US policies on genocide.

The Importance of Presidential Leadership

"Nothing is more central to preventing genocide than leadership—from the President, Congress, and the American people," stated the 2008 report of the US Task Force on Genocide Prevention.[22] According to Laurence Woocher, a member of the project's team, this assertion was repeatedly voiced during consultations with current and former officials, from the rank and file to the most senior.[23] Expounding the views of the Task Force, Woocher wrote, "[A] demonstrable presidential commitment to an issue like preventing genocide sends a signal throughout the U.S. government bureaucracy and to the international community. Clear presidential priority, though not a panacea, tends to tilt internal and external debates in favor of more robust action."[24] A policy directed by the White House had therefore the best prospect of overcoming inertia, caution, and the almost inevitable intra-bureaucratic power plays.[25]

The significance of the presidency to humanitarian responses was highlighted by others also. "There is no substitute for political will in the conduct of American foreign policy, which can only be manifested through presidential leadership," wrote Andrew Natsios.[26] According to Natsios, "Neither media pressure nor clever administrative innovation can substitute for consistent presidential leadership in complex emergencies. . . . Pressure from the media may force the president into tactical initiatives in a catastrophe, such as the Rwandan refugees in Goma, or eventually in Bosnia, but it cannot substitute for an American commitment to international leadership in complex emergencies more generally."[27] Although the president may not get to hear of emergencies until they are "well along in their deadly slide toward chaos," the president *is* the one to set foreign policy tone.[28] John Shattuck argued likewise that strong public support for US action in cases such as Bosnia and Rwanda was unlikely, unless inspired by the president. In these circumstances the president had to explain to the American people that "the redefinition of US national interests includes the prevention of Human Rights and humanitarian disasters that might destabilize the world."[29]

Finally, in his study of six US interventions during the 1990s, including Rwanda, Bosnia, and Kosovo, Robert DiPrizio concluded that the greatest influence on America's responses had been the presidency itself. Since few humanitarian crises had threatened vital national security interests, he wrote, lack of consensus over appropriate policy gave the president wide discretion in deciding the American response.[30]

While discussing the same factor—the power of the presidency to influence US responses—the commentaries cited above referred to different policy tools in the arsenal of American presidents. The first is the president's prerogative to set policy priorities *internally* within his or her administration—generally through verbal or written directives. As pointed out by Donald Snow, the extent and potency of this power was not a given but depended on the personalities, status, prestige, management styles, and other characteristics of individual presidents.[31] A second instrument of power is the president's constitutional privileges of making policies.[32] Within this scope is included the president's role as commander in chief, with powers under the US Constitution to commit American forces to an armed conflict.[33] A third tool is the ability to mobilize or discourage international will for action, based on US clout and the personal standing of the president. And the fourth is the ability to influence domestic opinion, among others via public discourse.[34] As the most pertinent to the policy-opinion nexus, this final instrument constituted a key focus for the research presented in the following chapters.

THE EXPLANATORY POWER OF OFFICIAL DISCOURSE

Murray Edelman, a constructionist pioneer in the social sciences, made the point that it is language about political events rather than the events themselves that people experience.[35] More than a decade later, robust constructivist and poststructuralist challenges to the academic field of international relations opened its research agenda to the study of ideational elements in the form of ideals, identities, motives, norms, and culture.[36] This trend increased the attention to the benefits and challenges of analyzing discourse.

Given the often-confidential nature of foreign policymaking, the study of government decisions, especially in relation to contemporary and recent events, depends heavily on publicly available content such as press releases, speeches, executive and congressional records, public debates, interviews, and media reporting and commentary. While these sources are easily accessible, having to rely on their credibility could pose various difficulties for scholars. Particularly challenging is the fact that in pursuit of political objectives official rhetoric is often employed for manipulating audiences, including hiding the intentions of speakers or of the power structures behind them.[37] This reality led to debates about researchers' ability to capture political motives through discourse analysis. Legal scholar Fernando Tesón noted in this context that conversations about humanitarian interventions in the Security Council, the General Assembly, and (back then) the Organisation of African Unity—including attempts to justify actors' policy positions—were not as reliable indicators to the real motivations of states as were their actual deeds.[38]

On the other side of the argument, historian Michael Hunt highlighted the insights that *could* be gained from the analysis of political discourse: "Public rhetoric," he wrote, "is not simply a screen, tool, or ornament. It is also, perhaps even primarily, a form of communication, rich in symbols and mythology and closely constrained by certain rules. To be effective, public rhetoric must draw on values and concerns widely shared and easily understood by its audience. A rhetoric that ignores or eschews the language of common discourse on the central problems of the day closes itself off as a matter of course from any sizable audience, limiting its own influence."[39] Expressing similar ideas, poststructuralist scholar Lene Hansen argued that it will be extremely unlikely and politically unsavvy for politicians to express and legitimate foreign policies without taking into account how relevant themes are being represented in the wider public sphere.[40] Both claims have supported the view that as political discourse is not created in a vacuum, its study can teach us some things about the normative environment in which it is articulated, and about the cultural norms, values, and attitudes to which it tries to appeal. Thus, by studying past efforts to legitimate US policies in relation to cases of genocide and the responses to these efforts, we can gain important insights about the normative and cultural environments in which these efforts were undertaken. We can also find out which constraints and imperatives to action were invoked or avoided in official discourses, by whom, and to what likely effects. It is in these contexts that the method of framing analysis becomes useful.

The Sources and Effects of Framing

Framing analysis can help us study the role played by words like "genocide" in forming people's attitudes toward particular conflicts or situations. Thoughts about genocide are less likely to come up spontaneously in one's mind, unless some association has been made between the term and the event. This association could have been invoked by a politician in verbal or written communiqués or produced by a journalist in a news report, commentary, or other form of media discourse. It might have been raised explicitly or implicitly—the latter by summoning related words, concepts, or symbols that can trigger these connotations. The activation of these associations or habitual schemas is part of what framing is about.

Robert Entman defined framing as the process of "selecting and highlighting some facets of events or issues and making connections among them so as to promote a particular interpretation, evaluation, and/or solution."[41] He identified two main classes of media frames: substantive and procedural. Procedural framing, which occupies much of the news these days, deals mainly with evaluations of political actors' legitimacy.[42] Substantive frames deal with two or more of the following functions in relation to political events, issues and actors: problem definition, identification of causes, conveying moral judgement, and endorsement of remedies.[43] From among these four, Entman assigned the greatest importance to problem definition, which "often virtually predetermines the rest of the frame," and to remedy endorsement as it "directly promotes support (or opposition) to public policy."[44]

Even with the social media revolution, majorities of Americans continue to receive most of their information about foreign crises from traditional mainstream news media outlets.[45] Public opinion is thus influenced by selected, framed, and reported highlights of events, issues, and problems.[46] Under these conditions, it is easy to understand how the data get mediated twice, thrice, or even four times over. Facts about an event are experienced firsthand by someone: a local witness to the event, aid worker in the field, journalist, and so forth. The information is then interpreted internally, recounted to others and reinterpreted until it reaches the public and is reinterpreted once more by those who watch, listen, or read it. Entman thus pointed to the diminishing semblance between the information and the realities in the field the lower down the "cascading chain" a story travels.[47]

The significance of the relationship between the framing of information and the formation of public attitudes has long been acknowledged.[48] Studies have shown that whoever controls the framing of a conflict—its origins, causes, parties, fatalities, policy options, and imperatives or constraints to action—is well positioned to influence the preferences of the citizenry and potentially their ability and motivation to endorse or oppose official policies.[49]

These types of questions are dealt with by academics within the field of public opinion research, situated at the confluence of four disciplines: political science, sociology, psychology, and communications.[50] In this multidisciplinary environment, methods such as framing analysis, which originated in media studies, have become tools of choice for scholars from different backgrounds wishing to examine interactions between publics and policymakers.[51]

Public Salience and Media Effects

In democratic systems, the visibility of far-off crises may be crucial to the motivation and ability of domestic actors to influence policy decisions about them.[52] Agenda setting research has established causal relationship between the salience of a topic in the news and its salience to the American public.[53] Crises that do not attract media attention tend to be largely invisible to publics and consequently to politicians.[54] In the absence of hard interests in relation to a crisis, policymakers often prefer to contain the moral imperative to save "others" rather than risk acting upon it. Therefore Benjamin Valentino argued that the most significant barrier to US intervention in Rwanda was the indifference exhibited by the American people.[55] Even after a crisis had become visible, the volume, intensity, "quality," and duration of media coverage would continue to affect its salience. As discussed in Chapter 6, the sidelining of the Darfur story by the US media in favor of Iraq, Afghanistan, and the "war on terror" coverage diminished the willingness and ability of both the public and politicians to push for stronger policy responses.[56] Importantly though, media attention does not always translate to political will for action. National security adviser Brent Scowcroft had made the point in relation to the US response to the Kurdish refugee crisis in the spring of 1991, purportedly an outcome of a CNN effect. "We were actually quite cynical about media's impact," he noted. "Media are too fickle," and their attention to any given crisis can therefore be ridden out by policymakers.[57]

Along with media interest, the salience of a crisis can also be influenced by how it is framed by the executive branch, the existence or absence of political opposition to the official frame (the "indexing" factor[58]), the amount of time politicians allocate to talking about it, and the predispositions and attitudes of the public itself. Importantly, these relationships may be described as circular, in the sense that each of the key actors—the politicians, the media, and the public—has the power to increase or reduce the salience of the crisis for all other actors.

Moral concerns can also influence public salience, but their effects are difficult to measure. According to John Mueller, the American public pays little attention to international affairs and especially to distant man-made tragedies. His list of foreign policy events that significantly diverted public attention away from domestic issues did not include a single humanitarian crisis.[59] Similarly, in their analysis of three decades of national polling data, Page and Bouton found that American citizens had ranked the importance of altruistic foreign policy goals consistently lower than a range of goals involving direct self-interest.[60] For example, in a 2002 poll they had studied, the goal of "promoting and protecting human rights in other countries" was ranked fifteenth out of twenty "very important foreign policy goals."[61] The question to ask is to what extent these findings also apply to the arguably more intensely normative situation of genocide. Chapter 4 addresses these relationships.

STUDYING POLICYMAKERS' PERCEPTIONS OF MASS AND ELITE ATTITUDES

Having established the rationale for studying the official legitimation of US policies and the effects of different factors on the opinion-policy-media relationship, we can now turn to the second part of the question: that is, how politicians assess predispositions and attitudes of the American public toward genocidal or allegedly genocidal crises. Before moving forward with the exploration, it will be useful to have a clearer picture of the composition, study, and effects of public opinion.

Public opinion may be seen as the clustering of shared opinions of groups of individuals, complex, multilayered, multifaceted, and fluctuating as they tend to be.[62] The importance of studying opinion was recognized already in the eighteenth century, but systematic measuring did not begin until the early twentieth century, and systematic academic research until the 1950s.[63] The demand had originated from governments, reformers, and intellectuals wanting to know more about the states of mind of their citizenries.[64]

American presidents were early to identify the value of the polls. During the 1930s, Franklin D. Roosevelt employed pollsters to measure public attitudes on a variety of policy issues and even took part in the formulation of survey questions.[65] Nowadays, public opinion is seen as a key factor in competitions over political power and influence, a force that politicians, interest groups, and other actors try to manipulate in order to propagate ideas, influence priorities, and pass legislation.[66] In these efforts, cost-benefit calculations and expectations of latent public reactions feature high on agendas. Highlighting the significance of latency, V. O. Key argued in a seminal treatise on public opinion and American democracy that in the "practice of politics and government, latent opinion is really about the only type of opinion that generates much anxiety among policymakers."[67]

While the term "public opinion" can refer to both elites and the general public, it is used more commonly in relation to the latter.[68] Hence, in situations where confusion could arise in this book, we refer to "mass opinion" and "elite opinion" instead.

Going Public

Media scholar Shanto Iyengar has noted that the practice of bargaining and accommodation between rival political parties has long since fallen out of fashion in Washington, as elected officials prefer now to "go public" instead.[69] To be sure, competitions over leaders' popularity have become permanent phenomena, overshadowing substantive debates.[70] According to presidential scholar Richard Brody, the personal popularity of a US president is "a political resource that can help him [or her] achieve his program, keep challengers at bay, and guide . . . expectations about the president's party's prospects in presidential and congressional elections."[71] Policy issues have thus become opportunities for a serving president to assert power or for political opposition to advance counter-policies and undermine the president's standing. In Iyengar's words, "A president who attracts high marks from the American public can use personal popularity as leverage to get policy agendas passed. . . . Conversely, when the president's opponents sense that majority opinion is on their side, they seize the opportunity to push their own policy agendas."[72]

Presidential popularity is measured by opinion polls in ongoing assessments of the president's approval rating and overall job performance. Periodical surveys are also conducted of his or her handling of foreign policy and the economy.[73]

In summary, while the measuring of public opinion has been motivated more by self-interest than by a genuine desire to improve the match between policies and the will of the people, the bottom line remains that what American citizens think about foreign policy can and often does matter to administrations. The question is to what extent and under what circumstances.

The Opinion–Foreign Policy Gap

During the first part of the twentieth century, the conventional wisdom advocated by prominent (realist) thinkers was that the American public should not be trusted as an active participant in, and contributor to, the formulation of foreign policies. These experts viewed the public as disinterested, ill informed, emotional, capricious, and unable to see the long-term requirements of the national interest.[74] However, during the final decades of the century, some new research began portraying public opinion not only as consistent over time but also as coherent, sensibly structured, and rational.[75] Among other things, these findings focused attention on broad divergences between the foreign policy attitudes of official America and the preferences of the citizenry. Based on one explanation, policymakers tended to ignore or override the wishes of the public; according to another, they frequently misread them.

Ignoring or Misreading the Public? In a study titled *The Foreign Policy Disconnect* (2006), public opinion scholars Page and Bouton identified significant discrepancies between the preferences of the American public and those of US officials in relation to a broad range of foreign policy items. They found that public majorities had taken opposite positions to those of most policymakers in *one-quarter* of the issues examined.[76] This ostensible disregard for the preferences of the public had rarely been penalized in the ballots, and accountability was seldom exacted.[77] The researchers offered a number of explanations for US governments' successes in getting away with ignoring the public. These included the costs and mediated nature of foreign-policy-related information, the unequal distribution of political influence among the citizenry, and some other deficiencies in the US two-party system.[78] Page and Bouton noted also that the pressures on foreign policies had originated much more from special interest groups—multinational businesses, nongovernmental organizations (NGOs), and others—than from ordinary citizens.[79]

A different explanation for the incongruities between opinion and policy was offered by Kull and Destler (1999). Based on findings from studies conducted by them and by others, policymakers and other elites had often misread citizens' attitudes.[80] The analysis undertaken in the following chapters applies both explanations (misreading and ignoring the public) to the opinion-policy dynamics over Rwanda and Bosnia during the 1990s and to the case of Darfur in 2004.

Tying Together Theory and Methodology

Relationships and mutual influences between opinion and policy constitute the analytical and methodological hubs around which the empirical work carried out for this study has evolved. The exploration of key aspects of this association therefore has served an important purpose. Past studies established causal links between the salience of a foreign crisis to the American public and the attention, prioritization, and treatment that it is likely to receive from policymakers.[81] Other studies have described an inverted process, whereby policymakers and political elites seek to control public attention, perceptions, attitudes, and policy preferences toward a crisis, mostly by influencing how it is covered and framed by the news media.[82] These upward and downward processes are depicted in the information-centered model in figure 2.1, which draws on Robert Entman's Cascading Network Activation model.[83] The model offers a blueprint for the enquiry undertaken in the following chapters.

Explaining the Model

Absent direct experience of foreign crises, ordinary citizens rely on the news media to provide them with the information they need for "knowing" and "understanding" events and for forming opinions and policy preferences in relation to them.[84] The main sources of information for the media

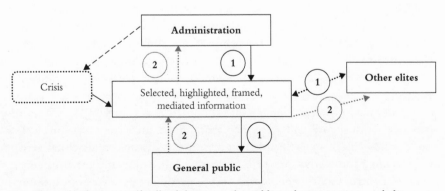

2.1. Flow of information/feedback between the public, administration, and elites.

are government officials, though depending on the case, information from journalists, NGOs, and other actors on the ground may also be used.

1. *Downward flowing information*—Political elites in the United States contend continuously over influencing frames in the news.[85] The information about foreign crises flows mostly downward, from political elites and (or through) the media to the citizenry. In trying to "manage" the public (and political opposition), officials may use agenda setting (e.g., reducing the media salience of a thorny policy, or increasing the salience of a desirable one), persuasion, and propaganda.[86] Notably, in contending over frames, elites are trying to influence the very same frames that (as explained below) end up affecting them and thus create an iterative (circular) flow in the model.[87] These processes are investigated in the next chapter in relation to crises of the 1990s and then in the chapters on Darfur.

2. *Upward flowing information*—Policymakers and other governing elites cannot know "the full reality of public thinking and feeling."[88] To assess citizens' opinions and policy preferences, they rely on a variety of indicators, including opinion polls, feedback from Congress and the news media, and manifestations of public behavior.[89] Elites can learn about mass opinion from the media in at least two ways: by reading or listening to reports that tell them "what the public thinks," or by assessing the media's coverage of an event (on the assumption that dominant news frames, crisis salience, and volume of coverage both reflect and affect current public views).[90] In the second part of the model then, information about mass and some elite opinion flows upward to government officials and other political elites, mainly through the media.

How can insights from the model be used to address the questions pursued in this book? First, I analyze official representations of genocidal or alleged genocidal crises by examining what information was "pushed" to the public domain and how this information was framed at different times by American presidents or other White House and State Department officials. In the case of US Darfur policy I use the downward process to study variances in official depictions of material and/or ideational "problems" allegedly posed by the crisis. I then look for divergences in their public representation of the challenges that the crisis was ostensibly creating for America, both before and after the official genocide determination. I also explore how inaction or insufficient action was justified and which actors were blamed for the failures to act. Finally, I examine any other attempts made to control public agendas or advance particular policy options. Studying these issues could help to reveal intentions and policy objectives pursued at the time by the Bush administration and to provide greater appreciation of the wider cultural context that had informed the framing of the crisis by the administration or by other actors. Better understanding of these normative and cultural contexts and cues could enrich our understanding of policymakers' conceptions about the underlying factors that influence Americans' responses to genocide, one of the key objectives in this study.

Assuming the lenses of policymakers could help us explore the significance of the term "genocide" to policy decisions in yet another way: that is, by studying the upward flow of mediated information about public attitudes and behaviors (i.e., the second part of the model). Examining this information could help us to assess how administration officials might have interpreted these indicators in the 1990s and during 2004 and to what extent these interpretations affected their decision making.[91]

The next chapter begins to explore the official rhetoric–policy gap by contrasting invocations or omissions of the term "genocide" in presidential discourses with official actions or inaction. Questions addressed include the following: How reflective of reality have the depictions of alleged gaps between official rhetoric and official behavior been? When and how has the term "genocide" been used in or omitted from US presidents' discussions of ongoing events? How important has this discursive element been to efforts to legitimate or justify official policies to the American public, compared to other frames? And what can these findings teach us about US administrations' perceptions of the significance of the label?

CHAPTER 3

Words versus Deeds in America's Relationship with Genocide

THE FAILURES by successive US administrations to carry out or lead effective responses to genocide attracted over the years numerous criticisms, domestic and foreign. High on the list was the gap between moralizing official rhetoric about the "heinousness" of the crime and the need to act, compared to the meagerness of the actual responses. In *"A Problem from Hell"* Samantha Power quoted some such speeches by American presidents, which according to her analysis effectively committed the United States to upholding the promise of "never again."[1]

To learn more about the motives and significance of these discourses, in this chapter I explore a two-part question. First, under what circumstances, in what ways, and to what ends did US presidents invoke the term "genocide"? And second, when and why did they avoid doing so: (1) during the Cold War; (2) in relation to Bosnia and Rwanda, when the Clinton administration (and the Bush administration over Bosnia) would have wished to justify, legitimate, and win domestic support for policies of inaction; (3) after Srebrenica, when Clinton was left with little option but to support a military intervention; and (4) in relation to Kosovo, a situation over which the Clinton administration would have wanted to win public support for NATO's aerial bombings of Serbia. The data examined cover public discourses of US presidents between 1949 and 2000. They were drawn predominantly from the extensive and well-regarded archives of the American Presidency Project at the University of California, Santa Barbara, as well as from some other sources.[2]

PRESIDENTIAL DISCOURSES DURING THE COLD WAR

As far as I could ascertain from the data, in the twenty-six years between 1951 and 1976 the word "genocide" appeared in the public communications of American presidents on only three occasions.[3] From 1977 to the end of the Cold War in 1989 (thirteen years), the number of presidential references

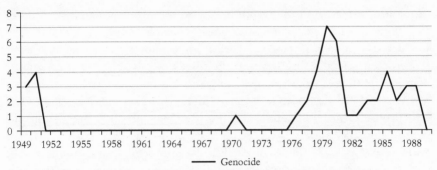

3.1. American presidents—mentions of "genocide" during the Cold War.

to the term increased to forty-seven—nineteen of them in speeches or comments made by President Jimmy Carter (1976–1980).

Carter on Cambodia

In September 1979, during a presentation of the final report of the President's Commission on the Holocaust, Carter declared, "Out of our memory . . . of the Holocaust we must forge an unshakeable oath with all civilized people that *never again* will the world stand silent, *never again will the world . . . fail to act in time to prevent this terrible crime of genocide. . . .* We must harness the outrage of our own memories to stamp out oppression wherever it exists. We must understand that human rights and human dignity are indivisible."[4] Righteous as it was, the speech masked a disconnect between President Carter's celebrated human rights foreign policy agenda and his administration's willful neglect of the genocide/politicide that had recently ended in Cambodia.[5] Cold War norms, geostrategic interests, the shadow of the Vietnam War, and the absence of diplomatic or economic relationships with Democratic Kampuchea (Cambodia) were all said to have led US administration officials to the conclusion that there was little they should do to try to halt the atrocities.[6] What the United States *could* do, however, was to speak out, in Carter's own words, not to "stand silent."

At different times, senior officials did speak out about "speaking out." Richard Holbrooke, then assistant secretary of state for East Asia and Pacific affairs, stated in July 1977, "We cannot let it be said that by our silence we acquiesce in the tragic events in Cambodia."[7] In February 1978, Warren Christopher, deputy secretary of state, noted, "[We] will take every suitable opportunity to speak out, lest by our silence we seem to acquiesce in the unspeakable human rights abuses that are occurring there."[8] Yet references to genocide were missing. It had taken Carter a whole two years and three months into his presidency to invoke the label in relation to Cambodia:[9]

"America cannot avoid the responsibility to speak out in condemnation of the Cambodian Government, the worst violator of human rights in the world today. Thousands of refugees from Cambodia have accused their Government of inflicting death on hundreds of thousands of the Cambodian people through the *genocidal* policies it has implemented over the past 3 years."[10] Based on a search of the archives, this also may have been Carter's first reference to "genocide" in any public speech.[11] But despite his strong language, another year and a half had to pass before the president again referred to a "tragedy of a genocidal proportion" in Cambodia and, two days later to a "deliberate attempt to decimate a population in the form of genocide."[12] These times, however, the denunciations of an alleged starvation of the Cambodian people were directed not at the recently ousted genocidal regime of the Khmer Rouge—still disingenuously supported by the United States[13]—but at America's archenemy, Vietnam, which had taken control of the land. The shift was evident also in the number of public references Carter had now made to the situation. Whereas since entering office in early 1976 to the defeat of the Khmer Rouge (January 1979) the president had mentioned the situation in Cambodia on twenty-six occasions, over the next two years his discussions of Vietnam-controlled Cambodia (1979–1980) more than doubled to fifty-five instances.[14] This newly found interest in Cambodia's plight gave credence to the later claim that the Carter administration—similar to its predecessors under Ford and Nixon—had lacked sufficient concern for the fate of its people, to overcome the muffling realpolitik effects of Cold War calculations.[15]

Reagan—Accidental Champion of the Genocide Convention

A few years later, at the International Convention of B'nai B'rith in September 1984, President Ronald Reagan took to the issue of genocide:

> With a cautious view, in part due to the human rights abuses performed by some nations that have already ratified the documents, our administration has conducted a long and exhaustive study of the convention. And yesterday, as a result of that review, we announced that we will vigorously support, consistent with the United States Constitution, the ratification of the Genocide Convention. And I want you to know that we intend to use the convention in our efforts to expand human freedom and fight human rights abuses around the world. *Like you, I say in a forthright voice, "Never again!"*[16]

Over the years, different presidents, from Truman to Nixon to Carter, had besieged the US Senate to consent to ratifying the convention, but never with enough resolve and muscle to challenge a small but influential conservative opposition within the legislature. As documented by Power, Reagan's speech had been no more than a political tactic in the run-up to the November 1984 presidential election, and as such yielded no results.[17] However, almost a year later, in April 1985, an impending public relations disaster following a glitch in the preparations for a presidential visit to West Germany was said to have forced Reagan to change course, back up his earlier words with deeds, and finally push the convention through the Senate.[18] The treaty was approved, albeit with significant reservations, and signed by the president on 4 November 1988—a staggering forty years after the United States had helped to ensure its adoption by the United Nations.

During his two-term presidency Reagan spoke about genocide more freely than past presidents had, although nearly always post hoc. On different occasions he eluded to the "Armenian genocide," the "genocide in Cambodia,"[19] the "virtual genocide" of the Miskito Indians in Nicaragua, and to "Stalin's genocide."[20] One time he associated the "genocide" in Cambodia with a pledge of never again, but the context was the communist threat and the undertaking—as with Carter—no more than an abstract promise to denunciate:

> *Never again will we shrink from denouncing* the terrible nightmare totalitarianism has wrought: occupation of an entire section of Europe, *genocide* in Cambodia, boat people in Vietnam, a bloody invasion of Afghanistan, and everywhere the suppression of human rights and growing want from economic failure. *We will not remain silent* when, in Afghanistan, yellow rain is dropped on innocent people, solemn agreements are flagrantly broken, and Soviet helicopters drop thousands of "butterfly" mines, which maim and blind Afghan children who pick them up thinking they're toys. We will *condemn* these crimes and work for international *repudiation.*[21]

Although he invoked genocide on nineteen separate occasions and the Holocaust a record seventy-eight times,[22] Reagan still avoided any meaningful actions in response to the genocides or other mass atrocities, which had taken place during his presidency in Indonesia, El Salvador, Guatemala, Burundi, Iraq, Sudan, Uganda, and elsewhere.[23]

In summary, despite the proliferation of mass atrocities throughout the Cold War, American presidents' invocations of the term "genocide" were rare and far apart. The context was nearly always procedural or commemorative, often in relation to the Holocaust.[24] The audiences also were generally sympathetic to the vision of some meaningful US action on genocide.

When pledges to act *were* made by a sitting president, they were abstract and related to hypothetical scenarios. No Cold War president invoked genocide in relation to a still ongoing situation or used it to mobilize public support for direct action.[25] During these decades, US backing of "friendly" dictatorial regimes entailed turning a blind eye to atrocities committed by them or even complicity in the acts. And since atrocities on the other side of the bipolar divide were being perpetrated with Soviet and Chinese acquiescence or by their very hands, the prospects for US-led humanitarian interventions into these situations were dimmer still. In all fairness, it could be argued that had the genocide label been invoked by the United States during the Cold War to stimulate action, the prevailing norms and anxieties of the time would have made the effects negligible compared to the communist nuclear threat. Summoning the term could have increased the visibility of the crisis, but not necessarily the pressure to do much more.

POST–COLD WAR DISCOURSES

George H. W. Bush

The presidency of George Bush Sr. saw the end of the Cold War and the beginning of a "new world order." In his public speaking Bush invoked the term "genocide" much less frequently than Carter and Reagan had done: four times in four years. Twice he used the label in the context of the ongoing crisis in Bosnia, but both times without confirming the linkage.[26] He also helped to introduce the desensitizing term "ethnic cleansing" into the Balkan discourse, using it three times during his last year in office.[27]

On 16 June 1991, the president declared at a dinner in honor of Holocaust survivor and Nazi hunter Simon Wiesenthal that his visit to Auschwitz had left him with the decision "not just to remember but also to act." He pledged America's eternal vigilance for justice, peace, and human rights throughout the world. As your president, he added, "I say there is no room in America for indifference. The Holocaust must never be dehumanized or dismissed. We pledge it will also never be forgotten."[28]

However, from mid-1992, as the crisis in Bosnia was gaining salience and images from Bosnian Serb–run concentration camps were broadcast on the evening news, it became apparent that the limited engagement policy adopted by Bush would not reflect the principles advocated in his earlier speech. Prominent to the policy were fears of quagmire and casualties, sparked by Vietnam analogies, which had affected the thinking of senior officials, from the White House to the Pentagon.[29] These fears led to a firm rejection of any US troop contribution to the international efforts to reduce the violence.[30] Earlier claims by President Bush after Operation Desert Storm that the demons of Vietnam had been dispelled did not apply to Bosnia apparently.[31] When asked how he could watch the killings without using America's might to end the suffering, the president invoked Vietnam, quagmire, and risks of casualties and argued that "ancient tribal rivalries" would not be resolved by sending American troops.[32] Instead, he highlighted the American relief efforts and his own leadership in setting a no-fly zone.

Despite or perhaps because of the strong criticism leveled at the administration by different media outlets, civil society groups, engaged members of Congress, and some junior and midlevel Foreign Service officers, the word "genocide" was excluded almost entirely from the rhetoric of senior administration officials.[33] President Bush referred to the civil war as a situation, a crisis, a conflict or even more emotively as a true humanitarian nightmare, a human tragedy, acts of barbarism, and a cruel war—but not as genocide.[34] Toward the end of his term, just before leaving office, Bush quietly oversaw a US vote in favor of a UN General Assembly Resolution that equated Serb ethnic cleansing practices to genocide.[35] However, a US genocide determination on the crisis was withheld, allegedly so as not to drop a "hot potato" into the lap of the incoming Clinton administration.[36]

President Clinton's Genocide Rhetoric

Bill Clinton had presided over American politics during most of the 1990s. In foreign policy, these post–Cold War years were highly contentious. The collapse of the bipolar order resulted in an explosion of internal strife, which advances in media technology had made more visible to the US public and thus harder to ignore. At the same time, with the communist threat gone, existential concerns no longer held in check domestic contestation of official policies.[37] Under these conditions, the administration was facing greater challenges than in the past to explain, legitimate, and justify its actions (or inaction). As Clinton's presidency spanned the ongoing civil war in Bosnia, the genocide in Rwanda, ethnic cleansing in Kosovo, and high-profile emergencies in Somalia and Haiti, these crises had to be dealt with within the parameters of an international system already engaged in humanitarian intervention debates.

Bosnia. Before taking office, Clinton had adopted an interventionist stance on Bosnia as a presidential candidate. Criticizing US inaction, which he saw as a weak spot in the foreign policy of the Bush administration, Clinton argued, "If the horrors of the Holocaust taught us anything, it is the high cost of remaining silent and paralyzed in the face of *genocide*. We must discover who is responsible for these actions and take steps to bring them to justice for these crimes against humanity."[38] Elsewhere on the campaign trail he asserted that "history has shown us that you can't allow the mass extermination of people and just sit by and watch it happen." He then added, "I think the United Nations, with the United States' support, needs to consider *doing whatever it takes to stop the slaughter of civilians*, to investigate under international law whether there have been any human rights violations. . . . *We may have to use military force.* I would begin with air power against the Serbs to try to restore the basic conditions of humanity."[39] Once in office, however, Clinton shifted his rhetoric a number of times, commensurate with changes to his objectives and perceived interests.[40] Following the example of Bush, he was soon referring to the situation in Bosnia in less emotive terms as a conflict, the Balkan war, and a few times as ethnic cleansing.[41] His discourse and that of other administration officials helped reconstitute the civil war as the product of ancient hatreds (the "Balkan discourse") and hence a conflict that the West could not and therefore should not try to resolve.[42]

But during the 1993 inauguration of the US Holocaust Memorial Museum in Washington, DC, the theme was once again Holocaust remembrance, with Clinton acknowledging historical failures and the need to combat denial of past and future holocausts:

> Even as our fragmentary awareness of crimes grew into indisputable facts, far too little was done. Before the war even started, doors to liberty were shut. And even after the United States and the Allies attacked Germany, rail lines to the camps within miles of military significant target were left undisturbed. . . . The evil represented in this museum is incontestable. But as we are its witness, so must we remain its adversary in the world in which we live. So we must stop the fabricators of history and the bullies as well. Left unchallenged, they would still prey upon the powerless; and we must not permit that to happen again.[43]

Pressed by journalists the following day over parallels between his speech and the ongoing ethnic cleansing in Bosnia, Clinton resisted the "Holocaust" frame: "I think the Holocaust is on a whole different level. I think it is without precedent or peer in human history. On the other hand, ethnic cleansing is the kind of inhumanity that the Holocaust took to the nth degree. The idea of moving people around and abusing them and often killing them solely because of their ethnicity is an abhorrent thing. . . . I think you have to stand up against it. I think it's wrong."[44] When challenged over his critique of President Roosevelt's decision not to bomb the railway lines to Auschwitz, Clinton pointed out that during the Holocaust the United States was already at war with Germany. Going to war over the "ethnic cleansing" in Bosnia was not a viable option, he stressed.[45] During the next two years Clinton was persistent in refusing to uphold the spirit of his early moralizing rhetoric, even as devastating genocide was unfolding in Rwanda.

Rwanda. In interviews after the end of his second term, Clinton described his administration's inaction over Rwanda as one of his greatest regrets as president.[46] "We couldn't have saved all of them," he said at one time, "[but] we could have saved as many as 300,000 lives. . . . I have no defence."[47] During the genocide itself, Clinton and other senior administration officials would not get involved in the management of the crisis, nor discuss it often publicly.[48] In the sensitive political climate, so short a time after the infamous "Black Hawk down" incident in Somalia, military intervention was never debated.[49] Even a *non*-American deployment was eschewed, for fear it might end up requiring a US rescue mission, as had happened in Somalia. Modest policy responses discussed by the midranking bureaucrats assigned to the crisis were discarded or blocked by the Pentagon.[50] Additional explanations for the American inaction, pointed to since, included the absence of "hard" national interests, a silent public, distractions by other crises, and the Pentagon's view that nothing short of a full-scale military intervention could stop the genocide.[51]

One study of the US Rwanda policy concluded recently that the main objective behind the administration's rhetoric during the genocide was to alleviate public unease about lack of action. Its author, Kia Guarino, argued that in providing distractions and avoiding classifying the crisis as genocide, the official discourse helped mitigate and almost eliminate public demands for humanitarian military intervention.[52] Early on, senior officials had managed to avert domestic attention away from the genocide by framing the story around the extraction of compatriots and other foreign nationals.[53] During that brief period, expressions of official concern for Rwandan lives were avoided.[54] Insinuations in Clinton's rhetoric about the historical roots and protractedness of the conflict were used similarly, though more subtly than in relation to Bosnia, to reduce the perceived urgency to act and to lower public expectations for US involvement.[55] While use of the genocide label was avoided for as long as possible, once the scale of the atrocities had become widely apparent Clinton could not ignore the topic completely. Consequently, in the few times he did address the events, the president was said to have made "empty promises laden with heavy emotional terms" other than genocide.[56] He then invoked Somalia to help defend his policy.[57]

The strongest defense for American inaction in Rwanda was provided by Presidential Decision Directive 25 (PDD-25) on US involvement in peacekeeping operations, released on 3 May 1994, one month into the genocide. Under the revised policy, US assistance to UN peacekeeping became conditioned on the fulfilment of a set of requisites, drawn from the Weinberger and Powell doctrines. They included advancing US interests, clear objectives and exit strategy, congressional and public support for the action, acceptable costs (and risks), and a direct link between US participation and the prospects for mission success.[58]

From the start to the end of the genocide three months later, Clinton and his White House staff made thirty-one public references to Rwanda.[59] In only two of them did they use the term "genocide" or "genocidal" to describe the events. The first reference was made during a White House conference on Africa, two months and three weeks into the genocide (27 June 1994). Clinton's acknowledgment of the word seemed almost incidental: "The daily reports from Rwanda, of course, remind us of the obstacles we face. There we have provided material, financial, and statistical support for the U.N. peacekeeping mission, more than $100 million in humanitarian relief. We've insisted that those who are committing *genocide* be brought to justice. And we supported the French decision to protect Rwandans at risk."[60] Notably, the reference had come *after* genocide had already been acknowledged by various NGOs (e.g., Human Rights Watch on 19 April), the CIA (internally, 26 April), the head of the UN peacekeeping mission in Rwanda General Dallaire (late April), the US Department of Defense (internally, 9 May), the UN Security Council ("acts of genocide," 17 May), and the US Secretary of State Warren Christopher (publicly, 10 June).[61] The second presidential reference to genocide was inserted in a White House statement concerning the closing down of the Rwandan embassy in Washington, released three days before the genocide had ended. It read, "The United States cannot allow representatives of a regime that supports *genocidal massacre* to remain on our soil."[62] Two additional references were made by the White House, shortly after the war: in a 29 July press briefing by National Security Adviser Anthony Lake, and in a letter from Clinton to Congress (1 August) about US assistance to Rwandan refugees.[63] These brought the total number of presidential "genocide" references on Rwanda during the whole of 1994 to four.

Srebrenica. The US dithering over Bosnia continued even after the letdown on Rwanda. A turning point was finally reached after a failure to stop genocidal massacres in the supposedly "safe" area of Srebrenica, which began in 11 July 1995. In the following days a systematic killing campaign of an estimated eight thousand Bosnian Muslims, mostly men and boys, was met with indecisive international responses. As with Rwanda, fears of the risks of military intervention were said to have been largely behind the reluctance to undertake stronger measures to protect the survivors and to prevent subsequent atrocities in other safe areas.

It took a critical mass of international, domestic, and in-house pressures to convince the administration that nothing short of a military response was going to save it from a major political embarrassment.[64] On 29 August 1995, in response to a high-casualty bombing attack on the city of Sarajevo, NATO forces under US leadership launched a series of air strikes against the

Bosnian Serb forces.[65] The campaign lasted three weeks and resulted in Serb capitulation and an imposed peace agreement, negotiated in Dayton, Ohio, and signed in Paris on 14 December 1995.[66] In the weeks following Srebrenica and up until the NATO campaign, Clinton had tried to assign the failure to intervene to the UN and to his European allies—a move that set off a short but tense period in America's relationship with NATO.[67] Scrambling for further damage control, Clinton then tried to pin some of the responsibility on the Bush administration, arguing that the decision to let the Europeans deal with "the first major security crisis on the European Continent at the end of the cold war" had predated his presidency.[68]

Once the NATO bombing was under way, the administration provided Congress with a short list of arguments to justify the policy shift. The intervention, it noted, was in response to the "tragic and inexcusable" attack on Sarajevo, "the latest in a series of BSA [Bosnian Serb Army] attacks on unarmed civilians in the safe areas," which had breached the terms outlined in the NATO ultimatum. It had been authorized by and was consistent with UN Security Council and NATO resolutions.[69] Therefore the strikes constituted an "appropriate and necessary" response to the Bosnian Serbs' actions, intended to reduce the threat to Sarajevo and deter further attacks on other safe areas.[70] Ignoring a growing number of genocide references to Srebrenica in public discourse, Clinton and his staff continued to avoid the term.[71] In the twelve months following the fall of the safe area, the White House made ten public references to Srebrenica (401 refs to Bosnia), but none of them mentioned genocide."[72] It wasn't until four years later, in March 1999, that Clinton finally used the "G word" to describe the massacres carried out in the safe area, as part of his efforts to justify NATO's bombings of Serbia over the crisis in Kosovo.[73] It took eight more years after that for an authoritative determination to be made on Srebrenica (by the International Court of Justice) as the only legally recognized genocidal massacre of the civil war.[74]

From Rwanda to Kosovo. On 25 March 1998, four years after the genocide in Rwanda, Clinton traveled to Rwanda's capital Kigali and in the airport issued a post hoc quasi-apology to the survivors: "The international community, together with nations in Africa, must bear its share of responsibility for this tragedy, as well. We did not act quickly enough after the killing began. . . . We cannot change the past. But we can and must do everything in our power to help you build a future without fear, and full of hope. We owe to those who died and to those who survived who loved them, our every effort to increase our vigilance and strengthen our stand against those who would commit such atrocities in the future—here or elsewhere."[75] Justifying US inaction based on the argument of a widespread failure to comprehend the extent of the violence until it was too late, Clinton stated, "It may seem strange to you here but all over the world there were people like me sitting in offices day after day after day, who did not fully appreciate the depth and the speed with which you were being engulfed by this unimaginable terror."[76] Still, the lessons from Rwanda and Bosnia may have revealed a new Clinton, closer in rhetoric to his period as presidential candidate but now more determined to put words into action. In February 1999, after months of escalating violence between the ethnically Albanian Kosovo Liberation Army and Serb police and militia in Serbia's province of Kosovo, the United States and its NATO allies handed Serbia's president Milosevic a strongly worded ultimatum (according to some too strong) to retreat his forces.[77] On 24 March 1999, after negotiations had failed, NATO began bombing Serbia. This time it took seventy-eight days of intense air attacks (to 10 June) to convince Milosevic to pull his forces out of Kosovo.[78] By then, however, a retaliatory ethnic cleansing campaign by Serbia had driven 1.3 million Albanian Kosovars out of their homes. NATO's high-altitude strikes that were intended to minimize casualties for the interveners not only were ineffective in preventing the ethnic cleansing but also inflicted serious casualties and suffering on the Serb civilian population.[79]

Before, during, and after the bombing Clinton invested time and efforts, first in legitimating and then in justifying the intervention—much more so than over Bosnia in 1995. Probable reasons for the increased efforts by the White House include the much smaller number of casualties in the lead-up to the intervention, the absence of UN Security Council authorization for the air campaign, and the fuzzier link to America's national interest.

The administration's term of choice for the events was once again "ethnic cleansing"—though this time more appropriately. While the "G word" was mentioned on ten separate occasions during the campaign, the context was indirect and the references did not depict the crisis itself as a case of genocide.[80] It was only after the Serb capitulation, once criticisms of the bombings had begun gathering momentum, that Clinton stepped up his rhetoric and on three separate occasions described the motives behind the intervention as attempts "to reverse *genocide* and ethnic cleansing."[81]

Genocide, Ethnic Cleansing, and Holocaust Analogies under Clinton

During their term, President Clinton and his White House staff made 117 separate references to genocide. Yet despite the sharp increase in usage compared to the Cold War years and to Bush's presidency, they seldom applied the label to ongoing crises or to threatened situations.[82] From 1993 to 1996, 1,023 public references to Bosnia by Clinton and his staff had

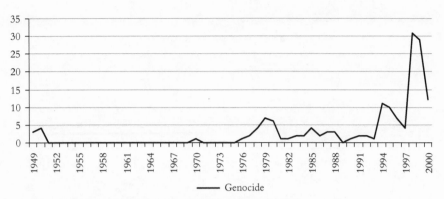

3.2. Mentioning "genocide" during and after the Cold War.

correlated with but one reference to genocide in the context of the civil war.[83] In the case of Rwanda, 59 presidential references to the country in the whole of 1994 correlated with 4 references to genocide, all belated.[84] During 1999, 454 references to Kosovo correlated with 17 references to genocide—14 indirect and 3 post hoc references to Kosovo as genocide.[85] However, not one of the three constituted an official US genocide determination on the crisis.

The administration's preferred term for Bosnia and Kosovo had been the deceivingly sterile, baggage free, and legally harmless "ethnic cleansing" (see figure 3.3, next page).[86] Between 1993 and 1996 Clinton and his staff applied this term to the Bosnian crisis on 59 separate occasions and during 1999 in relation to "Kosovo" 140 times.[87]

Notably, the employment of "ethnic cleansing" did not always appear coordinated. That is, in Bosnia it was invoked not only when the administration had wanted to avoid intervention but also *after* it was dragged into one. In Kosovo, the phrase described the events more accurately than the genocide label. Also, as the association with "aerial intervention" had already been made in Bosnia, the official thinking in relation to Kosovo may have been that the term would be appropriate for the task.[88]

The Holocaust appeared in the Clinton White House rhetoric 144 times.[89] When *inaction* was the preferred policy, the term was rarely linked to a contemporary crisis.[90] For instance, when the association was raised over Bosnia in April 1993, President Clinton rejected it outright.[91] During these periods, the context of invoking the Holocaust included commemoration events, the inauguration of the Holocaust Memorial Museum in Washington, DC, and references to a "nuclear holocaust."

In periods when intervention *was* the preferred official policy, the administration did make use of Holocaust analogies, but only after the

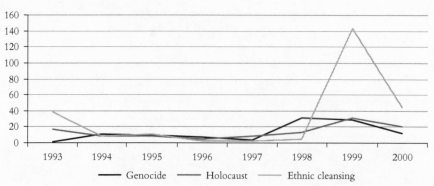

3.3. Clinton mentioning "genocide," the "Holocaust," and "ethnic cleansing."

intervention had ended, such as during and after the negotiations of the
Dayton Peace Agreement to mobilize public support for sending US peacekeepers to the Balkans. In less than three months (late October to mid-
December 1995) Clinton and his staff made references to concentration
camps, death camps, barbed-wire fences, and the Holocaust itself at least
eight times.[92] The absence of Holocaust analogies during the short lead-up
to the Bosnia intervention could be explained by the existence of broad
consensus for military action, which reduced the need to justify the
campaign.

Similarly, in the three months after the commencement of the Kosovo
intervention Clinton invoked Holocaust analogies in relation to the crisis
no fewer than twelve times, often alluding to the European context.[93] In
contrast to his rejection of the early association with Bosnia, he now argued,
"Though his [Milosevic's] ethnic cleansing is not the same as the ethnic
extermination of the Holocaust, the two are related, both vicious, premedi-
tated, systematic oppression fuelled by religious and ethnic hatred. This
campaign to drive the Kosovars from their land and to, indeed, erase their
very identity is an affront to humanity and an attack not only on a people
but on the dignity of all people."[94]

Exceptionalist Language: Linking Values and Interests

Among America's presidents, Bill Clinton was most adept at integrating
"exceptionalist" rhetoric into his public speeches and comments.[95] He used
it to legitimate the projection of American power during different events,
including NATO's intervention in Bosnia, the deployment of US peacekeepers to the embattled region, the later extension of their mandate, and
the intervention in Kosovo in 1999. These missions, Clinton argued, were
not only about protecting US interests but also about upholding American

values, defending the defenseless and advancing the cause of peace.[96] He also used exceptionalist language to argue for the indispensability of America's leadership—albeit selective and conditional—in the pursuit of global freedoms and world peace.[97]

Clinton's address to the nation on the eve of the 1999 NATO Kosovo campaign included two main rationales for the attack: American values and American national interests. This framing reminds us of Trout's proposition from Chapter 2, that to achieve foreign policy legitimacy presidents must make a case for the desirability of their policies by having them appear to embody and enhance core national values and national interests.[98] Strung together, interests and values were a recurring theme in the discourses of American presidents.[99] In Clinton's rhetoric they were employed to justify both strong and weak policies in relation to man-made humanitarian crises.[100] On 3 May 1994, one month into the genocide in Rwanda, the president spoke of the need to assume the obligations and risks of a post–Cold War global leadership based on US national interests and "clearly stated values."[101] While his abridged definition of the American national interest was to protect the land, the people, and the way of life of the nation, he did not stop there. Describing America as the world's most powerful nation, its oldest democracy, and "the most daring experiment in forging different races, religions, and cultures into a single people," Clinton declared that the United States had an interest to serve as a "beacon of strength and freedom and hope" to the world.[102] In November 1996, Clinton again invoked values and interests, this time to justify his decision to renew the US peace-keeping mission in Bosnia: "The United States cannot and should not try to solve every problem in the world, but where our *interests* are clear and our *values* are at stake, where we can make a difference, we must act, and we must lead. Clearly, Bosnia is such an example."[103] Six months later he reiterated the same principle in a speech in West Point: "We have to embrace our role as the decisive force for peace. You cannot and you should not go everywhere. *But when our values and interests are at stake*, our mission is crystal clear and achievable, America should stand with our allies around the world who seek to bring peace and prevent slaughter. From the Middle East to Bosnia, from Haiti to Northern Ireland, we have worked to contain conflict, to support peace, to give children a brighter future, and it has enhanced our security."[104] Then in the lead-up to the Kosovo bombing (26 February 1999) Clinton famously declared, "The question we must ask is, what are the consequences to our security of letting conflicts fester and spread. We cannot, indeed, we should not, do everything or be everywhere. But where *our values* and our *interest* are at stake, and where we can make a difference, we must be prepared to do so."[105] Speaking to American veterans later in the campaign (14 May 1999) he argued that resolving the conflict was not only the moral thing to do but also the right thing in terms of strategy, practicality, and (national) security. To support the latter, Clinton invoked terrorism, radicalism, the danger of setting a new precedent, and the risks of mass refugee flows and regional destabilization in Southern Europe, which inevitably would have led to a US intervention.[106]

Clinton's "Doctrine" and Legacy

After the Kosovo campaign, Clinton's publicly expressed views on America's role in the world became increasingly daring. In a speech to NATO troops in Macedonia following the surrender of Milosevic he announced, "If we can then say to the people of the world, whether you live in Africa, or Central Europe, or any other place, if somebody comes after innocent civilians and tries to kill them en masse because of their race, their ethnic background or their religion, and it's within our power to stop it, we will stop it."[107] While other administration officials quickly backed away from the alleged implications, his remarks added impetuous to what was becoming known as the Clinton Doctrine.[108] When asked two days before the speech whether there was such a thing as a Clinton Doctrine, the president responded,

> I think there's an important principle here that I hope will be now upheld in the future—and not just by the United States, not just by NATO, but also by the leading countries of the world, through the United Nations . . . that *whether within or beyond the borders of a country, if the world community has the power . . . we ought to stop genocide and ethnic cleansing.* . . . That is what we did, but took too long in doing, in Bosnia. That is what we did, and are doing, in Kosovo. That is, frankly, what we failed to do in Rwanda, where so many died so quickly—and *what I hope very much we'll be able to do in Africa, if it ever happens there again.*[109]

As Kosovo was to be Clinton's last major man-made humanitarian crisis, the question remained whether the hard-learned lessons that he seemed to have internalized would outlive his presidency. The answer was soon to follow.

Clinton's Legacy. In October 2000, presidential candidates Governor George W. Bush and Clinton's vice president Al Gore attended a televised foreign policy debate at Winston-Salem, North Carolina. In response to a question on the use of force, both contenders supported five out of eight major US interventions of the previous twenty years: Panama, Grenada, Iraq in 1991, Bosnia, and Kosovo the year before. Both of them also supported a sixth intervention (Lebanon and Haiti, respectively),[110] leaving Somalia as the only contentious intervention for the two. However, in a follow-up question about the 1994 genocide in Rwanda, both candidates professed support for Clinton's policy of nonintervention. Bush's answer was, "I think the [Clinton] administration did the right thing in that case. . . . It was a horrible situation. No one liked to see it on our TV screens . . . they made the right decision not to send U.S. troops into Rwanda."[111] Notably, this was not an off-the-cuff response. Several months earlier Bush had argued in an interview, "We should not send our troops to stop ethnic cleansing and genocide in nations outside our strategic interest. I don't like genocide and I don't like ethnic cleansing, but the president must set clear parameters as to where troops ought to be used and when they ought not to be used."[112] When asked what he would do if another Rwanda were to take place during his presidency, Bush said he would work with world organizations and encourage them to act but would not commit US troops.[113]

Back in the presidential debate, Bush again pointed to strategic interests as the central element to any decision involving the use of US troops.[114] If the military were to be deployed, both the mission and an exit strategy had to be clearly understood. In situations like Rwanda his preferred engagement would include early prevention efforts (supported by an early warning system) and continued US support for improving inter-African intervention capacities.[115]

Initially in the debate Gore had argued that intervening to stop genocide and "ethnic cleansing" was a fundamental American strategic interest, supported by American values.[116] Such a view, he suggested, was not shared by Bush.[117] Still, he conditioned his support for intervention on other factors, without specifying what they were. In relation to Rwanda though, his position was barely distinguishable from that of Bush:

> I do not think that it [Rwanda] was an example of a conflict where we should have put our troops in to try to separate the parties for this reason. . . . One of the criteria that I think is important in deciding when and if we should ever get involved around the world is whether or not—*if our national security interest is involved, if we can really make the difference with military force, if we've tried everything else, if we have allies*. In the Balkans we had allies. . . . In Africa we did not . . . because we had no allies and because it was very unclear that we could actually accomplish what we would want to accomplish by putting military forces there, *I think it was the right thing not to jump in, as heartbreaking as it was*. But I think we should have come in much quicker with the humanitarian mission.[118]

As argued in the introduction, the concurrence by both candidates in support of the nonintervention in Rwanda was, or at least should have been, troubling. Four years after the genocide, public discourses in the United States were suggesting a near consensus over a moral failure of the Clinton administration in Rwanda. Therefore the candidates' positions exposed potential gaps between public opinion and official policy in relation to genocide; or did these gaps exist in effect between *professed* public opinions and *actual* public attitudes concerning America's role and responsibilities in the world?

THE USE AND AVOIDANCE OF THE GENOCIDE LABEL

Considerable attention has been paid in this chapter to rhetorical displays of political leadership, particularly in relation to the use of the term "genocide." What significance have past US administrations attributed to the influence of the label, and what can we say about their motives in invoking or avoiding the term in public discourses? To address these questions, I studied presidential speeches made before, during, after, and between some of the most well-known genocides or purported genocides of the past decades. My analysis contrasted the use of the "G word" against policies of the time, in the assumption that presidents' rhetoric would have been constructed to support official objectives. Two primary factors stood out in the analysis: context and administrations' calculations against or in favor of interventions.

Context

When Cold War presidents engaged in genocide rhetoric it was mostly when the venues, timings, audiences, interests, and other contexts had been favorable. After the Cold War, the proliferation of internal conflicts and the rise in public support for humanitarian interventions forced President George H. W. Bush and later Clinton to contend with more foreign policy emergencies and less deferential public and media. Outside remembrance days, invocations of genocide reflected at times bitter public debates, at least more so than in the preceding period.

Inaction as a Preferred Policy

The evidence examined supported findings from previous studies, according to which when nonintervention was the preferred policy presidents had intentionally avoided using the genocide label, to escape the moral and legal responsibilities associated with the term. Yet moralizing rhetoric short of genocide was still used in their discourses, particularly after the Cold War. To maintain "ethically correct" postures of commitment to action while in fact seeking legitimacy for weak policies, speeches had to be structured to resonate with dominant cultural norms, but without overly inciting the public or locking the administration into risky commitments.[119] This was achieved by using other phrases and imageries, such as "ethnic cleansing." Remaining unclear are the scale, frequency, and degree of importance assigned by administrations to the term, and consequently to its use or circumvention, in line with a preferred policy.

As I argue in the conclusions to the book, no government—certainly no American government—would openly admit indifference to genocide, however distant or irrelevant to its perceived interests. Raphael Lemkin's efforts and those of others had conferred on the term a clout compelling enough to discourage such public admissions. The Bush–Gore presidential debate therefore offered an important opportunity to look beyond appearances. That both sides felt safe to present prudent but ethically "thin" positions in such a forum suggests a presumption on their part—correct or mistaken—that the American people would endorse or at least abide by these views.[120] I continue to explore this important question in Chapter 4 in the context of public attitudes versus public behavior.

Strong Action as Preferred Policy

The analysis has shown that even when intervention *was* favored, the Clinton administration—one of the only post–World War II administrations forced to intervene militarily in situations of distant atrocities—had barely used the genocide label to legitimate its policies. This held true in relation to Bosnia when delays and hesitations finally gave way to the decision to intervene. In regard to Kosovo, Clinton had rarely used the label in his otherwise rigorous efforts to justify the campaign, and when he did it was indirectly and without naming the crisis itself as genocide. Only after the intervention had ended and Clinton came under fire over its management did he and his staff apply the genocide label to the crisis. In all, the term was used much less frequently to justify interventions and deployments of troops than ethnic cleansing or even Holocaust analogies were.[121] Finally, while Clinton did employ exceptionalist rhetoric as part of these efforts, no evidence was found to suggest that he or other presidents before him had tried to couch America's relationship with the term "genocide" in exceptionalist terms or imagery.

From Somalia and until Kosovo, Clinton's engagement with mass atrocities had been described as "intervention-reluctant."[122] In the case of Bosnia it would have been politically unsafe to invoke the genocide label so soon after the failure to act in Rwanda. Clinton could have found himself having to also explain why a genocidal massacre of eight thousand civilians in Srebrenica had justified an intervention that he had avoided in the preceding three and a half years, despite a death toll of more than ten times that number. But then again the answer may be much simpler: with domestic and international public opinion on his side and Security Council authorization in his possession, Clinton did not need the genocide label to win legitimacy.[123] After more than three years of robust media coverage, the American public already had a sufficient grasp of the situation, the actors, and the stakes involved.

In Kosovo, without a Security Council seal of approval and with only a fraction of the casualty estimates in Bosnia to highlight the seriousness of the situation, the circumstances were different. Invoking genocide could have provided the administration with a useful imperative and powerful narrative. However, one could argue that as a genocide determination on the crisis might not have passed legal scrutiny, it would have been a risky argument to make.[124] When asked in an interview about his reluctance to determine genocide in Kosovo, Clinton gave a blurry response:

> *I try to be hesitant in using it* [genocide]. There is no question that a few thousand people have been murdered because they were Kosovar Albanians. There's no question about that. . . . There's no question that what he [Milosevic] was doing constitutes ethnic cleansing and that he was killing and uprooting people because of their ethnic heritage. There is no question about that. And I think that not only he, but others who are in decision-making positions, have to be held accountable for what they've done. And of course, this whole war crimes tribunal that's been set up to review what happened in the Balkans will have to review those facts. *But the main thing I want to do is, whether [or not] the [genocide] label belongs on it, is to stop it if we can.*[125]

The message seemed to be something like: a genocide determination would have to be made by the courts, but this should not constrain a US decision to act. During the rest of his second term, Clinton did use the label a few more times to argue that the United States and the international community had a moral obligation to prevent atrocities and protect human rights.[126]

A MYTH OF OFFICIAL COMMITMENT

Samantha Power cited well-meaning speeches in well-chosen venues to portray a continuity of presidential rhetoric allegedly "strong" on the pledge to respond to genocide. However, in the years following the publication of her award-winning book, this narrative developed into a myth. In reality, no American president has ever fully committed the United States to the project of confronting genocide, not even Clinton in the last year of his presidency—or more recently Obama, who in August 2011 declared preventing mass atrocities and genocide a national security interest and a core moral responsibility of the United States.[127] Such a commitment would have contradicted a core principle of American foreign policy: retaining the freedom to choose actions case by case, based on dynamic circumstances and potentially changing interests. In the rare occasions when presidents did invoke the label, their rhetoric was moralizing but mostly devoid of meaningful commitments. No concrete promises were made—particularly not in relation to military action. In the first post-Clinton presidential debate, contenders from both sides of the political aisle had kept his Rwanda policy—the epitome of inaction— soundly intact.[128] No successor to Clinton—Republican or Democrat—would have intervened if the exact same scenario were to occur again. Clinton and his staff seemed to have been the only ones truly moved by the consequences of their fatal decision making at the time of the genocide.

Overall, the genocidal or non-genocidal nature of the crisis situations explored in this chapter seems to have played a minor role in administration officials' efforts to push policies of intervention *or* nonintervention to the American public and to Congress. Absent clear legal obligations on states to act in a particular way or ways to halt the crime, the moral imperative to prevent or stop genocide was either avoided or sidelined by different circumstances and other concerns.

To better understand how policymakers perceived the moral clout of the genocide label in the public sphere, we need to look at domestic reactions to the term during the same periods. What attitudes did the American public communicate to its leadership in relation to the "genocidal" dimension of crises? How did citizens respond to the events? How were the opinions and behavior of the public interpreted by administration officials, and what were their effects on official actions? Building on past studies, the next chapter offers a preliminary examination of these questions.

CHAPTER 4

Domestic Responses to Genocide

PUBLIC OPINION VERSUS PUBLIC BEHAVIOR

THIS CHAPTER continues to explore imperatives and constraints to America's responses to genocide, focusing on the US public and
its influences on official action. So far, public opinion has been portrayed as
a likely vehicle for advancing the moral sway of the genocide label, but also
as an absent actor in debates over policies. Except for a few voices, wrote
Samantha Power in *"A Problem from Hell,"* a society-wide silence during
most genocides of the twentieth century caused US officials at different levels to assume that the political costs of getting involved exceeded the costs
of remaining uninvolved.[1] Her conclusion that the battle to stop genocide
was lost in domestic politics added considerable import to her "missing
actors" finding. On the other hand, and in seeming contradiction to Power's assertions, national opinion polls from the last three decades have indicated majority citizenry support for strong US responses to genocide.
Therefore the question to ask is this: if the public did endorse strong action,
why was it silent in the face of official inaction?

In this chapter I argue that to understand the effects of the public on US
policies we need to explore in greater depth underlying causes for the divergences between Americans' professed opinions and their actual behavior. As
the chapter's findings show, a correlation may have existed between administrations' inaction on genocide and how officials interpreted the opinion-
behavior gap.

Based on past research, US policymakers' reading of the citizenry relies
on intermittent monitoring of news media coverage, congressional actions
and discourses, and, to a lesser extent, opinion polls.[2] In this chapter we use
the same indicators to learn how administrations might have understood or
misread the public during some of the alleged genocides of the 1990s, how
they interpreted incongruities between public opinion and behavior, and
what effects these interpretations might have had on their policy decisions.
The focus of the analysis thus shifts from the executive branch to the
intended audiences of its rhetoric: mass opinion, legislators, journalists, and

other elites. The case studies analyzed include the interventions in Bosnia (September 1995) and Kosovo and the "noninterventions" in Bosnia (1992–mid-1995) and Rwanda. While better understanding of public attitudes and their effects is likely to account for only part of the story, in a global village increasingly dominated by populist agendas, this part could prove to be at certain junctures a pivotal one.

Notably, national polls in the United States have paid only modest attention over the years to the influence of the genocide label. As a result, the polling data available to us precluded a more in-depth treatment of the topic, including the demographic characteristics, political preferences, and geographic distribution of respondents. A more consistent focus in future polls on the themes explored would help further this understanding.

OPINION AND BEHAVIOR AS REFLECTIONS OF ATTITUDES

How committed have Americans been to the promise of "never again"? By "committed," I refer to the extent of efforts, risks, resources, and sacrifices—personal or communal—that the general public and elites were willing to make, take, or invest to prevent or stop genocide. Additionally, we want to know which factors motivated or impeded these commitments and whether it is possible for the purpose of this study to separate the effects of the genocide label (potentially one of these factors) from those of other elements.

In 2005 McFarland and Mathews published a study of a related but broader question concerning Americans' commitment to protecting human rights. Using surveys and polls, they identified marked differences between a strong principled public support for the idea of defending human rights abroad and a considerably lower willingness to commit the means to achieve this goal.[3] How reflective could polls be of public attitudes to intensely moral themes such as genocide? And can their findings be used to understand and predict public behavior? According to social psychology theories, attitudes as hypothetical mental constructs cannot be discerned directly but must be inferred from self-reports of individuals or from their behaviors.[4] This complexity adds to the methodological challenges already facing our analysis. For example, a *New York Times* editorial from the days of the civil war in Bosnia may teach us something about elite opinion at the time. But in addition to reflecting opinion, could this editorial be said to manifest also elite *behavior*? One objective of this chapter is to try to clarify relationships and distinctions between expressed opinions and behaviors as indicators of attitudes within and between the general public and the elites. Another is to try to learn how administration officials' interpretations of those indicators influenced US responses and nonresponses to the civil war in Bosnia and to the genocide in Rwanda. In "public behavior" we include such activities as attending protests and rallies, writing letters, and signing petitions, whereas elite behaviors are manifested more through editorial writing, public speaking, and other related activities. Voting in elections obviously pertains to both.

PUBLIC OPINION IN THE UNITED STATES DURING BOSNIA, RWANDA, AND KOSOVO

During the 1990s the American public was often seen as a mitigating factor in official policy decisions about humanitarian interventions, owing to its purported unwillingness to place US troops in harm's way.[5] However, a number of studies conducted by Steven Kull and colleagues between 1999 and 2003 challenged these perceptions in favor of a more interventionist view of the citizenry.[6] The findings from these studies, among the very few to pay specific attention to the effects of the genocide label, are reviewed hereafter.

In a 2002 article titled, "American Public Opinion, the Media and Genocide Prevention," Kull argued that Americans had been consistent in supporting the proposition that genocidal behavior creates a strong moral imperative for US action.[7] These views, he observed, had manifested most clearly in the discussion of hypothetical scenarios but were evident also in relation to the crises in Bosnia, Rwanda, and Kosovo. Challenging conventional wisdom about the predominance of hard interests over moral imperatives in deciding policies, Kull wrote, "The whole concern about 'national interest' is the lowest concern. If you give the public a series of arguments related to why we should or should not go into a peacekeeping operation, national interest arguments get the lowest score. The high scores are always in the nature of humanitarian concerns for people being killed and so on and arguments based on genocide occurring are often the strongest of all."[8] A year later, in a retrospective study of US polls conducted during the Bosnian civil war, Kull and Ramsay determined that survey statements that favored a military intervention in the crisis had enjoyed greater public support than statements against intervention.[9] Among the interventionist statements, those that emphasized humanitarian concerns had attracted the highest level of public support.[10] The support was particularly strong when the crisis was described as "genocide" and the intervention as multilateral (rather than unilaterally American). Earlier, in his 2002 article, Kull also noted that polls that tested associations between the Bosnian crisis and the terms "genocide" and "the Holocaust" had returned positive results:

> In a March 1994 CNN/USA Today poll, 63 percent of the respondents found "what Serbian forces are doing to other ethnic groups in Bosnia"

to be very or somewhat similar to "the Holocaust which occurred in Nazi Germany during World War II." In an April 1994 PIPA poll, 62 percent agreed that "The Bosnian Serbs' effort at 'ethnic cleansing' through killing Muslims is essentially a small version of Hitler's genocide against Jews. The United States should be willing to risk some of its troops in an effort to stop this genocide." In the July 1994 PIPA poll, 76 percent agreed (53 percent strongly) that "the current situation in Bosnia, with Serbs carrying out ethnic cleansing of Muslims, falls into the category of genocide."[11]

In the July 1994 poll, 65 percent of respondents had also agreed with the statement that when genocide is occurring the United States together with the United Nations should intervene always or in most cases with whatever force is necessary to stop the genocide.[12] Also, 23 percent had supported the statement that the United States should intervene only when American interests are also involved, and only 6 percent believed that the United States should never intervene. Conducted during the late stages of the contemporaneous genocide in Rwanda, the same poll showed a 62 percent citizenry support for a multilateral deployment of troops, including Americans, to both Bosnia and Rwanda.[13] Yet when asked in a follow-up question (which helped to untangle the influence of genocide from those of other factors) how a genocide determination by the United Nations would have affected their backing of a military action, respondents' support for intervention rose from 62 to 80 percent in relation to both crises. Focus groups conducted in parallel to this poll reported similar attitudes by their participants.[14]

Opinion support for intervention in Rwanda manifested in other polls as well. Kull summarized these findings in a 2002 conference paper, again challenging the conceptions of public aversion to military responses to the genocide:

> Polling that was carried out just before and during the civil war [in Rwanda] suggests that the public would have supported U.S. participation in a UN intervention there. In May 1994, when the conflict was getting going, CNN found a plurality of 45 percent that supported intervention. By July, when the civil war was really underway, 60 percent said that they favored the U.S. participating together with other countries in a peacekeeping force to set up safe havens in Rwanda and 61 percent said that they favored contributing to a UN force of 20- to 100,000 troops to occupy Rwanda and forcibly stop the killing. This last poll . . . also found that the public was ready to be galvanized by coherent leadership from the top. If the President and Congress had both aligned themselves with the goal of intervening to stop the

killing, another 15 percent said that they would then support it, bringing the level of support up to around 75 percent.[15]

In contrast to a strong *elite* backing for Clinton's inaction during the genocide,
the general public continued to profess in the following years retrospective
support for the notion of intervention.[16] For example, in a poll conducted in
1995, 74 percent of respondents thought that the United Nations should
have forcibly gone into Rwanda and set up safe zones; 62 percent would
have had the United Nations go in with a large military force to occupy the
country and stop the killings.[17]

Public support for US intervention in genocide continued to manifest
after Rwanda and Bosnia, even though polling questions did not often separate the effects of the label from those of other factors. For example, in
June 1996, 78 percent of respondents to a Program on International Policy
Attitudes (PIPA) poll agreed (50 percent strongly) that the United States
should contribute to UN peacekeeping because "if we allow things like
genocide or the mass killing of civilians to go unaddressed, it is more apt to
spread and create more instability in the world so that eventually our interests would be affected."[18] A few years later Kull argued in a hindsight analysis of the intervention debate over Kosovo (relying on a PIPA poll from
May 1999) that Americans' support for the use of force was "heavily influenced" by their belief that what was taking place was genocide: "Sixty
percent said that they considered the Serbian attacks on ethnic Albanians to
be a form of genocide. What is particularly interesting is that 69 percent
found convincing the argument: 'The Serbs' effort at ethnic cleansing
through killing many ethnic Albanians and driving hundreds of thousands
of them out of Kosovo is a form of genocide. The U.S. has a moral obligation to join in efforts to stop this genocide.'"[19] Support for action continued
to manifest into the new millennium. In a March 2001 Pew poll, 74 percent
agreed with the statement "In the future, the U.S. and other Western powers have a moral obligation to use military force if necessary, to prevent one
group of people from committing genocide against another."[20]

Different Wording, Different Results

As noted earlier, the level of public support for humanitarian interventions was a contested issue during the 1990s. For example, in a 1994 piece
published in *Foreign Affairs,* Andrew Kohut and Robert Toth cited various
polls that portrayed Americans as largely averse to the idea of a US military
intervention in Bosnia.[21] While their data did not go beyond December 1993, Kohut continued to argue even after the civil war had ended that
at no time was there majority support for the idea that "the United States
had a responsibility to do something" about the fighting.[22]

Then how should we account for the variances among the different studies and views? One explanation offered by Kull and Ramsay referred to the inclusion or omission of certain elements from the wordings of survey questions, which according to them led to substantive differences in polls' outcomes. Particularly significant were divergent depictions of burden sharing, the type of actions to be taken, and the prospects for mission success.[23] For example, the inclusion of the word "multilateral" in questions about ground intervention in Bosnia had increased support from an average of 43 percent in six different polls to 62 percent in four others.[24]

A complementary explanation, which focused specifically on the omission or inclusion of the genocide label in survey questions, was offered by Kenneth Campbell in *Genocide and the Global Village*. The contradicting results, wrote Campbell, were caused by "ambiguous characterizations" of the conflicts in Bosnia, Rwanda, and Kosovo as civil wars, or ancient feuds, for which "peace" and "conflict resolution" were the stated objectives. By neglecting to relate the genocide label to these crises, policymakers had missed the important point "that the public has not applied its Vietnam reluctance [i.e., risk of casualties or quagmire] to core goals such as genocide."[25] According to Campbell, when survey questions were "more accurately framed as 'genocide'" the responses obtained were radically different.[26]

Although supported by most of the data presented so far, Campbell's explanation could be challenged by some other results. For example, in a 1993 Roper poll fewer than half of the respondents supported the use of a military force "to overthrow a foreign government that practices *genocide*, to stop an invasion of one foreign country by another, or to intervene in a civil war to protect innocent lives."[27] While these responses seem to suggest a weak effect of the genocide label, it could also be argued that the reference to "genocide" in the poll was explicitly associated with the "overthrow" of a foreign government—not a very popular policy option in the early 1990s.[28] In another possible though indirect challenge to the significance of the term, 77 percent of respondents to a 1999 poll had supported international military intervention, including by the United States, to stop a government from committing *atrocities* and killing a significant number of its own people.[29] Hence, even though the word "genocide" was not mentioned, the broad support for intervention paralleled and in some cases even exceeded results from other polls that did use the term "genocide." Once again, the lack in data has made it difficult to draw clear conclusions, since a strong public support may well have existed for intervention, regardless of the term used.

So far the discussion has emphasized several key points to bear in mind. First, most available polling data from the 1990s seem to indicate in hindsight majority support in the US public for multilateral interventions in genocide—both in general and in relation to specific events. However, we still don't know how this professed support was interpreted and to what extent it had been taken into account by American policymakers. Power, for one, argued that in relation to Rwanda the existence of a domestic constituency for intervention became clear only after the genocide had ended.[30] During the events, views *against* intervention—particularly among the elites—were much more visible.

Second, the exploration helped to identify some of the complexities involved in studying gaps between mass and elite attitudes, several of which had been highlighted by Kull: "In every case [Bosnia, Rwanda and Kosovo], the public was faced with a situation in which the elite was divided about whether intervention was a good idea, the government did not take a clear position on whether genocide was in fact occurring, and military authorities were questioning whether success of the operation was likely. If any one of those three factors . . . had been different, then there is strong evidence that there would have been a clear and strong majority supporting participation in a multilateral intervention."[31] These manifestations of active opposition to intervention in the higher echelons of American society should be kept in mind as we turn from professed attitudes to public behavior. In examining studies that tested the claim of society-wide silence in relation to Rwanda and Bosnia, we next attempt to get a sense of how mass and elite opinion had conducted themselves during the events and how their actions had been interpreted by policymakers and the media.

PUBLIC BEHAVIOR: A SOCIETY-WIDE SILENCE?
Rwanda

Notwithstanding the many conflicts that had raged invisibly under the radar of Western media after the Cold War, America's muffled reaction to the genocide in Rwanda is widely recognized as an extreme case of "bystanding to genocide." Furthermore, and as demonstrated below, it was also a situation of society-wide silence. To explain the official inertia and obfuscation that typified the behavior of the Clinton administration, analysts pointed to congressional silence, deficiencies in media reporting, obstructions by the Pentagon, and absence of protests or other pressure from mass and elite opinion.

Media Coverage. According to Power, the media's reporting of the genocide had provided almost immediately causes for alarm for anyone watching the news or reading the elite papers. In the *Washington Post* the events were front-page stories on 9 and 10 April, in the *New York Times* on 10 and 16 April. On 19 April the *Post* cited a determination of genocide on the events by Human Rights Watch and death toll assessments of 100,000 civilians. A week later, much higher casualty assessments by the Red Cross and Oxfam (100,000–300,000 and 500,000, respectively) also made it into the news.[32] Although the story was not being ignored, a combination of circumstances and other factors had hindered the volume and quality of the coverage. To begin with, the suddenness of the events had caught the international media unprepared, with only a handful of journalists inside Rwanda. The cordon imposed by the perpetrators and the risks on the ground had made sure that there were no more than fifteen journalists present in the country at any one time.[33] This shortage reduced the amount of video footage coming out of the country and consequently the prospects for a meaningful CNN effect. The coverage was also affected by other more conspicuous "media events," such as the O. J. Simpson trial, Bosnia's civil war, the crisis in Haiti, and the first post-Apartheid elections in South Africa. These stories attracted more public and media attention than the violence taking place in the little-known country of Rwanda.[34]

Retrospective critiques of the media's shortcomings also focused on errors of content. Melissa Wall, Linda Melvern, and others lambasted the initial failure of many journalists to understand the political nature of the violence and the widespread misuse of clichés like "ancient tribal hatreds" that had dominated early reports.[35] Political communication scholar Piers Robinson pointed to the "dismal performance on the part of Western media who presented the genocide as a 'cease-fire breakdown' and simply another round of unstoppable tribal blood-letting."[36] Political scientist Allan Kuperman wrote, "The media must share blame for not immediately recognizing the extent of the carnage and mobilizing world attention to it. They failed to report that a nationwide killing campaign was under way in Rwanda until almost three weeks into the violence. By that time, some 250,000 Tutsi had already been massacred."[37] In remote parts of the world where Western governments do not invest significant resources in intelligence assets, argued Kuperman, "the news business is relied on to serve as a surrogate early-warning system. In Rwanda, it did not fulfil this role."[38] He pointed to four substantive lapses of the media: mistaking the genocide for a civil war; reporting that the violence was subsiding when in fact it was escalating; grossly underestimating the death toll—sometimes by a factor of ten; and failing to report on what was taking place beyond Kigali.[39]

Elite Opinion, Congressional Behavior. Other voices to shape public attitudes had come from editorial boards and op-ed writers in the elite print media. In a stark contrast to those on Bosnia, wrote Power, op-eds on Rwanda were silent for three months: "Silent, ignorant, and prone to accept the futility of outside intervention."[40] Even though the term "genocide" did make it into *Washington Post* and *New York Times* editorials, the message by the end of April was something like: this seems to be genocide, but all that the world can do is "stand aside and hope for the best."[41]

Historian Stephen Wertheim also pointed to editorial despondency. To justify their support for the US policy of nonintervention, he wrote, editorials in the *Washington Post*, *New York Times*, and *New Republic* invoked lack of national interest and intervention risks and questioned the ability of military measures to "resolve complex political problems."[42] At no time did any of the editorials link the possibility of a US intervention to the genocidal nature of the events. According to Wertheim, though, even after the reality of genocide had been acknowledged, public pressures for armed intervention remained inconsequential.[43]

Not only were the editorials silent on intervention, but according to Robinson their trivialization of the events (as a regular round of tribal bloodletting) reduced for the public the sense of responsibility and desire to "do something."[44] In the absence of elite dissent, few voices were heard to challenge or criticize the official policy, further reinforcing the determination inside the Clinton administration to minimize their engagement with the conflict.[45] When asked, some policymakers and legislators had the public in mind. "Make more noise," said national security adviser Anthony Lake to representatives from Human Rights Watch who wanted to know what else they could do to change the policy.[46] Similar sentiments were expressed on Capitol Hill, where a near absence of congressional dissent was constraining public and media pressures.[47] Senate majority leader Bob Dole, who at the time had been campaigning for a US intervention in Bosnia, argued that the United States had no national interests in Rwanda, and once the American nationals living there were evacuated, the United States should end its involvement.[48] Power highlighted a host of factors that had combined to deter a congressional push for action, including objections from the Pentagon, the effects of Somalia, the likely costs, the absence of attractive policy options, failure to understand what was going on, not hearing from the constituents, the higher salience of Haiti, and absence of an American angle to the story after the evacuation and of a Tutsi diaspora to lobby for action. As a result, a few isolated attempts by members of Congress to push back against the sham policy were easily deflected by the administration.[49]

Somalia, Not the Holocaust. As discussed in the previous chapter, the belated capitulation of the White House to the appropriateness of the genocide label in Rwanda did not lead to meaningful behavioral changes among the elites, the media, or the general public, at least not until after the genocide had ended and a communal sense of guilt had prompted the United

States to orchestrate a humanitarian rescue mission for the masses of Hutus fleeing Rwanda to Goma, Zaire.[50] As pointed out by Power, the analogy that had gripped Americans' imagination was Somalia, not the Holocaust.[51] It was Somalia that had shaped responses to the events, agreed Wertheim, but underneath it was the absence of a normative commitment to stop genocide.[52] "Americans did not yet feel their government had a duty to attempt forcible intervention to stop genocide. . . . Existing humanitarian interventionist impulses did not amount to a principle, far less a policy, that genocide must be stopped, simply by virtue of being genocide."[53]

The Effects of a Society-Wide Silence. It should be clear by now that the domestic mood in the US during the genocide did not come across as supportive of an American involvement. According to Power, officials throughout the system were making their decisions with one eye trained on what the public would abide. But none of the indicators they had been monitoring—"op-ed pages of the elite journals, popular protest, or congressional noise"—made them apprehensive about the political costs of doing so little.[54] Consequently, as soon as the evacuation of US nationals was complete, one week into the genocide, the Clinton administration turned its attention to other matters. The president never assembled his top policy advisors to discuss policy options, nor were other high-level meetings convened. A weak statement by Anthony Lake constituted the only proclamation from a senior official on the ongoing crisis. As hundreds of thousands of innocent civilians, including children and babies, were being hacked to death, the United States failed even to engage in nonmilitary responses, such as invoking and denouncing genocide, threatening prosecution, supporting the UN forces on the ground, expelling Rwanda's ambassadors to the United States and United Nations (during the genocide), or electronically jamming hate-radio incitements carried out by the perpetrators.[55] Instead, the administration played a key role in withdrawing the only willing rescuers in Rwanda: the UN peacekeepers. It also prevented, together with the United Kingdom and China, the inclusion of the term "genocide" in a diluted UN Security Council (UNSC) presidential statement, issued 30 April 1994.[56]

CNN Effect? Despite the consensus on the international media's failure to cover the genocide, disagreements existed over the consequences of these failures. Journalist and scholar Linda Melvern wrote, "In the years since the [Rwandan] genocide, the shortage of accurate media coverage has been placed high on the list of reasons for Western inaction. One international report concluded that the Western media's failure to adequately report that genocide was taking place, and thereby generate public pressure for

something to be done to stop it, had contributed to international indifference and inaction, and possibly to the crime itself."[57] In contrast, according
to media and public affairs scholar Steven Livingston, media coverage does
not decide interventions. The most it can do is to increase the prospects for
a reversal in public support—for example, in response to mounting casualties.[58] In Rwanda, he wrote, a low media salience had reduced the potential
for a CNN effect.[59] The prospects for a media-induced policy change during the genocide were dismissed also by Robinson. Although the "distance
framing" by the media did support official inaction, he argued, a strong
official certainty *against* intervention would have still precluded a policy
reversal, even if the coverage had been more empathetic.[60]

Bosnia

In contrast to Rwanda, the US dynamics over Bosnia between 1992 and
1995 were characterized by strong periodic pressure for some form of action.
These spikes in domestic reaction helped to affect changes to American
policies on at least three occasions: (1) the Bush administration's decision to
extend logistical support and later intervene in another crisis, in Somalia
(August–November 1992), allegedly to avoid having to intervene in Bosnia;
(2) the Clinton administration's threat to bomb Bosnian Serb forces around
Sarajevo (1994), which led to their temporary withdrawal; and (3) NATO's
aerial bombing campaign against the Bosnian Serbs, which ended the war
(1995). These three decision-making junctures are discussed next.

Bosnia to Somalia (July–December 1992). During the early months
of the Bosnian civil war the Bush administration had framed the crisis as an
intractable, tragic, but unavoidable explosion of "ancient hatreds" that could
lead the United States—if it chose to intervene—into a Vietnam-style
quagmire.[61] According to Jon Western, most Americans had accepted that
frame. Members of Congress and the news media initially deferred to the
administration's superior knowledge of the events. The few who thought
otherwise lacked the organizational and political base to mobilize public
opposition to the official narrative and policy.[62] However, in August 1992,
the administration's frame was increasingly being challenged by independent reports, including the discovery of Bosnian Serb–run concentration
camps.[63] Domestic pressures ensued that favored a US intervention or at
least the lifting of the arms embargo that had disadvantaged the Bosnian
Muslim side. Media reports began applying Holocaust metaphors and imagery to the crisis, changing the frame from a spontaneous burst of violence to
a systematic campaign organized by radical Serb nationalists.[64] The coverage boosted public support for international airstrikes and even for sending
US ground troops as part of a UN intervention.[65] In the months that

followed, the pressures from the media were heightened by criticisms from Democratic presidential contender Bill Clinton, NGOs, State Department dissenters, congressional liberal humanitarians, hard-line interventionists, and other foreign policy elites critical of the Bosnia policy.[66] The Bush administration and the Joint Chiefs of Staff led by Colin Powell found themselves having to defend the official position again and again.

One solution to the pressure was to deflect attention from Bosnia by changing gears in the US response to the Somali crisis, which had been unfolding since 1991.[67] On 14 August 1992, President Bush authorized a limited logistical air support for the UN mission in Somalia. Modest as the step was, it is said to have resulted in a 66 percent drop in the coverage of Bosnia in the evening news during the second half of August compared to the first half.[68] On 25 November 1992, after an abrupt about-face by the Joint Chiefs, President Bush ordered a ground deployment of US forces to Somalia. These changes to the administration's policy were alleged to have been induced by pressure from the public and by a desire to sidestep a much riskier intervention in Bosnia.[69] Domestic political imperatives therefore might have helped to counterbalance the absence of "hard" national interests for intervention in Somalia.

The Sarajevo Marketplace Massacre (5 February 1994). Another spike in public response came more than a year later, following a mortar attack on a market in Sarajevo that killed sixty-eight Bosnian civilians and wounded over a hundred. According to Piers Robinson, extensive coverage of the event by the US print and electronic media combined with policy uncertainty to produce a strong CNN effect and consequently another change in US policy.[70] An American ultimatum that included a threat of the use of force, led the Bosnian Serbs to withdraw their heavy weapons from the hills around Sarajevo and averted the fall of the city.

The NATO Air Campaign after Srebrenica (July–November 1995). On 11 July 1995, the town of Srebrenica—one of six "safe zones" that the UN undertook to protect—fell into the hands of advancing Bosnian Serb troops. NATO's "close" air support—constrained by ineffectual command and control procedures and a reluctant UN chain of command—proved powerless to deter or stop the attack.[71] A resident UN peacekeeping force of six hundred Dutch personnel was overrun and, under questionable circumstances, chose to cooperate with the Serbs.[72] In the following days up to eight thousand Bosnian Muslim men and boys were mass murdered in what later was determined to have been the only genocidal massacre of the civil war.

After Srebrenica, pressures for action descended on Clinton from as far and wide as Congress, the United Nations, NGOs, the US media, and America's

European allies. A coalition of elite and grassroots organizations—activists, journalists, op-ed columnists, religious organizations, former administration officials, and members of Congress from both parties—all "erupted in unison, making life unbearable for the White House."[73] Holocaust analogies and invocations of "genocide" began reappearing in the op-ed pages of the elite press, next to and at times together with angry realpolitik critiques. Senior commentators and other heavyweights to criticize the administration included Anthony Lewis, George Will, Charles Gati, Newt Gingrich, Jacques Chirac, Richard Holbrooke, George Soros, and Scott Simon. However, unlike during 1992, the main targets of the criticism this time were not the Serbs but the United States and its allies—the moral gist being that together with the Europeans "the United State was *again* allowing genocide to proceed."[74] A coalition of twenty-seven human rights NGOs issued a press release demanding a humanitarian military intervention—some of them for the first time ever. The proclamation noted, "Force must be used to stop genocide."[75] The media's reporting highlighted the failure of the West to defend Srebrenica and empathized with the victims. More than three years into the civil war, this coverage, coupled with policy uncertainty, produced, according to Robinson, another CNN effect and a third change in US policy.[76] While the invocations of genocide and Holocaust analogies did not create the CNN effect, they almost certainly helped to reinforce it.

Domestic politics played a key role in the policy change. With Senate majority leader Bob Dole, a main contender for the 1996 presidential election, appearing bent on setting Srebrenica as a central policy issue, this was in Power's words "the first time in the twentieth century that allowing genocide came to feel politically costly for an American president."[77] The image said to haunt Clinton the most was of US ground forces coming under attack while assisting a UN withdrawal. Earlier, he had committed to send troops if UN peacekeepers became stranded and in need of extraction. Making matters worse, America's European allies had threatened to withdraw should Congress lift the arms embargo from the Bosnian Muslims— and this was indeed happening. Harnessing a broad Democratic dissent, Dole led a successful bipartisan campaign to unilaterally revoke the embargo. On 1 August 1995, the bill was passed by both Houses with a veto-proof margin.[78] Attacked from all sides, Clinton was said to face a crisis of American leadership.[79]

Within days the administration had rushed through already ongoing preparations for a policy change. On 29 August 1995, in response to another high casualty bombing of Sarajevo, NATO forces, led by the United States, began a series of air strikes against the Bosnian Serb forces.[80] As told in

Chapter 3, the campaign lasted three weeks and resulted in Serb capitulation and a peace agreement.

Many recurring and case-specific factors had combined to influence Clinton's decision to intervene: the domestic and international consensus for action; the need to reclaim America's leadership, repair NATO's credibility and improve the relationship with the alliance; Bob Dole's commitment to Bosnia; and the risk of being asked to evacuate the UN peacekeepers. Other incentives included the low risk to interveners in high-altitude aerial bombings; the fact that, having left Serb-controlled areas, UN troops could no longer be used as collateral damage; optimistic assessments of the prospects of success (Croat victories over the Serbs had served to refute alarmist assessments from the Pentagon); declared French readiness to intervene that had undermined the strategy of hiding behind European and United Nations' reluctance to act; and a desire to deter future perpetrators.

That so much leverage was required to tilt the scales is nothing short of discomforting. Still, the important question is how instrumental the US public's anger over the failure to stop a genocidal massacre in Srebrenica was for the policy change. A definite answer has been hard to come up with. What can be said is that invocations of genocide and Holocaust analogies helped mobilize the media, Congress, political elites, and to some extent the citizenry for a popular revolt against three and a half years of largely ineffective policies, of strategic failures that saw a crisis, allegedly marginal to the United States, turn into one that had threatened the nation's interests and unnerved the presidency.

OPINION VERSUS BEHAVIOR

The evidence examined thus far appears to back the claim of a professed US public support for strong action on genocide.[81] If the polls were to be trusted, most Americans would have even supported dispatching US ground troops for such a purpose, especially as part of a multilateral, UN-authorized mission. Yet the analysis also confirmed the existence of a gap between public opinion and public behavior—particularly, but not only, in relation to Rwanda. The voiced support for a robust response to the genocide did not translate into large protests, mass rallies, petitions, letter writing campaigns, or other grassroots actions.[82] In fact, given the elite support for US *inaction*, public behavior or its absence could have been read by the Clinton administration as acquiescence and, years later, by Power and others as an example of society-wide silence. As noted, the silence continued even after the administration had stopped eschewing the term "genocide," suggesting a low impact of the narrative. Still, as Clinton's acknowledgment was belated and a little more than a side note amid rapidly moving events, it could have been easily missed or belittled by the media and consequently by the public, particularly since the legitimacy of the label was no longer being questioned at that time.

There was no society-wide silence over Bosnia. As discussed, domestic pressures for stronger action began as early as August 1992 with the discovery of the concentration camps, escalated again in February 1994 after the Sarajevo marketplace massacre and in the aftermath of Srebrenica in July 1995. Even outside these peaks, different factors combined to sustain media, elite, and general public interest in the crisis. Highly influential was the direct personal exposure of some journalists, members of Congress, and even administration officials to the suffering on the ground. Emotive catch-phrases in the reporting such as "the worst atrocities in Europe since World War II," emerging from the modicum of media access to the region, had their effects also. The public's engagement with the story included periodic pressures for action that did make a difference but that until Srebrenica could not tip the scale in favor of a meaningful military intervention.

Two primary reasons for the stronger pressures over Bosnia were the duration and speed of events—three and a half years, compared to three months in Rwanda—and the location—Europe versus Africa.

In the case of the former, it takes time to mobilize a community for a cause, and unless a constituency already exists, then in the absence of other strong imperatives for action, relying on the public to affect a quick policy change from inaction to action would be overly optimistic. As to the latter, while not surprising it was still vexing to concede that the mass killing of *white* Europeans—albeit Muslims—generated much stronger identification and empathy in Americans than the extermination of many more black Africans.[83] Third, putting on the table aerial strikes rather than a high-risk ground intervention boosted public support for action in Bosnia, whereas in Rwanda intervention by land was presumed to be inescapable. Public assertations about the manageable risks of ground intervention in Rwanda were made only after the genocide. Consequently, the gap in relation to Bosnia was more about public attitudes versus government priorities than between public opinion and public behavior.[84] Inconsistencies between opinion and behavior were influenced possibly more by fluctuations in crisis salience and wordings of survey questions than by gaps in the policy preferences of the citizenry.

Manifestations of public behavior do not necessarily reflect public opinion and vice versa, particularly in relation to an intensely normative policy issue such as responses to genocide. Clearly, it is easier to express moralistic views than to follow them up with deeds. The more the public is led to believe that translating moral values to action could be costly or risky for the United States, the more reluctant it is likely to be to act on these values.

A critical question then is who gets to inform the public about what the costs and risks of alterative policy options are and whom the public trusts enough to receive this information from.

A final factor to consider in relation to the divergence between Rwanda and Bosnia is that of opposing signals from mass and elite opinion. In the case of Rwanda, America's elites objected to military intervention; in relation to Bosnia, many of them supported some form of strong action. The media coverage of elite dissent over Bosnia may have increased the sense in the general public that something could and should be done to stop the killings.[85] Obviously there was not much time for similar attitudes to develop over Rwanda. A question for further research then pertains to the spread of attitudes across mass and elite opinions and their respective influences on policies.

Understanding the Opinion-Behavior Gap

What factors accounted for the opinion–behavior gap? Some elements have already been discussed whereas others have not. In the case of opinion, Americans' exceptionalist view of their nation had stood in sharp contrast to a growing number of US "failures" to stop genocide. At the personal level therefore, "morally correct" responses to polls may have reflected conscious or half–conscious attempts by the respondents to uphold a righteous self–image. But when it came to taking action (i.e., behavior), standing up to government policies would have required sustained efforts and commitment that most citizens may have been reluctant to invest, particularly when not knowing exactly what to do. Other inhibitors to active dissent included doubts about the effectiveness of a US involvement; self–skepticism about the citizenry's ability to affect policy changes; the absence of political leadership to galvanize the opposition; flawed media coverage; the effects of compassion fatigue; reluctance to bear likely risks and costs of military interventions for humanitarian purposes; and deliberate official framing of information in line with preferred policies. A last constraint on public involvement to mention has been the low identification and hence little empathy experienced by the American citizenry in many past situations for the suffering of distant "others."

On Empathy. Sociopsychological studies of the motives behind individual personal donations to help victims of natural and human–caused disasters have offered important insights into the causes and effects of identification with and consequent empathy toward strangers. Predictably, identification has featured high in decisions to give to charities. The strength of identification was found to depend on such factors as the number of victims, levels of physical and psychological proximity between donors and victims, and in–group outgroup relationships.[86] Other decision factors included knowledge of the event and familiarity with its whereabouts, mutual influences of social groups, views concerning international responsibility, and perceptions about victims' commitments to improving their situation.[87] Important insights were gained also by studying differences in donors' attitudes between natural disasters and human-caused atrocities. Persisting preferences to support the former over the latter were found to reflect assumptions often made by donors about the blameworthiness of victims. That is, in contrast with "perfectly blameless" images of natural disaster victims, the complexities inherent in violent conflicts had raised questions, particularly among uninformed donors, about a possible culpability of the victims in the violence. Significant also may have been the sense that while donations directly responded to the needs of natural disaster victims, they could not address the underlying causes of mass violence in any significant way.

Analyses of donation decisions offer but a narrow perspective on public reactions to mass atrocities. Their main value is in identifying potential directions for further research, such as the roles of identification and empathy.[88] For example, important research by Paul Slovic and others has suggested that while high numbers of casualties could capture the attention of governments and the media, it may have a numbing effect on publics.[89] In experiments, ordinary citizens have shown greater willingness to make charitable donations to one distant victim over two, and to two victims over four. By the time the number of victims had reached thousands or more, their plight had become a statistic.[90] The strongest empathy is generated in the human mind toward a single individual, and so as large-scale atrocities are less easy to personalize in media reporting they may attract lower levels of empathy from the public. Add "compassion fatigue," that is, audiences (mainly in the West) switching off in response to the frequency of the stories, the unpleasantness involved in hearing about the suffering, and frustrations over re-erupting violence, and the difficulty to harness active citizenry support for action becomes clearer.[91]

Misreading or Ignoring the Public? In Chapter 2, I alluded to two likely explanations for the discrepancies between official policies and public preferences, which I had labeled misreading and ignoring the public. Were Americans' attitudes toward Bosnia and Rwanda misread at the time by policymakers, as per Kull and Destler's findings presented in this chapter? Or were they ignored, as suggested by Page and Bouton as part of the "disconnect" theory (Chapter 2)? Two plausible and mutually inclusive scenarios may describe the opinion-policy relationship in our context: (1) administration officials had misinterpreted the polls as well as other indicators and concluded that the public did not favor intervention; (2) officials had concluded in some situations that the public *did* support strong action, but believing that the risks and costs outweighed the potential benefits and fearing a future reversal in domestic support for intervention, they ignored these signs and decided to manage the public instead. Either way, studying public *behavior* as a key indicator of public attitudes would have led officials to conclude in most cases that inaction was not likely to incur prohibitive political costs.

"READING" THE PUBLIC ON GENOCIDE

The genocidal character of the civil war in Rwanda was acknowledged by the Clinton administration, quietly, grudgingly, belatedly, but before the genocide had ended. In the case of Bosnia, this did not happen. However, in contrast, domestic pressures for robust US action had been periodically strong in relation to Bosnia but absent over Rwanda, even after the genocide label was officially recognized. Considering the wide range of factors that contributed to the inverse association between the two crises, the significance and extent of the term's impact on American foreign policy during the 1990s remains uncertain. Faced by contradictory signals from the citizenry, officials' readings of the public were likely affected by the imports they themselves had assigned to different indicators of professed attitudes and behaviours of mass and elite opinion. In the case of Rwanda, for example, prioritizing behavioral indicators over expressed opinions of the public would have led the Clinton administration to conclude—in hindsight justifiably—that the political costs of inaction could be managed. Such a prioritization was therefore consequential. Looking ahead, real time study of decision makers' analyses of domestic attitudes should be assigned greater attention. In particular, closer attention should be paid to anticipated public behaviors as dominant indicators of the effects of public opinion on US policies. The making of the Darfur policy, explored in the next two chapters, adds additional insights to our understanding of the relationship between opinion, behavior, and policymaking in the context of responses to a distant genocide.

CHAPTER 5

America and the First Genocide of the Twenty-First Century

THE FLARE-UP in Darfur in early 2003 had arrived at a time of change in the discussion of international responses to domestically perpetrated mass atrocities. After a decade of intervention debates and continued failures to act, NATO's unauthorized air campaign in Kosovo (1999) was alleged to have introduced, post facto, a new if contentious approach to the tension between legality and morality concerning action. The UN Commission assigned to investigate the intervention described it in hindsight as illegal but legitimate.[1]

It may be argued that the decision to use force reflected not substantive changes but a rare accord between moral imperatives and the interests of power: that is, fears of a regional escalation and others. However, the intervention did establish two significant precedents. First, for good or bad, neither Russia's veto power at the UN Security Council (UNSC) nor the restrictions imposed by the UN Charter on unauthorized uses of force were able to protect Serbia's president Milosevic from a military response to his transgressions. Second, it was shown that when championed by influential actors, moral arguments could help advance a popular legitimacy for strong action—at least in some parts of the world. Although legitimacy may not necessarily result in action, it is an important requisite for mobilizing political will. At the end of the day it had become clear that the international order *is* malleable to the devices of power, even if sometimes in unexpected directions.

While Kosovo's repercussions were being debated, the "Responsibility to Protect" initiative, co-sponsored by UN secretary-general Kofi Annan and the Canadian government, was gaining international traction. However, the optimism inside the humanitarian interventionist camp was soon to diminish, once America's so-called just war in Iraq began to lose whatever legitimacy it had had at its early stages. Under these conditions, the international response to the erupting violence in Darfur—on the heels of a supposedly winding down genocidal civil war in Sudan between the North and the South—was anything but preordained. By the second quarter of 2004, as Western media's coverage of the crisis was beginning to grow, the first humanitarian intervention debate of the twenty-first century was about to begin.

FROM THE GENOCIDE CONVENTION TO DARFUR

More than half a century passed between the signing of the Genocide Convention in the UN General Assembly and Colin Powell's determination of genocide on Darfur. Yet even after the determination had been made, the actions taken by the Bush administration were still too weak to halt or significantly curb the violence in this western region of Sudan. This chapter explores the determining factors, influences, and circumstances that had surrounded the formulation of the US Darfur policy during 2004. It offers a timeline of reactions to the crisis before, during, and after the September genocide determination—from the White House, the State Department, and Congress, but also by media outlets, civil society organizations, and key actors outside the United States. The inquiry covers discourses about the nature of the crisis; the US interests involved; alternative policy options and the benefits, costs, and risks they portended; and different perceptions of America's moral, legal, and political obligations to help stop an ongoing genocide.

RESPONSES TO DARFUR

Early Warnings

The violence in Darfur erupted in April 2003, following a surprise rebel attack on a Sudanese Army station at El Fasher Airport. The assault was carried out by insurgency groups, mostly from ethnically African tribes of the region—disgruntled after decades of political and economic marginalization by the political center in Khartoum.[2] The government retaliated aggressively, among other things by training and arming local militia mainly composed of ethnically Arab tribesmen known as the Janjaweed ("men on horses"). It then unleashed the Janjaweed against the "African" villages of Darfur, which it had accused of supporting the insurgency.[3] Overshadowed by the peace talks between the North and the South of Sudan, the evolving crisis remained invisible for months.[4] In July 2003 Amnesty International first broke the story in the West, warning of another crisis looming in Sudan and calling for an investigation of causes and solutions.[5] However, the report failed to make headlines—likely due to the "low" estimates of casualty numbers: still in the hundreds.

According to Gerard Prunier, the first foreign observer to grasp the real extent of the danger was Sudan expert Eric Reeves, who published an alarming analysis on the crisis on 8 October 2003.[6] In follow-up reports, on 24 November and 12 December, Reeves cited warnings of "ethnic cleansing" by foreign diplomats stationed in Khartoum.[7] On 18 December, Jan Egeland, UN undersecretary-general for humanitarian affairs, declared in a BBC radio interview that the humanitarian crisis in Darfur was being viewed by the organization as "probably the worst in the world."[8]

On 30 December, Reeves argued for the first time that the atrocities perpetrated by the Janjaweed militia and the Sudanese government had amounted to genocide. "Ethnic cleansing," he wrote, was being used as a "dangerous euphemism for genocide."[9] Over months, Reeves attempted to demonstrate the appropriateness of the genocide label in describing the events. He highlighted the ethnic identity of the target group, the systematic and deliberate nature of the violence, the number of casualties, and the complicity of the Sudanese government in the killings.[10] Western governments and the United Nations wished to avoid the genocide label, he reasoned, because of fear that a genocide determination would make inaction politically untenable for them.[11] Seeing few alternatives to military intervention, he believed that securing a genocide determination may be the only way to force the international community's hand. However, his attempts to attract media and public attention to the crisis were unsuccessful.

In early 2004 analyses of the US role in relation to the crisis, Reeves pointed to considerable delays in both rhetoric and actions by the State Department and President Bush's White House. On 21 January he argued that the United States and other international actors had been for months hesitant to call out Darfur, for fear of upsetting the North-South peace negotiations.[12] Six days later he wrote, "No voice is more powerful than that of the US; no silence more consequential."[13] In February, Reeves again criticized the State Department's "lack of voice": "So we are now hearing the deathly sound of silence on the part of the Bush administration. The one State Department statement on Darfur [16 December 2004] was both tepid and largely inconsequential—and it was now a month and a half ago. In the interim, the crisis has exploded."[14] Between early January and 7 April 2004 (the latter date marking President Bush's first and for a while only public statement on Darfur), no fewer than twenty-three increasingly alarming analyses were published by Reeves about the crisis.

Official US Responses

The US Department of State was made aware of the events in Darfur in October 2003, eight months after the eruption of the violence. The warning had come from senior USAID officials already engaged with the crisis.[15]

Two months later, on 16 December, the department issued an initial public statement on Darfur. The announcement cited reports of more than six hundred thousand internally displaced persons (IDPs), seventy-five thousand refugees in Chad, and as many as three thousand civilian casualties. It then called on the government of Sudan to "take concrete steps to control the militia groups it has armed, to avoid attacks against civilians and to fully facilitate the efforts of the international humanitarian community to respond to civilian needs."[16]

For a time, the Bush administration responded to the evolving crisis with quiet diplomacy and humanitarian efforts on the ground.[17] However, by the spring of 2004 the continued escalation, combined with the discovery of the crisis by Congress and the US media, led to a new, more confrontational US policy. On 3 February, USAID administrator Andrew Natsios issued a press release that contained estimates of more than a hundred thousand refugees in Chad, six hundred thousand IDPs in Darfur, and a total of three million people affected by the crisis. Speaking for the United States, Natsios warned of a looming human catastrophe and deplored what he had termed a continued pattern of indiscriminate attacks on civilians and gross abuses of human rights. He called upon all parties to abide by international humanitarian law and to facilitate immediate, safe, and unimpeded access of humanitarian organizations to all in need. The statement also included a vague US commitment to cross-border delivery of assistance: "The United States reaffirms its commitment to addressing the immediate protection and assistance needs of those in Darfur, as well as throughout Sudan, *including humanitarian cross border operations* if assistance cannot be provided through Sudan."[18]

On 11 March 2004, Charles Snyder, acting assistant secretary of state for African affairs, took to deriding the Sudanese government in testimony before the Subcommittee on Africa of the House International Relations Committee. "We have rejected the [Sudanese] government's claim that, while it may have originally supported the Jingaweit [*sic* Janjaweed], they are now out of its control," he said. "These militias are proxies for the government and Khartoum bears responsibility for their conduct, whether they say they have control or not."[19] According to Snyder, the Sudanese government had also been warned that the violence in Darfur would slow down the normalization process between the two countries, including the lifting of US economic sanctions long imposed on Sudan.[20]

Darfur Gets Public Attention

Between late March and early April 2004, a number of public statements—mostly in the context of the tenth anniversary of the genocide in Rwanda—began raising Darfur's visibility for the international media.[21] The first of these statements was made on 19 March by the UN resident and humanitarian coordinator for Sudan Dr. Mukesh Kapila. The crisis in Darfur, Kapila warned, was now "the world's greatest humanitarian and human rights catastrophe." "The only difference between Rwanda and Darfur" he said, was in "the numbers involved of dead, tortured and raped."[22] Speaking to the BBC Radio 4, Kapila noted, "I was present in Rwanda at the time of the genocide, and I've seen many other situations around the world and I am totally shocked at what is going on in Darfur. . . . This is ethnic cleansing, this is the world's greatest humanitarian crisis, and I don't know why the world isn't doing more about it."[23] In what could have reminded his listeners of the language of the Genocide Convention, he argued that more than just a conflict, this was "an organised attempt to do away with a group of people."[24]

On 31 March, in his opening remarks to the inter-Sudanese cease-fire talks in N'Djamena Chad, USAID official Roger Winter also warned of the repercussions of the rising death toll in Darfur: "Aside from the death, destruction, and long-term hostility that the conflict has already caused, our humanitarian experts believe that as many as 100,000 may die over the coming months in Darfur, even if a ceasefire is achieved this week. The toll will rise proportionate to any delays. The entire world will notice and react."[25] Back at the United Nations, after a briefing to the Security Council on 2 April, Undersecretary Egeland told reporters (again) that Darfur, which he now characterized as a case of "ethnic cleansing," was one of the world's worst and most neglected humanitarian crises.[26] The very next day, Human Rights Watch released a report that stated, "The Sudanese government is complicit in crimes against humanity committed by government-backed militias in Darfur."[27]

On 7 April, in a speech commemorating the tenth anniversary of the Rwandan genocide, Secretary-General Annan launched a five-point Action Plan to Prevent Genocide and highlighted Darfur as an urgent problem facing the international community. If humanitarian workers and human rights experts are denied free access to the region and to the victims, he said, the international community must be prepared to take swift and appropriate action. Not ruling out military action, he clarified,

By "action" in such situations I mean a continuum of steps, *which may include military action. But the latter should always be seen as an extreme measure, to be used only in extreme cases.* We badly need clear guidelines on how to identify such extreme cases and how to react to them. Such guidelines would ensure that we have no excuse to ignore a real danger of genocide when it does arise. They would also provide greater clarity, and thus help to reduce the suspicion that allegations of genocide might be used as a pretext for aggression.[28]

On the same day, the White House released President Bush's first public statement on Darfur. The communiqué condemned the atrocities and called on the Sudanese government to reign in the "local militias" responsible for the violence and to provide unrestricted access to humanitarian efforts. "The Government of Sudan must not remain complicit in the brutalization of Darfur," it concluded.[29] Less than twenty-four hours later, a US backed cease-fire agreement was signed in N'Djamena between the warring sides.[30]

American pressure continued. On 22 April, in an annual meeting of the UN's Human Rights Commission (HRC), the US delegation urged the assembly to condemn ethnic cleansing in Darfur and compared the atrocities to Rwanda's genocide. The US ambassador Richard Williamson told journalists, "Ten years from today the only thing that will be remembered about the 60th annual Commission is whether we stand up on the ethnic cleansing going on in Sudan."[31] Having failed to shake the HRC, Williamson was also the only one to vote against the weak concluding resolution that replaced a stronger draft initially submitted by the United States and the European Union.[32]

Following the increase in international attention, the handling of the US Darfur policy was reassigned to Secretary of State Colin Powell. On 18 May, in a speech to an audience of humanitarian NGO activists, Powell described Darfur as "one of the most serious crises on the face of the earth now."[33] He outlined US efforts in the region: getting aid in, logistically supporting the cease-fire monitoring teams, pressing the Sudanese government to reign in the "lawless" militia and ease humanitarian access, pushing the UN (Security Council) to issue a strong statement on the crisis, and mobilizing the international community for action. Addressing voiced concerns, Powell reassured the audience that Darfur would not suffer from the more prominent US-brokered North-South talks at Naivasha. "We have told the Government of Sudan that we will not normalize relations, even with an agreement at Lake Naivasha, until the crisis in Darfur is addressed," he said.[34] Similar pledges were frequently made by him in the months that followed.[35]

Oddly, a day after Powell's strong speech, the American public learned that the State Department had just removed Sudan from the list of countries considered uncooperative in the war on terrorism. Defending the decision, a State Department spokesman told the press that Sudan was removed from the list because of its "remarkable" information sharing with the United States, but that it was being kept on another list of state sponsors of terrorism.[36]

FROM ETHNIC CLEANSING TO GENOCIDE

On 23 May 2004, a report on the situation in Darfur by the well-respected NGO International Crisis Group reiterated the ethnic cleansing charges made by Mukesh Kapila, Jan Egeland, Human Rights Watch, and the US delegation to the UN HRC. "It is too late to prevent substantial *ethnic cleansing*, but if the UN Security Council acts decisively—*including by preparing to authorise the use of force as a last resort*—there is just enough time to save hundreds of thousands of lives directly threatened by Sudanese troops and militias and by looming famine," stated the report.[37] On 27 May, during a State Department briefing, Assistant Secretary Snyder ratcheted up the administration's rhetoric on the crisis, also referring to ethnic cleansing in Darfur.[38] Not long after, at a 7 June briefing prior to a G8 meeting, National Security Adviser Condoleezza Rice spoke about the disaster brewing in Darfur "for which the Sudanese government bears a lot of responsibility."[39] After the meeting, a mild joint G8 statement was followed up immediately by a much tougher one by the State Department: *We believe that the Government of Sudan is responsible for the humanitarian crisis and ethnic cleansing occurring there.* While all the parties to the ceasefire must end the violence and allow unimpeded humanitarian access to all those in need, the Government holds the additional responsibility of reversing the effects of the ethnic cleansing by supporting the voluntary return home of all displaced persons under conditions in which their security is assured."[40]

First UNSC Resolution on Darfur and More "Genocide Debate"

On 11 June 2004, fifteen months after the initial flare-up in Darfur, the UNSC finally passed a resolution on the crisis (UNSCR 1547). However, the resolution did little more than to express "concerns" about the situation and call for a cease-fire and a political settlement.[41] In an interview earlier that day with Marc Lacey from the *New York Times*, Powell was less restrained: "We kept pressing them [the Sudanese government] on a cease-fire, because there was little point in trying to get the aid in if there was nothing but violence at the other end of the aid pipeline, press them on bringing the Jingaweit [*sic*, Janjaweed militia] under control. Of course, they say that they're really not controlling them, but we have every reason to believe that these militias are being supported by various instrumentalities of the Sudanese Government."[42] Asked about the correct label for the crisis—"ethnic cleansing" or "genocide"—Powell refused to make a judgment: "These [rhetorical distinctions] turn out to be almost legal matters of definition and I'm not prepared to say what is the correct legal term for what's happening. All I know is that there are at least a million people who are desperately in need, and many of them will die if we can't get the international community mobilized and if we can't get the Sudanese to cooperate with the international community. And it won't make a whole lot of difference after the fact what you've called it."[43] The administration, he said, was already reviewing the question from legal and policy perspectives, but no decisions had yet been made about "whether all of the criteria that are used to make a determination of genocide have been met."[44]

On 15 June, in testimony before the Senate Committee on Foreign Relations, Subcommittee on Africa, USAID assistant administrator Winter added another ethnic cleansing characterization to the chorus.[45] However, two days later (17 June), in a surprise response to journalists' questions, Secretary-General Annan suddenly reversed his position on the nature of the crisis: "Based on reports that I have received, I cannot at this stage call it genocide," he said. "There are massive violations of international humanitarian law, but I am not ready to describe it as genocide *or ethnic cleansing* yet."[46] In a scathing piece the very next day, Eric Reeves accused Annan of expediently undermining any possibility of humanitarian intervention to stop the killing in Darfur. Noting that Annan's own undersecretary-general for humanitarian affairs had on more than one occasion labeled Darfur as ethnic cleansing, Reeves "wondered" whether the two men had been reading the same reports.[47] A week later (23 June), Pierre-Richard Prosper, US ambassador-at-large for war crimes, told Congress that the United States saw "indicators of genocide" in Darfur, but that the region must be "opened up" to the international community before this characterization could be confirmed.[48]

In a briefing the next day (24 June), State Department spokesman Richard Boucher pointed out that Darfur had been placed very high on Secretary Powell's agenda. The secretary had been conversing with Secretary-General Annan about the crisis for several weeks now, almost every day, he said.[49] According to Boucher, little progress had been made by Khartoum on the key issues of disarming the government-sponsored militias, easing travel restrictions on humanitarian workers, and reducing the violence. In fact, as many as twelve attacks by the Janjaweed had been reported over one week alone. When asked about "genocide" in Darfur, Boucher reiterated the department's stance: reaffirming "ethnic cleansing"; pointing to as yet insufficient evidence for a genocide determination; but in a distinct departure from the US rhetoric on Rwanda and Bosnia, refusing to rule out the possibility.[50]

Powell's Visit to Darfur—Efforts within a Narrow Self-Imposed Space for Action

During the last days of June 2004, the Bush administration pledged more humanitarian aid to Darfur, issued a joint (tepid) US–EU Declaration on the crisis, and dispatched Secretary Powell on a high-profile visit to Sudan (29 June—1 July).[51] The trip had attracted considerable attention from American and international media. On the way to Khartoum, Powell was asked by a journalist why it was so difficult to get the world to pay attention to catastrophes like Darfur and pointed back at the media:

> The United States has been in the forefront on this for a long time. . . . But sometimes people have to see it, they have to read about it, they have to see it on television . . . you have got to touch their consciences; you have got to touch their emotions. . . . *So, I want to bring attention to this* . . . by going out and seeing these camps . . . there are just so many other things going on in the world that tend not to make it as newsworthy as it should be. . . . [Events like Darfur do not] always make page one of a newspaper or the first two minutes of the evening news.[52]

In the months following the visit, Powell remained consistent in his public position: Darfur was a catastrophe to which only disarming the Janjaweed militias could offer a real solution.[53] "We have to fix the security situation in order for the humanitarian situation to resolve itself," he said.[54] Better humanitarian access was crucial to save lives but would not provide a lasting solution. The internally displaced and refugees had to leave their camps and go home, sooner rather than later; but for this to happen, the provision of security was essential.[55] Considering the size of the region, the logistical challenges, and the difficulty to put together a strong enough peacekeeping force, it was the Sudanese government that had to make this happen. "I cannot see, in my own mind," said Powell, "where . . . a peacekeeping force with the capability to sustain itself over such a large area would come from. So I believe the solution has to rest with the [Sudanese] government doing what's right."[56] Responding to a question on whether in light of the lessons from the Rwandan genocide the US military should be used to take out some bandits on horseback, Powell reiterated, "Right now, this is a matter for the Sudanese Government to handle. . . . This is a very large area. It is not a simple matter to think that there—you know, it is not a simple military solution that is at hand."[57]

Two kinds of leverage were needed to pressure Khartoum, said Powell: a threat of international sanctions and withholding the reestablishment of economic and diplomatic ties with the United States.[58] However, these pressures had to be continually "calibrated" to maintain both Sudanese cooperation and international legitimacy.[59] Overstretching the rope would be risky.

While arguing publicly that his visit to Khartoum had bought the international community assurances of cooperation, Powell continued to dodge questions about what the United States would do if Sudan did not meet its promises.[60] Since Khartoum had armed the militias, he responded on one occasion, they could disarm them. "[T]here [is] enough incentive for them. . . . And we're making it clear to them that there will be consequences if [they don't]."[61] While insisting that the United States would be satisfied not with promises but only with improved conditions on the ground, he claimed also that the effort had to be international, not solely of the United States.[62]

Military Intervention?

In a State Department press conference back in April, USAID administrator Natsios had been asked about the possibility of a military intervention for the delivery of humanitarian aid to Darfur but refused to endorse such an option. There were no alternatives to a successful implementation of the 8 April N'Djamena cease-fire agreement, he said.[63] Then, on 30 May, two former State Department officials in the Clinton administration, Susan Rice and Gayle Smith, published an op-ed in the *Washington Post* in which they called for stronger US involvement in Darfur through the Security Council. Their list of proposed actions included travel and financial sanctions, an oil embargo, the imposition of a no-fly zone, and an international humanitarian military intervention, supported by the United States. While arguing that America's overstretch in Iraq and elsewhere had made it necessary to recruit troops from European and other "capable" African countries, they did call for urgent military planning of a unilateral US intervention as a last resort.[64]

But as the complexities on the ground and the risks involved were becoming clearer, an outright military intervention was ruled out by most observers—mainly due to fears of casualties or failure but also for some the belief that not all nonmilitary options had been exhausted.[65] According to some sources, Defense officials in Washington were admitting as late as July that no immediate plans were being drawn for US troop deployment to Darfur, not even to support the delivery of humanitarian aid.[66] Speaking on 16 August about the risks of intervention, Powell cautioned, "This place is the size of—it's about 80 percent the size of Texas, around somewhere approaching the size of France, very rough country, no roads to speak of, rainy season. It would not be a simple military matter, and frankly, the way to solve it is using the government's forces, not bringing in an outside force that the government might well feel is violating its sovereignty, and then you have a new conflict on your hands."[67] Three widely cited constraints to action were the logistical challenges, the threat to civilian populations if intervention was to lead to the suspension of humanitarian aid, and the ease with which a Western-led military response could be portrayed by the Sudanese government as "another assault on Arabs and Muslims."[68]

"Genocide Debate"

During and following his Darfur visit, Powell was repeatedly challenged by the media over the question of genocide—often with references to the US failure in Rwanda.[69] His frequent response was that such a debate would undermine efforts toward saving the people of Darfur. "What we are seeing is a disaster, a catastrophe, and we can find the right label for it later," he said. "We've got to deal with it now. That's my focus."[70] The next day he added, "What's the point of arguing about whether all indicators [of genocide] have been met or not. . . . To spend a great deal of time arguing about the definition of what the situation is isn't as important as identifying where the people are who are in need, getting the supplies they need to them, getting them hope in the form of supplies, but hope in the form of security and hope in the form that they'll be able to return to their villages in due course."[71] When told that for many the US reluctance to use the label hearkened back to Rwanda, he responded defensively: "I don't think we have a problem of a Rwandan nature, where tens of thousands of people were lined up and slaughtered en masse," he said. "That is not what our problem is."[72] He cautioned also not to expect too much of a genocide determination. It may increase public exposure, he said, but it would not confer new powers or authority on the United States and others wishing to help the Darfuri people.

> I can assure you that *if all of the indicators lined up and said this meets what the treaty test of genocide is, I would have no reluctance to call it that.* And the fact that we have called it—have not called it that is not based on reluctance. This is not Rwanda ten years ago; it is Sudan now. There are some 75 camps under international supervision now. Thirty more will be under international supervision and support in the next month or so. . . . Now, *if it was a genocide and it met all the tests and we declared it that, we would certainly increase international pressure.* But whether we would be doing more than we are now doing is a question that I can't answer. *It doesn't open any real new authorities to me or give me any additional powers or responsibilities that I'm not now executing.*[73]

His insistence, however, seemed to have been lost on some. For instance, in a 21 July piece, the *Christian Science Monitor* cited a refusal by several NGOs to determine genocide because this would "compel a no-holds-barred intervention."[74]

Domestic challenges to the administration's policy were intensifying. On 15 July, John Kerry, the Democratic nominee for the upcoming US presidential election, added his voice during a speech in Philadelphia:

> I believe in the value of American leadership in the world. Today, a massive humanitarian crisis is unfolding in Darfur, Sudan, where

300,000 people or more may die in the coming months. This administration must stop equivocating. These government sponsored atrocities
should be called by their rightful name—genocide. The government of Sudan
and the people of Darfur must understand that America stands prepared
to act, in concert with our allies and the UN, to prevent the further loss
of innocent lives. *The United States must lead the UN Security Council in
sanctioning the planners and perpetrators of genocide and authorizing an international humanitarian intervention. As president, I will bring the full weight of
American leadership to address this crisis.*[75]

This constituted a shift in the position of the Kerry campaign, which earlier
had refused to support the call for a genocide determination. The next day,
the press confronted the White House about the speech, only to receive
evasive responses from Press Secretary McClellan:

Q: Yesterday, Senator Kerry criticized the administration's approach to
Darfur, saying it wasn't aggressive enough. He said there should be
humanitarian intervention, and there should be a clearer label of genocide. He says you're equivocating.

McCLELLAN: It's nice that he's decided to talk about it in an election year,
and—because this administration has been acting on this humanitarian
and security crisis. We have been—we have been—for quite some time,
we have been—the United States is leading the way when it comes to
addressing this situation and bringing the international community's
attention to it.

Secretary Powell went to the Darfur region to see, first hand, for
himself, the situation there. We've seen some mixed results from the
government. We have urged the government to take action to address
the security situation and to help allow for the aid to get to the people
who need it. And we are continuing to lead the way for the international community in addressing this issue. We are pursuing a resolution
at the United Nations that will continue to focus attention on this issue
and make sure that the—that it is addressed.

We welcome—we welcome him, all of a sudden talking about it in
an election year. But We've been acting on this for quite some time, and
the United States is leading the way to address this situation.

Q: He says you're equivocating on the question of whether it's genocide.

McCLELLAN: He's saying a lot of things in an election year, but look at the
actions that we are taking.

Q: Well, do you believe that it's genocide in Sudan?

McCLELLAN: We've addressed that issue previously. Secretary Powell has
talked about it, I've talked about it in briefings. Regardless of what you
want to call it, it is a humanitarian crisis and a security crisis that needs

to be addressed immediately. And that's why Secretary Powell visited the region at the direction of the President to bring attention to this issue, as well as to urge the government of Sudan to follow through on what they have committed to doing.

Q: But it's not genocide?

MCCLELLAN: I just addressed that.[76]

A Genocide Determination by Congress

On 22 July, a congressional resolution labeling Darfur as genocide was passed unanimously in both Houses.[77] Behind the resolution was a bipartisan group of legislators and civil society groups, long active on human rights violations in South Sudan.[78] Earlier, two Republican lawmakers, Senator James Brownback (R-KS) and Congressman Frank Wolf (R-VA), had joined Congressman Donald Payne (D-NJ) to bring to Capitol Hill firsthand reports of visits they made to Darfur.[79] Representative Wolf was the first but far from last to raise the charge of genocide;[80] by June, members from both sides of the aisle were using the term. Before that, on 17 May, House Concurrent Resolution 403, which condemned the Sudanese government for attacks against innocent civilians in Darfur, was passed.[81] On 25 June, a bipartisan roster of fifty-two senators sent a letter to Powell urging targeted sanctions, a travel ban, the freezing of assets, and increased assistance to Darfur and calling for a UNSC resolution on robust monitoring and peacekeeping.[82] On 22 July the engaged legislators, supported by other congressional activists, succeeded in passing the unprecedentedly strong genocide resolution in both houses. Among other things, the resolution called on the White House to make its own genocide determination on Darfur and to fulfill its legal obligation under the Genocide Convention of referring the case to the UNSC. It also urged the administration "to seriously consider multilateral or even unilateral intervention to stop genocide in Darfur, Sudan, should the United Nations Security Council fail to act."[83]

A Second Resolution by the Security Council

Soon after, on 30 July, the UNSC adopted its second resolution on the crisis under a UN Charter, Chapter VII mandate.[84] The resolution placed an arms embargo on all nongovernmental parties fighting in Darfur and called on Sudan to lift all restrictions on humanitarian aid. It also demanded that the government of Sudan disarm the Janjaweed and bring its leaders to justice, giving Khartoum thirty days to comply. If the deadline expired, the council would then assess if the progress was sufficient to prevent "further actions/measures" (according to Powell, gentler terms for sanctions).[85]

In the lead-up to the vote, the difficulty to secure multilateral consensus without giving up on the effectiveness of the resolution—particularly

regarding the ultimatum of sanctions—was becoming increasingly apparent.[86] Powell later described the challenge: "Well, you know, the UN is not
one single organization, it is an organization of sovereign nations, and specifically in the Security Council, each nation brings its own sovereign
interest to that. Our job, when we put forward a resolution, is to write the
resolution in such a way that it gets the maximum number of votes."[87] On a
quick tour of the Middle East, Powell faced serious difficulties in persuading
a highly suspicious Arab media that the Bush administration was not targeting the Sudanese people, as it was believed to be doing at the same time in
Iraq. His rhetoric had shifted frequently from conciliatory to indignant to
forceful.[88]

The efficacy of the Security Council resolution, while signaling an
upgrade in the international response to Darfur, was still widely contested.
Grilled by journalists the day after the UN vote, State Department deputy
spokesman Adam Ereli had difficulties explaining why the threat of an arms
embargo did not include the government of Sudan and what the United
States and the Europeans could do in the future against a likely Chinese
veto.[89] According to Bellamy and Williams, informal consultations after the
adoption of the resolution had indicated to the United States that there was
no real support in the council for implementing sanctions if the Sudanese
failed to meet the demands.[90]

August 2004 saw a drop in Powell's public rhetoric on Darfur—from
sixteen references in July (out of a total of forty-seven public comments,
statements, and/or interviews) to four (though out of twenty-six).[91] The State
Department and the White House continued to engage with the crisis, but
at a lower intensity—mostly through aid and sponsorship of the peace
talks.[92] On 5 August, the *Wall Street Journal* published an op-ed on Darfur
written by Powell that highlighted US efforts and international leadership.[93]
The media, enacting its role, had still followed the story, but interest was
down.

On 26 August, a few days before the expiration of the UNSC ultimatum to Khartoum, the international community was informed of a new
round of political talks in Abuja, Nigeria, under the auspices of the African
Union (AU) and with US backing.[94] Needless to say, the ultimatum was
never acted upon.

AN OFFICIAL GENOCIDE DETERMINATION

Earlier in July, the administration had responded to the pressures it was
under by launching an investigation into the allegations of genocide in Darfur. The study was conducted by the State Department–appointed Atrocities Documentation Team (ADT), based mainly on interviews of Darfuri
refugees in neighboring Chad.[95] The data gathered by the ADT were then

corroborated against satellite images and other information sources. While waiting for the results, Powell warned again against raising false hopes about the effects of a genocide determination: "There should be no illusions about making a determination of genocide activities. It doesn't open any new avenues to you that we are not already using. *There is no obligation under international law for us to do more than we are doing now.* And if there is more that we want to do now, we don't need a declaration of genocide to do that."[96] In response to another question, he quizzed, "For us to call it [Darfur] genocide . . . imposes a stigma from the United States on that government [Sudan]. But will that stigma cause the government to pull back or will it cause the government take a more positive action of the kind we're looking for? . . . My judgment [of whether or not to call it genocide], though, will be based on the facts, not the politics of calibration, as much as the facts given to me by my experts."[97] On 9 September, Powell gave his now well-known testimony before the Senate Foreign Relations Committee. He first acknowledged the steps undertaken by Khartoum to ease the humanitarian relief efforts, engage in peace talks, and support the deployment of AU observers and troops to monitor the cease-fire. However, concluding that no meaningful progress had been made to improve the security environment by disarming the militias or arresting its leaders, Powell went on to say,

> Mr. Chairman, there is, finally, the continuing question of whether what is happening in Darfur should be called genocide. Since the United States became aware of atrocities occurring in Sudan, we have been reviewing the Genocide Convention and the obligation it places on the Government of Sudan and on the international community and on the state parties to the genocide convention. In July, we launched a limited investigation. . . . Those interviews indicated: first, a consistent and widespread pattern of atrocities: killings, rapes, burning of villages committed by Jingaweit [*sic*] and government forces against non-Arab villagers; three-fourths of those interviewed reported that the Sudanese military forces were involved in the attacks; third, villages often experienced multiple attacks over a prolonged period before they were destroyed by burning, shelling or bombing, making it impossible for the villagers to return to their villages. This was a coordinated effort, not just random violence. When we reviewed the evidence complied by our team, and then put it beside other information available to the State Department and widely known throughout the international community, widely reported upon by the media and by others, we concluded—I concluded—*that genocide has been committed in Darfur* and that the government of Sudan and the Janjaweed bear responsibility—and *genocide may still be occurring.* . . . We believe the evidence corroborates the specific

intent of the perpetrators to destroy "a group in whole or in part," the words of the Convention. This intent may be *inferred* from their deliberate conduct. We believe other elements of the convention have been met as well. . . . The totality of the evidence from the interviews we conducted in July and August, and from the other sources available to us, shows that the Jingaweit and Sudanese military forces have committed large-scale acts of violence, including murders, rape and physical assaults on non-Arab individuals. Second, the Jingaweit [*sic*] and Sudanese military forces destroyed villages, foodstuffs, and other means of survival. Third, the Sudan Government and its military forces obstructed food, water, medicine, and other humanitarian aid from reaching affected populations, thereby leading to further deaths and suffering. And finally, despite having been put on notice multiple times, Khartoum has failed to stop the violence.[98]

Invoking Article VIII of the Genocide Convention, Powell called upon the UNSC to launch an investigation into "all violations of international humanitarian law and human rights law that have occurred in Darfur." Nonetheless, he then went on to say,

Mr. Chairman, some seem to have been waiting for this determination of genocide to take action. In fact, however, *no new action is dictated by this determination. We have been doing everything we can* to get the Sudanese government to act responsibly. So let us not be preoccupied with this designation of genocide. These people are in desperate need and we must help them. *Call it a civil war. Call it ethnic cleansing. Call it genocide. Call it "none of the above." The reality is the same: there are people in Darfur who desperately need our help.*[99]

Stressing that the genocide determination had been made by the United States alone, Powell concluded, "Before the Government of Sudan is taken to the bar of international justice, let me point out that there is a simple way for Khartoum to avoid such wholesale condemnation by the international community, and that way is to take action—to stop holding back, to stop dissembling."[100]

The same day, the White House released a commensurate statement from President Bush, which read in part,

As a result of these investigations and other information, we have concluded that *genocide* has taken place in Darfur. We urge the international community to work with us to prevent and suppress acts of genocide. *We call on the United Nations to undertake a full investigation of the genocide and other crimes in Darfur.* The Government of Sudan has not complied with UN Security Council resolutions and has not respected the

cease-fire which it signed. The rebels are also guilty of cease-fire violations and failing to carry out past commitments. *It is clear that only outside action can stop the killing.* My Government is seeking a new Security
Council resolution to authorize an expanded African Union security
force to prevent further bloodshed. *We will also seek to ban flights by Sudanese military aircraft in Darfur.*[101]

On 21 September, President Bush reaffirmed his administration's genocide
determination in an address to the United Nations: "The world is witness-
ing terrible suffering and horrible crimes in the Darfur region of Sudan,
crimes my government has concluded are genocide."[102]

What Ought the United States Do in Relation to an Officially Declared "Genocide"?

On 9 September, the day of Secretary Powell's testimony in Congress,
John Kerry once again challenged the administration's Darfur policy. The
United States and the UNSC "must decide whether to take action to halt
the killing in Darfur or remain idle in the face of the second African genocide in 10 years," he said. "If I were president, I would act now. . . . We
simply cannot accept another Rwanda. The United States should ensure the
immediate deployment of an effective international force to disarm militia,
protect civilians, and facilitate delivery of humanitarian assistance in Darfur. The US should lead the United Nations to impose tough sanctions."[103]
The speech sounded bold, but in fact added little to the measures already
endorsed by the Bush administration. Even the call for international peacekeepers was not new, merely a stronger reiteration of the initiative pursued
by the United Nations and the United States to upgrade the mandate of the
AU's monitoring force in Darfur to peacekeeping. In fact, Powell had
already mentioned the proposal in public more than once.[104] After the official genocide determination, Kerry remained on the offensive: "Now that
the Secretary Powell has finally acknowledged that genocide is underway,
we all want to know one thing: what is President Bush going to do about it?
The toothless resolution the Bush Administration brought to the Security
Council is not an acceptable response."[105] Kerry was not the only one to
wonder how the United States would follow up on the determination.[106] A
new spike in media interest provided the administration with wider audiences, but with some difficult questions to field as well. Powell continued to
engage with the crisis, but as he had said would happen, no notable changes
were made to the official policy.[107] Securing approval for sanctions by the
Security Council had remained a challenge. Isolated calls for a nonconsen-
sual and likely non–UNSC-authorized military action were again discounted by Powell on the familiar grounds of risks and difficulties.[108]

Stymied by Sudan's refusal to upgrade the AU mandate, Powell stopped mentioning even the possibility of an all-African peacekeeping mission.[109] In effect, the protection of the Darfuri people was left by default in Khartoum's ostensibly antagonistic hands.

Assailed by the media, Powell engaged again in extoling the administration's achievements, adding now the genocide determination to the tally: "As you may have noticed, we're the only ones who have declared it is genocide. None of the other major nations of the world have done so. None of the international organizations have done so. We called it the way we believe it is, based on the work that we did."[110] While continuing to argue that the decision had been based on facts and not politics, he nonetheless highlighted its contribution to elevating the visibility of Darfur.[111] "I think We've done a lot by our designation of genocide to focus attention on the actions of the Sudanese Government," he said.[112] Another time he argued, "[The genocide determination] doesn't generate any additional action. It generates additional political pressure and elevates the degree of seriousness and rhetoric, but everybody ought to be doing what they can now, no matter what you call it."[113] To justify the failure in the Security Council, Powell began to point a finger at other members, albeit in a nonmoralizing, matter-of-fact tone: "Well, you know, the Security Council is a body of 15 nations, and we put forward a strong resolution but you already see that there are a number of countries on the Council that don't want to see a resolution that tough and we're going to have to work our way through this, as an international body."[114] Some of these countries just don't like sanctions, he said, while others had "commercial interests that they thought would not be well served if they voted against Sudan's interest."[115] Still, he refused to endorse any analogies to Rwanda or the Holocaust, arguing that the United States and the international community were doing much more in relation to Darfur.[116] Thanks in part to his high-profile engagement with the crisis and his genocide determination, most journalists who interviewed Powell seemed sympathetic to the US official line and willing to assign the failure to act to external actors—the United Nations or other countries.[117]

On 30 September, Senator Kerry and President Bush faced each other for a presidential debate in Coral Gables, Florida. In this compelling setting, Kerry's position was less forceful. He rejected the idea of sending American troops to Darfur, citing the overstretch in Iraq and the ability to deploy the AU force if supported by the United States. He did invoke, somewhat loosely, a moral US responsibility to act—a recurring element in President Clinton's rhetoric that had been largely missing in the discourses of the Bush administration: "As President, if it took American forces, to some degree, to coalesce the African Union, I'd be prepared to do it, because *we could never allow another Rwanda. It's a moral responsibility for us in the world.*"[118]

In his turn, President Bush highlighted some of his administration's efforts in relation to the crisis, but while reiterating his genocide determination, he likewise refused to commit US troops to the region.[119]

Two More UNSC Resolutions, Powell Resigns, Darfur Drops below Radar

On 18 September, the UN Security Council adopted its third resolution on Darfur (UNSCR 1564), once again under a Chapter VII mandate. The resolution repeated previous demands for a judicial Sudanese investigation of the crimes committed and *urged* (not demanded) the cessation of military flights over Darfur. The council had also consented to a US demand for an international commission of inquiry into violations of international humanitarian law and human rights law in Darfur. Included in the resolution this time was a mild threat of sanctions against Sudan's oil industry and certain members of Sudan's government.[120]

Based on a later interview conducted with US ambassador to the UN John Danforth, the American efforts to pass a stronger resolution had failed because of objections from China, Russia, and Algeria.[121] The three, together with Pakistan, also abstained at the final vote, further weakening the resolution by signaling that the council was divided on the matter. Despite projecting a forceful position in the lead-up to the vote, the United States chose not to join the strong statements made by two nonpermanent council members—the Philippines and Romania. According to Alex Bellamy, the American motivation was to try to preserve the unity of the council.[122]

As had transpired before, no marked progress followed the new resolution. While Khartoum was improving its cooperation with the humanitarian efforts, security remained an acute concern.[123] Some voices, including Powell's, began apportioning partial responsibility for the slow progress in the peace process to Darfur's rebel groups.[124] The media spike that followed the official genocide determination had soon dissipated. Sixteen public references to Darfur by Powell during September 2004 (out of a total of forty-nine comments, statements, and interviews) became six in October (out of a total of forty-five), four in November (of forty-three), and five in December (of sixty-one).[125] Questions from journalists had changed from "certainly I must ask you about Sudan," or "First, Sudan," to "One last question about Sudan."[126] In a mid-October interview with the Editorial Board of *USA Today*, America's largest daily newspaper, Powell did mention Darfur but was not asked a single question about the crisis.[127] Caught up in the home stretch of the 2004 presidential election, the Bush White House exhibited only limited interest in the situation.[128]

On 12 November, soon after President Bush won his second term in office, Powell "resigned" from his post as secretary of state and was preparing for the handover to Condoleezza Rice, scheduled for 26 January 2005.[129] It is difficult to appreciate the effects of the resignation on Powell's final days of handling the Darfur policy, primarily because on 26 December the Asian tsunami struck and everything changed. Despite a renewed escalation in violence during December, the crisis in Darfur was said to have dropped even lower below the radar of US and international media.[130]

For those eager to see progress on Darfur, the fourth UN Security Council resolution (19 November) was a bitter disappointment.[131] Its drafters did little more than echo old concerns and provide observations about the ongoing but ineffectual peace talks. With the Council shackled by threats of a Chinese veto and the AU and Arab League under the thumb of Sudan's allies, the AU Observer Mission's mandate remained limited to monitoring a nonexisting cease-fire and struggling to protect an inadequate flow of humanitarian assistance.[132] Despite promises from the United States and other powerful nations, the mission remained woefully and shamefully underresourced. Any upgrade to its make-up, size, or mandate required the consent of Khartoum, and obtaining this consent would take a few more years, many more political fights, and countless more fatalities.

TOUGH TALK, AND THEN . . .

This chapter explored discourses and actions of government officials and other domestic and international actors in relation to the crisis in Darfur. It looked at how these actors had framed the events, discussed costs and benefits of policies, and assigned credit and blame for action and inaction.

Compared with the 1990s, the US executive's response to Darfur constituted a mixed bag of old and new. Delayed reactions followed by evasions of declared positions were augmented by novel efforts—unrequited by other governments—to make the case for a concerted international action. Still, as in the past, the official priority continued to be "hard" interests first, everything else much later.

Secretary Powell's insistence that calling Darfur genocide would not lead to an upgrade of US efforts relied on a narrow legal interpretation of the Genocide Convention but constituted also a statement about the (in)significance of the term to political decision making. If the administration did not intend to upgrade its involvement, as admitted by Powell, it certainly would not have wished to be forced to do so over a genocide determination. Hence, long before the determination, Powell was already engaged in rhetoric that would allow him to sidestep a perceived US commitment to further action if "genocide" were to be invoked.

Unlike Clinton during the 1990s, President Bush and his staff avoided describing their efforts over Darfur as a moral responsibility of the United

States. The one to do so twice—presidential candidate John Kerry—did not follow his rhetoric with any meaningful alternatives to Bush and Powell's policy.[133] Absent political will to back up words with effective action, the tough language from the United States about the crisis—mainly from the State Department and Congress—could not make a significant contribution to halting the atrocities in Darfur, nor galvanize enough support for robust Security Council resolutions. Missing also were more palpable expressions of political leadership from President Bush—internal, domestic, and international—that might have further boosted the visibility of the crisis and Americans' willingness to bear greater costs and risks.[134] Despite Powell's good intentions and sincere efforts, no secretary of state could command as much public and bureaucratic attention as the US president.

In conceding that as the conditions on the ground precluded military intervention security in Darfur would have to be left in the hands of the Sudanese government—a government that, according to the United States, was guilty of genocide—Powell effectively exposed the unwillingness of the administration to do what was necessary to protect the Darfuri population. His account of the sticks and carrots meant to persuade Khartoum to do "the right thing"—that is, weak sanctions and a promise to restore diplomatic and economic ties—left the American policymakers with very little room for maneuver.[135] Internationally, the dynamics in the Security Council had made it clear to everyone that at least some of its members, including veto-yielding China and Russia, would not support the enforcement of any meaningful sanctions on Sudan. Powell's domestic damage control turned then to blowing the administration's own horn and, after the second disappointment at the UNSC, to rolling the blame unto other states.

Besides analyzing the framing and content of the administration's discourse, the inquiry also looked at the volume of coverage. Between October and December 2004, a drop in the frequency of Powell's public remarks suggested a possible decision to try to reduce the visibility and thus salience of the crisis. Earlier, from April to September, little was found to suggest that the administration was trying to talk down the crisis, reduce its salience, or downscale its involvement in it. In fact, if anything, it may have been the opposite. During these months, media interest and congressional "noise," together with an apparent desire to come to the rescue of the Darfuri people and a likely calculation that success was possible, had motivated the administration to pay greater attention to the events.

Still, in conveying to the public an image of substantial constraints, few obligations, and a limited set of policy options, administration officials likely saw their space for action as narrow: constrained by the conditions on the ground, international circumstances, and the modest resources they were willing or thought they were able to expend. Therefore, they kept the gap between rhetoric and action relatively small. Still, while the avoiding of promises for strong responses would have been domestically safer, the drawbacks were no less consequential. By unequivocally dismissing journalists' questions about a coercive response, Powell and other officials had weakened, likely, their leverage and made it easier for Sudan to resist the pressures. To be sure, the pitfalls of coercive diplomacy could lead to situations where you might be damned if you do but damned also if you don't. The one notable exception to the restrained US policy was the decision to issue the genocide determination. The motives for and implications of this decision are discussed in the following chapter.

Mitigating Political Risks

The main objective of this chapter was to learn how imperatives and constraints to the US policy on Darfur were integrated in or omitted from official discourses and public debates over America's legal, moral, and political obligations toward a situation described by the Bush administration as genocide. Despite the tragic outcomes of the failed response, the administration's relatively bold rhetoric and discernible efforts to muster international support for action were sufficient to portray Team Bush to the media and the US public in a favorable light and, following the genocide determination, to shift the blame to other actors. These few months of reprieve, before the crisis had become intractable and the general public had lost a sense of urgency, provided space for the State Department to try out a limited set of actions without risking significant political repercussions. Interestingly, at no time did the administration attempt to reduce public perceptions of US obligation to act on the argument of no American interest to do so—a valued claim of the past.[136] At the same time, to openly admit that the United States would not act to stop genocide due to cold political calculations would not have made for solid public relations either.[137]

The next chapter builds on these findings to construct a clearer picture of the constraints, imperatives, and other decision factors that had influenced the making of US policy on Darfur during 2004. Its emphasis is directed again toward better understanding the strengths and weaknesses of the genocide label, the genocide determination, and the significance of official interpretations of public attitudes.

CHAPTER 6

Determining Factors in the Making
of the US Darfur Policy

IN A STUDY of the United States and Darfur, Stedjan and Thomas-Jensen highlighted three key incentives for US administrations to decide to engage with mass human rights violations overseas: security concerns, economic interests, and domestic political considerations.[1] As this chapter intends to show, intervention in Darfur during 2004 offered the United States neither significant economic gains nor security advantages. In fact, it was likely the opposite. First, a lenient treatment of Khartoum was seen to serve a key US objective—ensuring Sudan's cooperation in America's war on terror. Second, improved bilateral relations would have taken the US government a step closer to lifting the ban that prevented American oil companies and other businesses from competing in the Sudanese market.[2] Third, good relationships were important for increasing the prospects of a successful settlement of Sudan's North-South civil war, a key electoral objective of the Bush administration.

Gaps in the information available to us make it difficult to reconstruct the full scope of incentives and constraints behind the making of the US Darfur policy. However, we can explore and assess the effects of the factors we *do* know about. In the first part of this chapter I outline seven constraints to strong action, two of them pertaining to the influence of the genocide label. Next, after examining motivations and competing impacts of the US genocide determination on the Darfur policy, I then reconstruct a rough approximation of how administration officials might have experienced public opinion and public behavior during 2004 in relation to the crisis. These factors and dynamics are then incorporated into a final analysis of US policy on Darfur.

CONSTRAINTS TO US ACTION ON DARFUR
Cooperation in the War on Terror
Commentators have pointed to the counterterrorism intelligence provided by Khartoum as a key constraint to a more forceful US Darfur

policy.[3] The effects were particularly significant owing to the centrality of
the "war on terror" theme in the 2004 presidential election later that year.[4]
The perceived value of Sudanese collaboration, wrote former NSC official
turned human rights activist John Prendergast, was strong enough to trump
humanitarian concerns for the administration.[5] Indicative of the attitude
was the already noted removal of Sudan from the US government's list of
States Uncooperative in the War on Terror, a decision announced in
May 2004 after Khartoum had already been accused of perpetrating ethnic
cleansing or even genocide in Darfur.[6]

The incoherence of the US Sudan policy was said to result partly from
its fragmentation into three separate tracks: intelligence cooperation, Darfur, and South Sudan. These were delegated to different government agencies, which operated at times at cross-purposes. USAID was tasked with
Darfur; the State Department worked on both the North-South negotiations and on Darfur but prioritized the former over the latter; and the CIA
was engaged in intelligence cooperation with Sudan.[7]

North-South Negotiations

A second constraint to the US Darfur policy was the administration's
interest in finalizing and then securing Sudan's Comprehensive Peace
Agreement.[8] Signed in January 2005, the accord ended two decades of
deadly civil war that included a genocidal campaign by successive governments in Khartoum against the ethnically African South. Strong pressures
from Christian groups in President Bush's core constituency and from
African American leaders, including the Congressional Black Caucus, had
brought the administration to invest effort, prestige, and diplomatic capital
in mediation and sponsorship of the agreement. Taking advantage of these
dynamics, the Sudanese regime was using the Comprehensive Peace Agreement as collateral against an interventionist US policy in Darfur.[9] Eric
Reeves wrote about the problem as early as 21 January 2004: "[A] suspension of or delay in the Naivasha process [the North-South peace negotia-
tions] gives wider scope for Khartoum to attempt to conclude the war on
its own savage terms, even as much of the international community hesi-
tates to speak honestly about the realities of Darfur for fear of upsetting the
Khartoum-SPLM/A peace negotiations."[10] The same tactics were highlighted by John Prendergast: "The [Sudanese] government wants to delay
the talks for as long as it can in order to continue its offensive in the western part of the country."[11] Prendergast criticized the international community's "quiet diplomacy" and urged the UK and US governments to
"make it clear to both parties that many of the incentives on the table
would be taken away."[12] Still, later promises by Powell that a North-South

peace agreement would not come at the expense of the Darfuri people were not kept.[13]

Iraq

A third factor behind the US dithering was the 2003 invasion of Iraq.[14] The American public's (justified) preoccupation with the war and its pro-tracted aftermath drew tremendous amounts of attention and resources from media outlets and politicians, leaving little to spare for Darfur.[15] No less influential, the resulting financial and military overstretch had all but precluded a simultaneous US-led intervention.[16] It was suggested that high-level Pentagon officials—longtime objectors to interventions for humani-tarian objectives—would not have supported sending troops to Darfur at such a time.[17] Finally, the attempts by the Bush administration to substitute a discounted WMD rationale for the war with a humanitarian pretext had weakened the moral standing of the United States, and consequently the international legitimacy for a US-led intervention.[18] Considering these cir-cumstances, Don Cheadle and John Prendergast's claim in their book about the US and Darfur that the American policy on the crisis was tailored to meet the limitations posed by Iraq might not be too far-off.[19]

International and Regional Backing for Khartoum

The support provided to Khartoum by China, Russia, and some non-permanent members of the UNSC was described earlier in the book.[20] Dip-lomatic backing also came from within the Arab League, the African Union, the Organization of Islamic Cooperation, and the Non-Aligned Movement and threatened to turn the international debate over Darfur into a West versus East or North versus South affair.

Sudanese Anti-intervention Campaign

Throughout 2004 the Sudanese regime carried out a counterinterven-tion campaign aimed at protecting its interests in Darfur. Tactics employed included leveraging economic and political interests of Security Council Members to ward off international sanctions;[21] agreeing to engage in peace negotiations to reduce the threat of intervention;[22] misrepresenting the vio-lence in Darfur as an extreme case of tribal conflict exacerbated by drought;[23] claiming that the situation was out of the government's control *despite* its best efforts;[24] playing the "sovereignty" card against external intervention; invoking African and Muslim solidarity to avert UN pressures;[25] using regional and anticolonial sensitivities ("African solutions to an African problem") to substitute a proposed UN peacekeeping mission with a weaker and easier to manipulate African Union observers' unit;[26] accusing the United

States of using false humanitarian pretexts to advance political interests, as it did in Iraq; closing Darfur to media to minimize the international community's knowledge of the situation and of the Sudanese government's involvement in the violence;[27] invoking Vietnam analogies to raise domestic fears inside the United States;[28] threatening to stir religious anti-Western animosity to weaken governments' motivation to send troops to Darfur;[29] impeding humanitarian relief operations, including encouraging or turning a blind eye to assaults on aid workers;[30] and staging mock demonstrations against a UN intervention.[31]

Put together these measures succeeded in spreading fears in many countries of the consequences of becoming embroiled in the crisis. It was argued that after years of testing the international community's resolve, the Sudanese government had learned to exploit the gap between rhetoric and action in responses to man-made atrocities.[32] Reportedly, the reluctance by the UN Secretariat and Security Council to take strong action against Khartoum was motivated by concerns about jeopardizing a future settlement or of risking further Sudanese obstruction of critical humanitarian aid work.[33] Remaining unclear, however, is how central these calculations had been to the UN inaction, as opposed to much less forgiving allegations of political expediency.[34] Either way, the outcomes for the civilian population of Darfur were still tragic. In almost a prophetic warning, former US ambassador to the United Nations, the late Richard Holbrooke, wrote in early April 2004 (without explicitly mentioning Darfur), "The lesson of each genocide is the same: The killing really takes off only after the murderers see that the world, and especially the United States, is not going to care or react."[35] It may indeed be argued that Sudan's successes in delaying, watering down, and disrupting the implementation of Security Council resolutions on the crisis have set a precedent that could undermine the council's authority and credibility in dealing with future situations. Perversely, these same concerns about the weakening of authority had been raised in the past *against* public shows of council disunity or of naming and shaming obstructionist council members.

The "Genocide Debate" and Fears of Overcommitment to Action

In a 2005 report to the UN Commission on Human Rights, special rapporteur on extrajudicial, summary or arbitrary executions Philip Alston alluded to the "genocide debate" on Darfur when he spoke of "excessive legalism which manifests itself in definitional arguments over whether a chronic and desperate situation has risen to the level of genocide or not." He then added, "While some insist that the term is clearly applicable and others vigorously deny that characterization, all too little is done to put an end to the ongoing violations. At the end of the day the international community must be judged on the basis of its action, not on its choice of terminology."[36]

Alston's apprehensions were echoed at different times by other scholars, experts, and diplomats.[37] "Genocide implies such enormous evil," wrote legal scholar Martha Minow, that the United States "would have had to be ready to commit as many troops, as much money, and as many diplomatic resources as might be necessary to stop it—with no assurances as to when or how such intervention would succeed."[38] Debating the use of the term should therefore not have taken such a high priority, as instead of reducing the impediments to mobilizing responses to Darfur the genocide determination may have increased them. The main obstacles to meaningful action reside elsewhere, Minow argued: in "apathy, fear, self-interest and perceived futility on the parts of national leaders and their constituents."[39]

According to David Scheffer, whether the genocide label had been applied to situations appropriately or not, some policymakers in the United States were still paralyzed by the presumption that any action on their part would obligate them, legally or morally, to a long-term commitment of significant resources.[40] The result, all too often, was an "intimidating brake on effective responses."[41] Scheffer listed various genocides and threatened genocides since the 1990s that had not been addressed appropriately by the United States, the United Nations, or NATO, arguably because of such concerns: the genocides in Rwanda, South Sudan, and southern Iraq; the Balkan wars; Burundi in 1993; the failure to use ground troops in Kosovo; and the ongoing situation in the DRC.[42] In Scheffer's opinion, the same fears had influenced also US unwillingness to take strong action on Darfur.[43]

Another commentator to express such concerns was legal scholar David Bosco.[44] In a 2005 piece in the *Washington Post* he argued, "The word genocide may be too powerful for its own good." Genocide conjures images of a "relentless and irrational evil that must be confronted massively," which are almost paralyzing. We are used to fighting crime, he wrote, but "genocide seems to require a crusade."[45] While genocide does carry a unique moral impact—and rightly so—Bosco warned that the concept and the interminable debate about its boundaries must not become the issue: "When the world chooses to immerse itself in terminology rather than take action, it does today's very real victims no good at all."[46]

The above concerns reinforce the possibility that notwithstanding the moral and legal imperatives for action triggered by the "G" word, invoking the term could increase political constraints on action.[47] However, it should be noted that once the official genocide determination had been made in the case of Darfur, the "genocide debate" in the United States had almost disappeared as a constraint to action—at least until March 2005 when the International Commission of Inquiry on Darfur issued its no-genocide determination.

The Commission on Darfur

One week after Powell's determination, a decision was taken by the Security Council to form a commission of inquiry that would investigate allegations of genocide in Darfur. Submitted in January 2005, the commission's findings were grave but fell short of determining that genocide was occurring or had occurred. Instead, the report concluded that crimes against humanity and war crimes had been committed that may have been "no less serious and heinous than genocide."[48] While no genocidal intent could be established in relation to central Sudanese government authorities, the report stated, it may have existed in individual cases—including among government officials. Yet such a determination should be made only by a "competent court" on a case-by-case basis.

The issuing of the report was followed by a short spike in the public debate over Darfur.[49] In one commentary in the *Chicago Journal of International Law*, legal scholar David Luban argued that the findings and the excessively complex language used to convey them had major consequences for international action.[50] Despite the commission's conclusion that the atrocities perpetrated were "no less serious or heinous" than genocide, he wrote, for the media—and consequently for the US public—this meant that the killings were not as "bad" as genocide, and both had lost interest in the crisis.[51] The UN, according to Luban, was also put in a difficult situation since "without the word 'genocide,' the mandate for action disappear[ed]."[52] He argued therefore that although the "no-genocide" declaration did not directly deflate the commitment to Darfur, it likely made the struggle more difficult by undercutting efforts of action groups to mobilize public and political support for their cause.[53]

THE GENOCIDE DETERMINATION ON DARFUR

As noted, the genocide-in-Darfur determination was the first of its kind in relation to an ongoing situation and had overturned a long-standing "unofficially official" US policy.[54] Presidents Ford and Carter refused to use the term for the killing fields of Cambodia; Reagan sidestepped it during the Anfal genocide in northern Iraq, as did both Bush Senior and Clinton in relation to Bosnia.[55] Regarding Rwanda in 1994, the Clinton administration took considerable pains to avoid applying the label to the "genocide of the Tutsi."[56] Having recently taken a political hit over Somalia, Clinton was adamant to avoid "another Somalia" at all costs.[57] Later, the president issued a public apology of sorts, and Rwanda was added to the list of failures to uphold the never again pledge.

Yet in 2004 legal experts in the Bush administration had concluded that acknowledging genocide in Darfur would not compel the United States to anything beyond calling "upon the competent organs of the United Nations to take such action under the Charter of the United Nations as they consider appropriate" (Article VIII in the Genocide Convention).[58] As recounted in Chapter 5, Powell's testimony resulted in short-lived heightened media coverage and political debates.[59] But as stated by Powell, no substantive change to US policy followed, a major blow for many in the nascent Darfur action movement who were hoping for an escalated US response.[60]

Outside the United States reactions were mixed. America's European allies continued to withhold their support for stronger action, rejecting the determination (France) or resorting to linguistic exercises to circumvent the legal repercussions associated with the term (Germany, the United Kingdom, and the European Union).[61] Still, according to some commentators the determination forced the international community to address the crisis more seriously.[62] For instance, an official British House of Commons report stated that the declaration had triggered an "explosion" of media coverage that pushed UN member states, including the United Kingdom, to take a firmer line on Darfur.[63] Eric Heinze also claimed that the determination had led to a "groundswell of controversies in world capitals."[64]

In the developing world the determination was received with distrust. The Arab League, the African Union, the Non-Aligned Movement, and even prominent dignitaries were siding with Khartoum.[65] Conspiracy theories on the motives behind the US decision charged the Bush administration with attempts to win back the African American vote in the upcoming presidential election, with trying to divert attention away from America's misbehavior in Iraq, and even with a plot to take over the rich oil fields in South (and allegedly western) Sudan.[66]

In the Security Council, no significant breakthroughs had followed. Several US-sponsored draft resolutions were watered down, mostly by China, with support from Russia and nonpermanent members Pakistan and Algeria. The resulting texts were described by critics as lukewarm, pitiful, or meaningless.[67] Although the council did at one point impose limited sanctions on some of the parties to the conflict, the language used was not strong enough to apply real pressure on Khartoum; nor were any of the threats to punish noncompliance followed through by its members.[68]

Motives behind the Determination

An important question is what had motivated the administration to make the unprecedented determination. One explanation offered by Prunier was that with the US presidential elections fast approaching, the White House could not ignore the mounting public pressure for some form of action. At the same time and given Sudan's prized collaboration with the United States in the war on terror, President Bush and Secretary Powell could not also disregard the intelligence community's opposition to antagonizing Khartoum. The need to compromise led then to an ostensibly powerful but in reality toothless determination of genocide.[69]

Prunier's theory was supported by testimony from the US ambassador to the UN John Danforth. In a BBC Panorama interview a few months after stepping down from his post, Danforth argued that the genocide determination was intended for "internal consumption within the United States."[70] At the time he did not believe the determination would make any difference outside the United States, nor was he consulted about it—a curious omission if the objective was indeed to change things at the Security Council.

A complementary explanation offered by Heinze was that having learned that a determination would not create a legal obligation to act, and realizing that the precedent of Iraq would lead many to object to another military intervention, the administration had decided to apply it as substitute for a more costly or risky US response.[71] Given the genocide debate on Darfur, reasoned Heinze, the United States was in no real risk of being accused of disingenuousness had it opted not to make the determination.[72]

There were other theories also. One, by Africa scholar Alex de Waal, tied the genocide determination to a purported desire by many Americans to redeem the United States of its failures to intervene in Rwanda and Bosnia.[73] Another, by Lorne Craner, assistant secretary of state on democracy, human rights and labor, was that after the Abu Ghraib and Guantanamo Bay prisoner abuse scandals the Bush administration was keen to reclaim its voice and authority on human rights issues, and showing leadership on Darfur was one way to achieve that.[74] Also raised was the incentive for President Bush not to go down in history as another US president who had refused to recognize genocide.[75]

Finally, some critics of the United States linked the genocide determination to the geopolitical struggle over energy resources between the United States and China. The United States, they alleged, was keen to push the international community to intervene in Darfur so that it could challenge China's extensive oil concessions in South Sudan. However, and as noted earlier in the chapter, better access to Sudan's oil might have dictated a more lenient treatment of Khartoum—the opposite of an intervention.[76]

Further insights into the motives behind the determination could be gained by examining the initial decision by the State Department to launch a genocide investigation. Interviews conducted by Kostas in November 2005 with two ranking officials involved in the process suggested that the department had surmised the existence of "indicators of genocide" *before* the investigation had begun.[77] According to Pierre-Richard Prosper, US ambassador-at-large for war crimes issues, the goal was to ensure that the administration had "solid information to support their . . . [genocide declaration], that could then become 'a catalyst for action.'"[78] Implicit in Kostas's account of the interviews was his understanding that both Prosper and Craner believed in and were in favor of a finding of genocide in order to generate wider support for action.[79] On the other hand, the two had also insisted that most of the department's staffers envisaged the investigation as a "clean legal and factual analysis," free of "policy considerations."[80] To be sure, these attitudes could have still differed from those held by higher ranking officials in the State Department, the White House, the Pentagon, and the intelligence agencies.

Legal Implications

My analyses of legal implications of the genocide determination on Darfur were published elsewhere.[81] As my findings have shown, back in 2004 prevailing interpretations of the duty to prevent in the Genocide Convention did not construe bystander behaviors of state parties as violations of international law. The International Court of Justice's ruling that a referral to the Security Council did not relieve states of the obligation to prevent, that states had to take all reasonable measures regardless of the prospects of success, and that the activation of the Genocide Convention required no more than a "serious risk" of genocide was not made until three years later, in 2007.[82] It should also be remembered that although couched in legal language, Powell's genocide determination was a political one.[83] A legal determination by a court would have carried greater authority but would have taken much longer to reach, if at all.[84]

The significance of the genocide determination and of all other factors examined in this chapter cannot be divorced from the contexts in which they operated, either as imperatives or as constraints to action. One of these contexts was related to the opinion-policy nexus. To tie together the two parts, we next integrate the chapter's findings thus far into the wider analytical framework of the study.

PUBLIC OPINION INDICATORS: INTERPRETATION
AND CONSEQUENCES

It was suggested in Chapter 2 that under certain conditions, interpretations of the policy preferences of the American public by government officials could influence the substance of policies. Research has found that these interpretations tended to form based on the monitoring of news media coverage, congressional discourse and conduct, and, to a lesser extent, opinion polls.[85] The analysis in Chapter 4 highlighted public *behavior* as another important gauge for public attitudes. The following section uses these four indicators to construct an image of how US officials might have read domestic public opinion in relation to Darfur back in 2004, commencing with how the crisis was covered by the media.

Media Coverage of Darfur

If the US media reporting on Darfur were to be the *only* indicator of domestic attitudes toward the crisis during 2004, it would have portrayed a morally minded but largely disconnected citizenry. First, it had taken the press a whole year just to pick up the story. Once it did, then—with the exception of the *Washington Post*, the *New York Times,* and to a lesser degree a few other elite papers—most print media rarely prioritized the coverage.[86] Outlets instead made use of wire services or freelance journalists to occasionally update on the situation. Reasons cited later by media studies included the high salience of Iraq and Afghanistan,[87] the coverage of the 2004 presidential election,[88] absence of a strong American angle to the story,[89] preoccupation with domestic infotainment news at the expense of foreign policy coverage,[90] budgetary constraints (e.g., the costs of the Iraq coverage),[91] lack of familiarity of American audiences with or interest in news from Africa,[92] claims that Darfur, and more broadly Sudan, were not the only tragedies taking place on the continent,[93] journalists' difficulty to get into Darfur,[94] purported slowness of the US media in covering mass killings when the victims are not white,[95] and difficulty to maintain interest in the story once the conflict had become protracted.[96]

Network reporting, from which most Americans were still getting their foreign news, was even more scant than the print media. According to a study by the American Progress Action Fund, the combined reporting on Darfur in the nightly newscasts of the three major networks for the whole of 2004 did not exceed twenty-six minutes (eighteen minutes on the ABC, five on NBC, and only three on CBS).[97] Equating these results with the coverage of some of the infotainment "hits" of 2004, such as the insider trading story about Martha Stewart, which received 130 minutes of network coverage, offers sobering insights about prioritization, crisis salience, and public exposure to news on distant atrocities.[98] Even though Darfur *was* the most visible African conflict in the US media during 2004, to those who relied on the evening news it was little more than an inconsequential blip on their screens. Critiques of the quality of coverage had pointed to downplaying the seriousness and humanitarian costs of the conflict and to a failure to provide sufficient context.[99] According to former White House and NSC official Harry Blaney, the story was presented episodically, "almost like some unstoppable natural disaster," and with little real analysis.[100] Linda Melvern argued that the print media had also failed to inform their readers of the targeted nature of the killings.[101]

Many commentators compared Darfur to Rwanda. In an early op-ed in the *Los Angeles Times* (April 2004), Carroll Bogert of Human Rights Watch invoked the media's failure in Rwanda, calling it a wake-up call and a warning not to miss the coverage of Darfur.[102] Contrasting the international coverage of the two crises, Melvern contended that in both cases the media had failed to report their scale, brutality, and underlying causes and to supply timely information about the (flawed) decision-making processes in the Security Council.[103] In an opposing piece though, Africa scholar Gerald Caplan argued that by mid-2004 the Darfur crisis had been covered by the media well enough for everyone "that counted" to know that an overwhelming political and humanitarian man-made disaster had befallen Western Sudan.[104] Darfur to him was different to Rwanda, of which the coverage had been minimal and distorted ("tribal savagery") and had left the public largely uninformed for many weeks. In all, the Rwanda comparison was used much more to enhance public concerns about Darfur than to allay them.[105]

Congress

As no compelling "hard" interests had initially existed for the United States in Darfur, the early congressional attention to the then invisible crisis was quite unusual. This attention had much to do with already established advocacy networks for South Sudan on Capitol Hill, which had been developed over the years in response to the long and bloody civil war between the Muslim North and the partly animist, partly Christian South. Once news about the new crisis broke out, many of these advocates extended their efforts to include Darfur. While most of the work was shouldered by a small bipartisan group of legislators—including fact-finding missions, speeches, drafting of resolutions, and so forth—their outstanding success suggested a robust congressional mind-set for strong action, or at least for a strong stance on the situation. The forcefulness of the congressional genocide determination and the unanimity in its adoption by both houses encourages also the likelihood of an influential role for the terminology of genocide in fostering that attitude.[106] Still, a more detailed study of discourse and other congressional dynamics during these critical months would be required to establish more clearly the nature and extent of the label's influence.

Opinion Polls

Darfur had not been a priority for pollsters during 2004. Only two polls were found that had focused on the crisis, both taken in early July just before the congressional genocide determination. Two other polls were conducted almost a year later, in June 2005, after the drop in public attention and after the no-genocide pronouncement by the UN commission on Darfur. The results have helped to shed some light on three points of interest: (1) principled public support for action on genocide; (2) public awareness of Darfur and perceptions about the appropriateness of the genocide label to the crisis; and (3) support for different types of US responses.

Genocide and Intervention Decisions. In 2004, the general proposition that genocide should not be allowed to occur continued to receive a high level of support in American society. According to a July 2004 Global Views poll (see next page, figure 6.1), 70 percent of the American public and 73 percent of political elites surveyed believed that countries should have the right to use military force to prevent severe human rights violations such as "genocide"— even in the absence of a UN approval (24 percent and 22 percent, respectively, objected).[107]

When UN-sanctioned responses were offered as an option, support rose even higher (next page, figure 6.2). A record 94 percent of American leaders and 85 percent of the public believed that the UN Security Council should have the right to authorize the use of military force to prevent severe human rights violations such as genocide (4 percent and 9 percent, respectively, had objected).

When the stated goal was framed as stopping a government from committing genocide, majority support existed even for the deployment of US troops. In all, 75 percent of the public and 86 percent of American leaders favored *as a principle* the use of US troops to stop a government from committing genocide and killing large numbers of its own people (22 percent and 7 percent, respectively, had objected; see figure 6.3, page 111).[108]

Even though the survey question did not specify whether the intervention would be unilateral or multilateral, the support was still significantly higher than in a parallel July 2004 Program on International Policy Attitudes (PIPA) poll, which focused specifically on Darfur (see below). Once again a visible gap seemed to manifest between principled and a crisis-specific support for action on genocide. It is clearly easier to commit to an ideal than to real action.

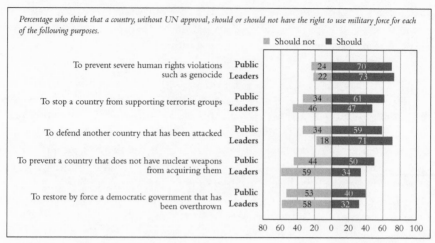

Percentage who think that a country, without UN approval, should or should not have the right to use military force for each of the following purposes.

6.1. Unilateral action—no UN approval. Source: Global Views, July 2004, Chicago Council on Foreign Relations (CCFR), 24.

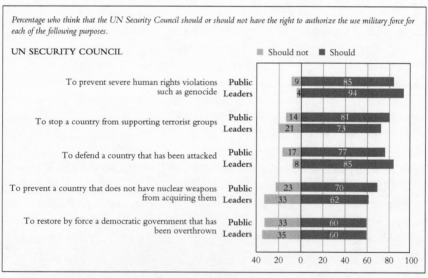

Percentage who think that the UN Security Council should or should not have the right to authorize the use military force for each of the following purposes.

6.2. United Nations Security Council—right to authorize/use force. Source: Global Views, July 2004, Chicago Council on Foreign Relations (CCFR), 24.

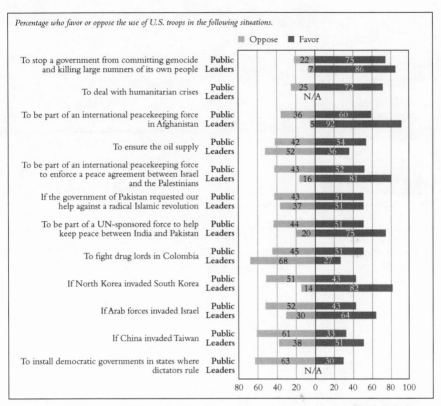

Percentage who favor or oppose the use of U.S. troops in the following situations.

■ Oppose   ■ Favor

		Oppose	Favor
To stop a government from committing genocide and killing large numners of its own people	Public	22	75
	Leaders	7	86
To deal with humanitarian crises	Public	25	72
	Leaders	N/A	
To be part of an international peacekeeping force in Afghanistan	Public	36	60
	Leaders	5	92
To ensure the oil supply	Public	42	54
	Leaders	52	36
To be part of an international peacekeeping force to enforce a peace agreement between Israel and the Palestinians	Public	43	52
	Leaders	16	81
If the government of Pakistan requested our help against a radical Islamic revolution	Public	43	51
	Leaders	37	51
To be part of a UN-sponsored force to help keep peace between India and Pakistan	Public	44	51
	Leaders	20	75
To fight drug lords in Colombia	Public	45	51
	Leaders	68	27
If North Korea invaded South Korea	Public	51	43
	Leaders	14	82
If Arab forces invaded Israel	Public	52	43
	Leaders	30	64
If China invaded Taiwan	Public	61	33
	Leaders	38	51
To install democratic governments in states where dictators rule	Public	63	30
	Leaders	N/A	

80 60 40 20   0   20 40 60 80 100

6.3. Support for use of US troops in various circumstances. Source: Global Views, July 2004, Chicago Council on Foreign Relations (CCFR), 29.

Public Awareness of Darfur and Appropriateness of "Genocide" Label. Based on the 2004 PIPA poll's findings, US public awareness of the crisis in Darfur was *very low* as late as July, shortly before the genocide determination by congress. A mere 14 percent of respondents have heard "some or a lot" about the situation "in a province of Sudan called Darfur" where "there is a conflict between the local black African Darfuris and the central government, dominated by Arabs." Twenty eight percent heard "not very much" and more than half, 56 percent, heard "nothing at all."[109]

Asked about the appropriateness of the term "genocide" to the events in Darfur, Americans' views depended greatly on their familiarity with the crisis (figure 6.4). A high of 87 percent support among the well informed had dropped to 46 percent among the least informed respondents.

When disregarding the low salience of the crisis to the public, the average support for the claim that Darfur *was* a case of "genocide" was at 56 percent (24 percent against and 20 percent did not know)—still a majority but not as robust.

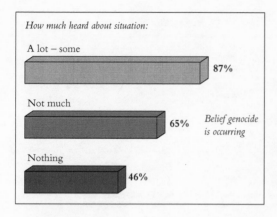

How much heard about situation:

A lot – some

87%

Not much

65%   *Belief genocide is occurring*

Nothing

46%

6.4. Genocide in Darfur? Awareness of the crisis (Program on International Policy Attitudes [PIPA], "Americans on the Crisis in Sudan," July 2004). Source: Steven Kull et al., "Americans on the Crisis in Sudan" (PIPA/ Knowledge Networks Poll, July 20, 2004), 4.

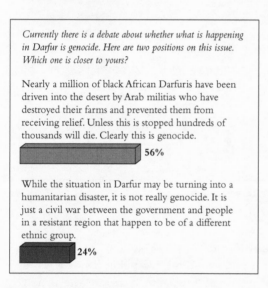

Currently there is a debate about whether what is happening in Darfur is genocide. Here are two positions on this issue. Which one is closer to yours?

Nearly a million of black African Darfuris have been driven into the desert by Arab militias who have destroyed their farms and prevented them from receiving relief. Unless this is stopped hundreds of thousands will die. Clearly this is genocide.

56%

While the situation in Darfur may be turning into a humanitarian disaster, it is not really genocide. It is just a civil war between the government and people in a resistant region that happen to be of a different ethnic group.

24%

6.5. Is genocide occurring in Darfur? (PIPA, "Americans on the Crisis in Sudan," July 2004). Source: Kull et al., "Americans on the Crisis in Sudan," 4.

As can be seen in the problematic design of the survey question (figure 6.5), the majority of respondents who had heard nothing about the crisis, or not very much, had been asked to make a genocide determination based on a reductionist description of the situation as "a million black African Darfuris [have been] driven into the desert by Arab militias who have destroyed their farms and prevented them from receiving relief."[110] The findings of this question therefore could have been easily challenged.

Support for Different Types of US Military Responses (2004–2005). Prior to the congressional and administration's genocide determinations, 69 percent of respondents to the July 2004 PIPA poll had said that if the United Nations were to determine "genocide" in Darfur, it had the obligation, together

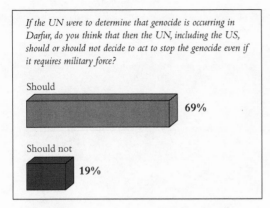

6.6. UN/US involvement in Darfur (PIPA, "Americans on the Crisis in Sudan," July 2004). Source: Kull et al., "Americans on the Crisis in Sudan," 3.

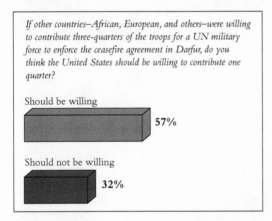

6.7. United States in UN peacekeeping (PIPA, "Americans on the Crisis in Sudan," July 2004). Source: Kull et al., "Americans on the Crisis in Sudan," 6.

with the United States, to act to stop it, even if this required the use of a military force (figure 6.6). While the numbers were not as robust as during the 1990s, the patterns remained the same.[111] Support for UN-imposed targeted sanctions on Sudanese officials was also high, at 68 percent (18 percent against).

Of the respondents to the same PIPA poll, 65 percent had supported the establishment of a UN peacekeeping force to enforce a recent cease-fire agreement in Darfur—provided that this was consented to by Sudan. When asked if the United States should contribute one-quarter of the troops if other countries had agreed to contribute the rest, majority support remained but had dropped a little to 57 percent (32 percent objected) (figure 6.7).

Polls on Darfur from June 2005. Another poll to survey the possibility of intervention in Darfur was conducted almost a year later, in June 2005, by International Crisis Group and Zogbi International. The results showed

I am going to read to you a number of steps that the U.S. could take to help stop the killings in Darfur. Please tell me if you strongly support, somewhat support, somewhat oppose, or strongly oppose each.

	Support★	Oppose★	Not sure
Cooperate with the International Criminal Court to help bring to justice those accused of crimes against humanity.	91	6	4
Impose tough sanctions on those Sudanese leaders responsible for controlling the militias.	81	12	7
Establish a "no fly" zone over Darfur to prevent aerial attacks on civilians and destroy those planes engaged in attacks on civilians.	80	13	8
Offer NATO logistical and troop support for an expanded African peacekeeping force.	76	18	6
Insert U.S. Soldiers on the ground.	38	55	7

★"Support" and "oppose" combine "strongly" and "somewhat."

6.8. A US action in Darfur? Source: International Crisis Group and Zogbi International, "Africa Briefing No. 26: Do Americans Care about Darfur?" (June 1, 2005).

	%
A: The U.S. should not tolerate an extremist government committing genocide or crimes against humanity and should use its military assets, short of putting U.S. troops on the ground, to help stop the humanitarian tragedy in Darfur.	84
B: The U.S. should not worry about genocide or crimes against humanity in places like Africa and should not antagonize powerful nations like China that support the government of sudan and its current policies.	8
Not sure.	8

6.9. Using US military assets. Source: International Crisis Group and Zogbi International, "Africa Briefing No. 26: Do Americans Care about Darfur?" (June 1, 2005).

significant public support for targeted sanctions (81 percent) and for a no-fly zone over the region (80 percent), but not for a unilateral ground operation by the United States (only 38 percent in favor, 55 percent against; figure 6.8).[112]

A related question posed by the poll was whether the United States should tolerate an extremist government committing genocide or crimes against humanity, or instead use its military assets, short of putting US troops on the ground, to help stop the humanitarian tragedy in Darfur. The latter option received a large majority support of 84 percent of the respondents (8 percent objected), echoing the familiar reluctance to mount intervention by land, but indicating a high support for the use of other military means (figure 6.9).

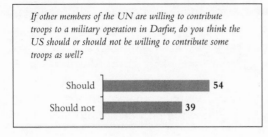

6.10. Contributing US troops to intervention in Darfur. Source: Program on International Policy Attitudes/Knowledge Networks, June 2005.

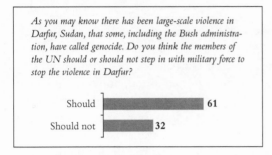

6.11. UN intervention in declared genocide. Source: Program on International Policy Attitudes/Knowledge Networks, June 2005.

Interestingly, a PIPA / Knowledge Networks poll conducted in the same month (June 2005) had returned a majority support for US troop deployment in a military operation *as part of a multilateral force*: 54 percent in favor (39 percent against).[113] Once again, mentioning the United Nations and multilateral cooperation may have made a notable impact on Americans' willingness to risk their own troops (figure 6.10).

Finally, reminding respondents the US genocide determination on Darfur (in another question) without explicitly specifying a US participation in the mission, attracted a higher 61 percent support for a UN military intervention (32 percent objected) (figure 6.11).

Learning from the Polls

The polls' results from 2004 and 2005 have continued to emphasize the significance of burden sharing and of international legitimacy for interventions in the calculus of the American public. However, the lack in more systematic polling, inconsistent or loose wordings of survey questions, and changes over time to domestic and international conditions, have made it difficult to draw clear conclusions about trends and variations in the significance of the genocide label for the public, or in the public's willingness to risk US troops to help halt a distant genocide. For instance, increasing American casualties in Iraq may or may not have been the sole reason for the decline in support for ground interventions by 2005.[114] At the same time, a reliance on a snapshot image of public attitudes at a particular moment as a dependable indicator for addressing dynamically changing events would have also been an overreach. In this example, the finding of low crisis visibility for Darfur in early July 2004, consequential as it may have been for decision making, would have likely changed soon-after in response to two genocide determinations and increasing casualties' estimates. Such changes could have easily altered responses to some survey questions, but as the next round of polls did not take place until June 2005, it would be difficult to know for sure.

US POLICY OF INACTION?

This chapter explored some of the elements that influenced America's responses to Darfur during 2004, with a focus on the motives behind and the consequences of the US genocide determination. The goal was to situate the effects of the term "genocide"—legal and moral, domestic and international, direct and indirect, "positive" and "negative"—within the framework of pragmatic and normative considerations that manifested at different levels of American society in relation to the crisis.

The evidence suggests that the efforts taken by the Bush administration in relation to Darfur were impelled by a political interest to alleviate domestic pressures, coupled with genuine aspirations to try to help the Darfuri people. However, these objectives were informed by keen attention to a set of constraints, some of them self-imposed. As argued earlier in the chapter, Ambassador Danforth's contention that the genocide determination was made for domestic consumption and the fact that he was not consulted about its details reinforce the possibility that US decision makers did not anticipate a breakthrough at the Security Council in its aftermath. To be sure, China and Russia's interests in Sudan, coupled with a long-standing commitment to the principle of state sovereignty were too well known in Washington to be overlooked. John Prendergast's disclosure, as a former staffer in the US delegation to the Security Council, of how these anti-interventionist attitudes had been exploited in the past by the United States and the United Kingdom to justify their own inaction supported his contention that the same had transpired also in the case of Darfur.[115] It could be argued therefore that the forceful US stand in the council was at least informed, if not encouraged, by the knowledge that a likely deadlock would allow it to gain positive domestic points without having to commit to meaningful but potentially risky or costly actions. A genocide determination could help alleviate domestic pressures, avert a stigma of bystander, and lead, hopefully, to a tougher international response—all this without taking significant political risks.[116]

To overcome the obstacles for action in the UN Security Council, the administration would have had to take one of two difficult courses of action:

apply or mobilize considerable pressure on Sudan or on China and others in the UNSC or bypass the council altogether—multilaterally or unilaterally. That it had attempted neither lends weight to the argument that the United States, like the rest of the international community, was either unable or unwilling to commit sufficient resources to meaningful action.[117]

Unable versus Unwilling

There is, however, an important difference between "unable" and "unwilling," and so it would be wise to avoid making generalizations about the role played by the United States. While critics have harshly and justly derided the Bush administration's insistence that it was doing all it could in relation to Darfur,[118] it is also true that during most of 2004 the United States was the most active of all UNSC member states in relation to the crisis. A May 2004 report by Human Rights Watch commended America's efforts, citing President Bush's statement of 7 April, congressional debates about the crisis, and attention-drawing visits to the region by USAID officials: "The U.S. government has taken the strongest public stance on Darfur of any individual government, with repeated statements condemning the human rights abuses and calling on the government of Sudan to address the situation."[119]

Citing Dr. Mukesh Kapila, a 2005 report by the International Development Committee of the British House of Commons also noted, "In late 2003 and early 2004, the U.S.A was the only member of the Security Council keen to press the GoS [government of Sudan] to fulfill its responsibilities to protect its own people. Many other countries were not in a mood to hear the concerns voiced by the U.S.A."[120] Two other manifestations of political will for action within the administration were the solitary US stand for Darfur during the annual meeting of the UN Commission on Human Rights in Geneva (23 April 2004) and the State Department's decision to launch the study that resulted in Powell's genocide determination.[121] Both efforts required dedicated involvement and good faith by officials at various levels, including in high-ranking positions.[122]

One of the reasons for the US failure to lead a meaningful international campaign on Darfur was the absence of clear alternatives to the use of force. As recalled, military action was rejected based mostly on constraints such as the war in Iraq and the risks and logistical challenges of long-term deployment in a vast and highly inaccessible region. The difficulties in Iraq had reduced not only the domestic focus on the crisis but also the ability and legitimacy for the Bush administration to champion another humanitarian crusade against a sovereign Muslim government. Without the "stick" of military intervention, the international community needed other means to dissuade Khartoum from using violence in Darfur, and these means had not been made available by states. It may be argued therefore that the absence of a strong leverage, or of political will to generate one, were at the core of the failure to stop the killings in Darfur.

Convincing powers like China and Russia to act against their own geopolitical interests is a tall order, even for the United States, and even when a strong case could be made to that end. While it might have been less challenging for the administration to try to contend with Khartoum than with its fellow P-5, the important point to make is that the United States should have done more, or at least attempted to do more, to stop the atrocities.

Still, compared to previous genocides, the US response to Darfur during 2004 did exhibit a discernible increase in the willingness of policymakers to engage with and invest efforts in trying to halt a faraway genocide.[123] Considering the absence of "hard" interests for US action, what could have accounted for the change? Arguably, the answer resides in domestic politics.

Domestic Politics

Based on this chapter's findings, a reading of public attitudes indicators would have suggested to the Bush administration in 2004 domestic support for a US leadership on Darfur. However, this support could have also been interpreted as qualified: that is, predicated on the perceived risks, costs, and available means of response. Despite the principled interventionist stance exhibited by the public in the polls, two competing indicators could have suggested to officials that maintaining a prudent policy of little action would not incur significant political costs. The first was the modest attention to the crisis by the media and consequently by the general public. Poll results, as noted, have shown that at the height of the debate (July 2004) only a small minority of Americans—14 percent—knew "some or a lot" about the situation in Darfur. In contrast, 28 percent knew "not very much" and 56 percent "nothing at all."[124] A second element that could have calmed the administration was a prevailing sense—particularly after Powell's genocide determination—that the failure to deal with the violence had not been the administration's fault. A *Washington Post* editorial articulated this view in late December 2004: "The United States has done more than any other country to control this catastrophe, which may already have claimed 300,000 lives. It has been frustrated by China and Russia, which have sold weapons to Sudan and used their muscle on the U.N. Security Council to undermine a push for sanctions; by the sluggishness of the African Union, which accounts for the slow deployment; and by the need to preserve diplomatic capital for the war on terrorism and for Iraq."[125] Both indicators could help to explain the by now familiar gap between a moral stance in the polls and the limited challenge mounted by the public to the deficient US policy.

Genocide?

Was genocide taking place in Darfur during 2004? The opinions of most well informed individuals at the time had sided with Congress and the State Department rather than with the UN Commission on Darfur. Statements to that effect were issued by Aegis Trust, Physicians for Human Rights, the Committee on Conscience of the US Holocaust Memorial Museum, the US Committee for Refugees, Africa Action, Justice Africa, Africa Confidential, "Yad Vashem," Genocide Watch, and numerous genocide scholars.[126] On the other hand, a number of prominent NGOs, most notably Amnesty International and Human Rights Watch, had rejected the appropriateness of the label—mostly on grounds of insufficient evidence for showing "State intent."[127] An alternative explanation offered was "counter-insurgency gone wrong."[128] Irrespective, many on both sides of the debate were calling for a shift of focus away from the definitional controversy to the crucial question of how to stop the violence.[129]

THE FAILURE OVER DARFUR

Despite its unprecedented rhetoric on Darfur, the United States—like the rest of the international community—had failed once again to uphold the pledge of "never again." President Bush's promise to himself that genocide would not occur "on his watch" was not kept. And if the events in Darfur during 2004 did constitute genocide—as was determined by the US government—then the Genocide Convention proved incapable of binding the United States to its promises. Still, in a departure from the past, the United States had made more efforts than other countries during 2004 to push for a meaningful response to the crisis. That it had failed had much to do with self-imposed restrictions on the risks and costs that America, and arguably Americans as well, were willing to bear to that end. No less to blame, however, was the unwillingness of other member states in the Security Council and in regional bodies to actively support these efforts. It may be argued therefore that this time the battle to stop genocide was lost more in international politics than in the US domestic sphere.

Driven by domestic pressures, the genocide determination did increase the salience of the crisis. But even such a proclamation by the world's foremost superpower could not make a meaningful impact on international political will. Not only that, but in an unfortunate twist of fate it helped to legitimate domestically a reticent US policy and made it easier for the Bush administration to evade riskier and costlier policy options. As noted by Seybolt, it proved to be a substitute for action instead of a call to one.[130]

Determining genocide without trying hard to stop it ended up producing a dangerous precedent for the future.[131]

There are a few measures short of full-scale military action that the United States could have taken in relation to Darfur. It could have pushed harder for bringing to a formal vote tougher draft resolutions, to force China and other supporters of Khartoum to choose between risking a public stigma of aiding and abetting a potential genocide and allowing these resolutions to be adopted.[132] For instance, the establishment of an enforceable no-fly zone over the region could have made significant differences in curbing the attacks on civilians. The United States could also have mobilized additional diplomatic and economic pressure on Sudan, including more significant targeted sanctions. As part of the efforts, more sustained attention could have been given to encouraging humanitarian-driven media reporting of the crisis inside the developing world—especially in Africa and among Arab and Muslim nations—to try to bolster public opinion for action. Finally, the United States (and the rest of the international community) could and should have provided much more support for the African Union Mission on the ground. The failure to do so even after the genocide determination had been made has been difficult to explain. It is hard to know, even in hindsight, which of these, or other measures, might have improved the situation for the people of Darfur. However, any efforts, successful or otherwise, to uphold President Bush to his not on my watch promise would have decreased the gap between official moral rhetoric and weak action. They also would have sent an important message to victims and survivors, to bystanders around the world, and to the perpetrators of this and any future mass atrocities—that genocide will not be left unchallenged.

Conclusion

DURING A PRIVATE meeting in May 2001, following their visit to the then highly volatile Burundi, members of the UN Security Council were asked by former Australian foreign minister Gareth Evans how they would act if genocide broke out in that country.[1] Based on the insider account of Singapore's ambassador to the council Kishore Mahbubani, the United States and all other P-5 delegates had made it clear that since their governments had no vital national interests in Burundi, they would not support a more proactive action than the one taken by the Security Council over Rwanda in 1994.[2] The nonpermanent members then declared that if the P-5 would not take the lead, they were not in a position to do so either.[3] The chasm between the international chorus of guilt after the genocide in Rwanda and the delegates' off-the-record positions now in relation to Burundi was as startling as it was revealing.

Governments are not in the habit of publicly rejecting the existence of an imperative to do "something" about genocide. Even staunch supporters of the nonintervention norm have been disinclined to openly espouse inaction. Debates instead have tended to revolve more around *who* and *how* to act than whether to. Despite this, international bystanding to genocide has coexisted expediently with moralizing rhetoric about the need to do just that: "something."

Over the years we have learned a few things about the incentives and disincentives for states to respond forcefully to mass atrocities. History has shown that unless governments identified significant security, economic, or other political benefits to action, the combined weight of recurring and situation-specific challenges was likely to dilute or even preclude meaningful measures. One major difficulty was the perennial gap between finite assets and the interminably competing demands on governments' resources. Amid these constraints, policymakers' decisions were dominated by conceptions of threats and opportunities to "vital national interests," but also by preferences for hard interests—domestic and geostrategic—and a reluctance to bear major political risks for low political gains.[4] Knowing this, perpetrators' incentives and resolve to carry out their misdeeds were often stronger than the impetus for would-be interveners to act.[5] And when the risks and other uncertainties of military interventions were added to the balance, the scales had tended to tilt sharply in favor of inaction.

Rather than question or challenge the preeminence of the national and other interests, the objectives of this project were to increase our knowledge and understanding of America's relationship with genocide by focusing on the little-explored interactions and mutual influences between American society—the elites, mass opinion, media, civil society, and other domestic actors—and the executive branch. As noted in the introduction to the book, in an age of ubiquitous social media, social networks, viral video clips, and now populist resurgence, a greater role for the citizenry in decision making on responses to genocide may be in the cards. The question is in which directions domestic policy trends would be taking US foreign policy. To provide context for such a debate, I summarize in this final chapter key findings and conclusions pertaining to the actors and factors that could shape, enable, or constrain political responses, including the consequences of labeling a crisis as genocide and other potential influences of public opinion on official policies.

THE SIGNIFICANCE OF OPINION-POLICY INTERACTIONS

At no time in the past were US policies on genocide determined solely by the voiced opinions of the American public or by administration officials' anticipation of its behavior. On occasion though such assessments did influence decision dynamics, most often when the disposition of the public was thought to echo views already held by policymakers or in situations of high policy uncertainty. The findings suggest that among the indicators used to infer public attitudes—that is, media coverage, congressional mood, opinion polls, and manifestations of public behavior—it may have been the latter one that yielded the strongest influence on policy.

The evidence points to recurring attempts by administrations to reconcile two potentially contradictory imperatives: a wish to discursively frame humanitarian crises in ways that would mitigate public pressures for risky or costly policies and the desire to protect the White House from accusations of bystander behavior. We say "contradictory" because if aroused, Americans were thought likely to condemn inaction; but if a military intervention were to fail or incur significant casualties, it was feared that the public would reverse its support for the policy.[6]

By default, most Americans were predisposed to overlook failures by their leaders to live up to the "never again" promise. While such pledges were likely sincere in the aftermath of genocidal events that did "shock the conscience of mankind," when it was time to act again, low prioritizations of distant crises in a reality of competing demands repeatedly ground mean-ingful action to a halt in favor of more pragmatic considerations. The unwill-ingness of successive administrations to respond robustly to these kinds of situations therefore constituted failings of omission. In some instances, the reluctance to invest significant resources in action may have been affected by misunderstandings of situations, in others by a wishful thinking that mod-est measures would suffice or that things would sort themselves out, unaided, or with only a little help.

When it came to the American public, professed majority views in favor of strong action on genocide tended to coexist with indifference or resignation to ineffective policies pursued by the United States. Therefore, voicing support for action turned out to be more a self-righteous assertion of values than a commitment to uphold them. Bystander behaviors may have originated in the State Department, the Pentagon, or the White House but did not stop there. To be sure, for ordinary citizens, distracted by everyday challenges and constrained by factors such as deficient media coverage, a short news life cycle, lack of leadership, low identification with victims, and disbelief in their own ability to make a difference, engaging with the injustices of the global village would not have been a small feat. This notwithstanding, the consequences of a "less than noisy society" pro-vided and continue to afford administrations considerable freedom in craft-ing morally thin policies. An important point to keep in mind is that foreign policy issues, particularly about distant humanitarian crises, seldom become salient enough to affect domestic politics in meaningful ways. The priority assigned by the public to the state of the economy, taxes, health, education, and high-level national security is well understood by politi-cians and informs their willingness to take into account public attitudes on less salient issues.

Legitimating Inaction

Overall, public opinion does matter to policymakers, for practical if not for other reasons. Managing it successfully could offer US presidents better approval ratings, a stronger hand in pushing legislation through Congress, and greater influence in presidential or midterm elections.[7] Faced with the need to reconcile poor conduct with high ideals, American policymakers have become adept at rhetorical management of the gap between the two. During the 1990s, threats of domestic pushback against ethically problem-atic policies were mitigated by combinations of half-measure actions, mor-alizing rhetoric, and purposeful framing of information. One strategy was to try to encourage a sense of a clash between "commendable but risky" humanitarian impulses and more "responsible" policy concerns. Another approach involved looking to ease the conscience of the citizenry about the

US failures to act. Official discourses aimed at legitimating inaction or weak policies were framed to manage salience, highlight risks and costs of action, control discussions of policy options, blame external actors for failures to act, or foster a feeling of inability to make a difference.[8]

Another modest way to try to reduce public pressures for action was to exclude the use of the genocide label from administrations' rhetoric. Some of the efforts made in this regard were described in Chapter 3. Unexpectedly, the findings have shown that deliberate omissions of the term also took place during times when the US government was pushing for interventions: for example, before and during NATO's aerial bombings in Bosnia and over Kosovo. To appear committed to some form of meaningful action, presidential discourses still employed emotive terminology; but these were less compelling and obligating than "genocide." Hence, the use or avoidance of the label proved to be less indicative of official intentions than anticipated. The term's exclusion from discourse was not always followed by noninterventions; invoking it (i.e., over Darfur) did not indicate intent to prepare the public for an intervention.

As shown, managing the potential costs of inaction was considered by administrations in most cases preferable to facing the risks of a failed intervention. Power famously wrote that "if everyone within the government is motivated to avoid 'another Somalia' or 'another Vietnam,' few think twice on playing a role in allowing 'another Rwanda.'"[9] Darfur was the exception. Benefiting from strong backing from within President Bush's core constituency in the evangelical right, the advocacy movement for action had wielded far greater political influence than its mere numbers would have allowed.[10] In fact, without the need to pacify this section of the electorate, the administration would not have prioritized Darfur anywhere near as much as it ended up doing.

As made evident throughout the book, discourse does matter, sometimes significantly. Like many other elements of foreign policy, domestic and international legitimacy is sought, gained, or lost through discourse. Building on social constructivist theory, Nicholas Wheeler argued: "It is a categorical error to posit a separation between words and deeds when thinking about how the social world hangs together; the former constitute the latter by establishing the boundaries of what is possible . . . words matter. The legitimating reasons employed by governments are crucial because they enable and constrain actions."[11] To be sure, as seen in Libya in 2011, international intervention (justified or not) can take shape with considerable speed when feasibility, key actors' interests, *and* legitimacy are all there. An important question raised in this study is how interests and feasibility could influence legitimacy, and vice versa.

From Shortage of Information to Sham Compliance

Lack of information was invoked by US policymakers during and in the aftermath of genocidal events to justify inaction and minimize political fallout. The dictum "we didn't know / understand / appreciate" after the Holocaust, Cambodia, and Rwanda continues to ring hollow in survivors' ears to this day. By managing the availability, framing, and substance of information, politicians could control public knowledge and perceptions of the scale, nature, and causes of atrocities as well as the risks, costs, and chances of success of alternative policy options.[12] While the haze of war and access restrictions resulted at times in genuine information gaps for countries with limited intelligence gathering capabilities, this had rarely been the case for official America. In the United States, argued Samantha Power, "someone always knew."[13]

In recent decades, the globalization of human rights concerns, technological advances in the news industry, and the proliferation of NGOs have helped to illuminate previously invisible and dark corners of the world. While these changes have led to a loss of credibility for the "lack of information" argument, the means for governments to justify inaction have not disappeared. As mentioned, one of the ways to deflect criticism was to carry out a range of limited measures aimed at generating the impression of a determined resolve to act.[14] In such situations states were technically complying with the imperative to do something, as they were "taking action," but in reality their compliance was sham.[15] The "sham compliance" frame could be useful to delineate the often fuzzy boundaries between passive inaction and deliberately deficient action. The distinction may seem minor, but if the intention in deficient action is to pacify the scruples of a public already predisposed toward looking the other way, then exposing these practices could be meaningful. Take for example President Trump's decision in April 2017 to fire fifty-nine Tomahawk missiles at a Syrian air base from which a chemical attack against Syrian civilians could have been launched. Clearly, this limited action was geared much more toward satisfying Americans' desire to feel that the United States was doing something than toward helping to resolve the widespread suffering in Syria.

THE FAILURE OVER DARFUR

Encapsulated in the Genocide Convention, the moral and legal pledges to prevent genocide have by now been endorsed by most states.[16] Yet it took more than half a century for a major power like the United States to translate these undertakings to an official determination of genocide and a referral to the Security Council. Even then the international community, including the United States itself, still shied away from committing to

sufficiently strong actions to stop the atrocities in Darfur. The Bush administration resigned to leaving the fate of the Darfuris, who according to its
own official determination were experiencing genocide, in the hands of the
government it had argued was behind the perpetration of the crime.

As the subject of an official genocide determination, Darfur constitutes
an important case for exploring the processes, events, and competing factors
that led another US administration to renege on its "never again" promise.[17]
Never before was the study of public attitudes, media coverage, and US
politicians' reactions to an ongoing situation of genocide so forthright.

Based on the findings, the efforts taken by the Bush administration
were impelled by a need to alleviate morally driven domestic pressures, but
at the same time by a desire to save lives. As noted, however, this political
will was constrained at all times by self-imposed limitations on action. In
terms of public attitudes, opinion indicators would have presented administration officials during 2004 with evidence of popular support for a strong
US policy. But as discussed in the previous chapter, the relatively low
salience of the crisis in the media, and consequently for the public, would
have indicated that avoiding robust action was also a possibility. How much
electoral weight was needed to tilt the scales in favor of more effective
action, and what would have led to the mobilization of such a critical mass?
The answer to these questions remains speculative. It was the hope of some
Darfur activists that the foundations laid by them would allow faster, wider,
and more influential public responses in the future.[18] That these aspirations
have so far not come true in relation to Syria and other contemporary man-
made tragedies is little more than a testament to the need to do much more.

As argued, the Bush administration's decision to score domestic points
through the genocide determination was likely influenced by the calculation that international actors' interests against intervention would shield it
from the risks and costs of military or other robust action. Yet the determination was also meant to intensify the pressures on Sudan.[19] As discussed,
the results were mixed. Issuing a genocide finding did increase the salience
of the crisis, and to a degree the pressure for action. But at the same time, it
also calmed the popular domestic demands to do more and shifted the blame
for the failed response to non-US actors. Between Powell's September 2004
determination and the "no proof of genocide" conclusion by the UN Commission of Inquiry in March 2005, invocations of the label were barely
challenged inside the United States. American action was thus constrained
not by a "genocide debate," as feared, but by self-imposed constraints and
by the failure of the determination to change hearts and policies overseas.
Consequently, stateside the administration was able to get away with a
moderately weak policy, even without a genocide debate to distract the
public.

Given the overall modest significance of Darfur to most Americans, it is unclear how realistic advocates' beliefs that the administration would upscale its response if the State Department's investigation had pointed to genocide, were. What *is* clear is that Powell and others in the department had actively sought to discourage such assumptions, either because they believed—as Powell had repeatedly argued—that the determination would not add new impetuous or powers to would-be interveners or because knowing that the administration was not going to upgrade its efforts anyway, they did not wish to expose themselves to morally charged accusations later on.[20]

The Distinctiveness of Genocide

In a forum on genocide prevention held in Stockholm in 2004, UN secretary-general Kofi Annan spoke about the need for "clear ground rules to distinguish between genuine threats of genocide, *which require a military solution*, and other situations where force would not be legitimate."[21] In contrast to this (later disavowed) distinction, the evidence examined in this book has pointed to more similarities than divergences between responses to genocide and to non-genocidal mass atrocities. First, notwithstanding the legal differences between genocide and other atrocity crimes in relation both to prevention and punishment, conferring the label on conflict situations had not necessarily resulted in stronger action.[22] In fact, an inverse ratio between interventions in non-genocides and noninterventions in genocide has challenged these assumptions.[23] The normative preeminence and significance of the label have thus been put in question, since if the "seriousness" of events were to correlate positively with the strength of responses, we might have seen more interventions to stop genocide.

Second, the similarities between genocide and other atrocity crimes extended also to the constraints to action. Out of *eighteen* recurring contributing factors to the international community's failures to prevent or stop mass atrocities examined in this study, only two were linked specifically to situations of genocide: (1) the effects of the "genocide debate" and (2) policymakers' reluctance to commit to action on genocide, for fear of having to bear the legal and moral obligations purportedly generated by the label. All other constraints had applied, often in similar ways, to non-genocidal events.

As a final point in this context, the impression arising from the data is that imperatives for action used discursively for anti-genocide advocacy campaigns had not differed significantly from those used in relation to non-genocidal situations. In contrast, the circumvention or adoption of "genocide" rhetoric in relation to crises by US officials *did* lead to different results, particularly in media coverage, public attention, and the robustness of civil society efforts to promote action. One cited example was the relative visibility of Darfur during 2004 compared to the deadlier but non-genocidal violence in the Democratic Republic of the Congo.[24]

The growing use of the broader term "(mass) atrocity crimes" may have circumvented some of the complications associated with the genocide label. Arguably though it did not preserve the latter's inimitable clout. Rather than write off the "G word," a more sensible approach would be to look for alternative means of harnessing its normative power as and when appropriate, while sidestepping the kind of debates that could "constrain or distract policymakers from addressing the core problems it describes."[25] For example, would "genocidal massacres," a terminology that includes the word "genocide" but may carry weaker legal implications offer some workable solutions for politicians and the media? This possibility and others like it invite more research.

OTHER OPTIONS FOR ACTION

It was held in the past that a genocide determination on a situation would add moral urgency to the imperative to act. However, there is a catch here. A legal genocide (or no-genocide) determination by a competent court takes a long time to issue, too long for a timely response to impending or occurring violence. On the other hand, a *political* genocide determination made by a state may take much less time but is more likely to face charges of bias and illegitimacy and, as happened in Darfur, could prove ineffective in the end.[26] What other ways are there for invoking stronger responses to mass atrocities? Convincing parties to an armed conflict to prioritize peaceful solutions requires in most situations the use of carrots, sticks, or a combination of both. In the case of Darfur, the Bush administration was criticized for not using more of its resources as leverage to help stop the killing.[27] To be sure, the Sudanese regime had succumbed on occasion in the past to strong external pressures.[28] In their study of the United States and Darfur, Stedjan and Thomas-Jensen highlighted leverage as the primary tool for conflict resolution from the outside.[29] Political will for action is insufficient if the means to act are not there, they wrote. Notably, for the purpose of this book "political will" should extend also to actors' willingness or unwillingness to invest the resources required for attaining this leverage. In other words, to argue that the Bush administration did not have sufficient leverage over Khartoum is to suggest that it was either unable or unwilling to devote the assets or capital required to generate such leverage. As fuzzy as it may be, the semantic distinction between unwillingness and inability is still an important one to make.

As was seen in the case of Darfur, obtaining authorization for robust international action when one or more of the five permanent UN Security

Council member states has strong interests against it can be extremely difficult. Placing the fates of war-torn societies at the mercy of the Council—one of the most powerful but at the same time politicized bodies—remains a recipe for disaster. One way to reduce the political expediency internationally is via blocs of like-minded states that are committed to push mass atrocity prevention agendas in the UN General Assembly, the Security Council, or regional intergovernmental bodies. Such efforts have been ongoing for some time now under Swiss leadership, but they require broader and stronger support from states.[30]

Labeling a situation "genocide" will not lead to momentous shifts in public attitudes or official calculations. Most Americans have learned to live with the gap between ideals and institutional practices, particularly in relation to policy issues that are of no direct or immediate and significant concerns to them.[31] After Iraq, it could take a long time before a US government dares risk a full-scale military intervention for anything other than strategic and easy-to-communicate vital American interests. Obviously, humanitarian imperatives have hardly fallen into this category.

One impediment to Americans' participation in the foreign policy making process arises from their aversion to reading, hearing, or watching the unfolding of depressing "news events" over which they have no control, or so are led to believe. A way to mitigate these effects of compassion fatigue is through more systematic challenging of disingenuous frames pushed to the public sphere by executive branch officials or by other self-interested actors. Increased visibility of credible alternative policy options could reduce the sense of powerlessness for the public and encourage more active participation. Notedly, this would hardly require additional efforts or resources, as such alternatives are regularly researched, compiled and made available to policymakers and the media in real time by human rights NGOs, however, are rarely given wide enough exposure and prominence.

Another way forward would be to institutionalize policy approaches that integrate longer-term imperatives for action with carefully thought through checks on coercive options.[32] Military alternatives should be reserved for extreme situations, be custom tailored for the specific needs, and meet thresholds of operational feasibility and balance of consequences. Past failures to act robustly through nonmilitary or limited coercive measures can often be traced to unwillingness by the United States and other key states to invest sufficient diplomatic, political, or economic resources to this end. Greater focus on these omissions and on expanding and improving the nonmilitary toolkit would make it harder for governments to hide behind half measures or pretexts of all-or-nothing choices.

APATHY OR EMPATHY

Senator William Proxmire fought longer and harder than most advocates for a US ratification of the Genocide Convention. In one of 3,211 speeches he gave on this topic over a period of nineteen years he pointed to ignorance and indifference as the two greatest "enemies" of success.[33] The same two sentiments proved detrimental to the willingness of the American public to concern itself with the suffering of "faraway others."

How keen were Americans to take part in policy debates over situations that cried for help but that, according to what they had been told, demanded considerable risk taking without clear benefits or guaranteed success? As revealed in this book, neither American exceptionalist values nor empathy could move the public or its representatives sufficiently to take the leap from the "never again" ideal to its implementation, from expressions of concern and condemnation to the willingness to bear the costs of action, from professed opinions to actual behavior.

So long as humanitarian interventions are presented to Americans, or are perceived by them, as all-or-nothing military campaigns, the constraints on the use of force discussed in this book will continue to outweigh imperatives for robust action. Before offering sustained support, Americans would have liked to receive assurances of high prospects for a mission success, low risks of casualties, multilateral sharing of burden, and international legitimacy for action. As some of these assurances were difficult—indeed impossible— to offer, the potential benefits of preventing, mitigating, or halting atrocities in far-off places could rarely secure strong, comprehensive, and sustained public backing. Altruistic sentiments were therefore weakened, morally driven pressures were moderated, and policymakers were provided with influential arguments with which to justify inaction. Accountability was also less likely to be sought by an anxious, undecided, or disinterested citizenry. Hence the process tended to stall not at the level of the principle but of its implementation.

CONCLUDING THOUGHTS

In a rebuke to the war in Vietnam and to American exceptionalism, Senator William Fulbright wrote in 1966, "We are not God's chosen savior of mankind but only one of mankind's more successful and fortunate branches, endowed by our Creator with about the same capacity for good and evil, no more or less, than the rest of humanity."[34] To be sure, the self-interests underpinning American foreign policy have been no different from those informing the policies of other states. It was the gap between righteous rhetoric and immoral actions that stood out so visibly in the case of the United States.[35] The Declaration of Independence, the nation's most cherished document, proclaims, "We hold these truths to be self-evident, that all men are created equal, that they are endowed by their creator with certain unalienable rights." While celebrated in speech, this universalist tenet has been far from scrupulously adhered to in practice by and within the United States. America's external transgressions, the products of considerable needs and sufficient power to pursue them, but at times also of greed, condescending attitudes, and a mythical yearning to export American values overseas, have earned the country a reputation far apart from some of the moralizing principles on which it had been founded.[36] In a similar vein, the double standards of violations of other nations' sovereignty, while aggressively defending its own, presented America and Americans to the world as hypocritical.[37] Fueled by these and other factors,[38] antipathy toward the US masked for foreigners well-intentioned and at times successful efforts to do "good" pursued by many Americans outside and sometimes within the US political establishment, in two World Wars and thereafter.[39]

Martin Mennecke once observed that "the only place where the 'G-word' seems to retain an aura of moral superiority . . . is within domestic politics, as seen . . . in the United States."[40] His assertion may well be factual; but as the findings of this book have shown, this "moral superiority" still failed to transform exceptionalist ideals into genuine policy commitments. Notably, while much of the criticism leveled against the United States has been warranted, political will for action in most other countries has not been any more openhanded; if anything, likely the opposite. Disregarding this fact, America's critics continue to focus their attention on its wrongdoings—past and present—and choose to ignore the misdeeds of others. The meaningful support provided by many states to the offending Sudanese regime over Darfur had reflected these omissions. Political scientist John Kane wrote in 2008, "The world will not let America be ordinary. It will always judge the faults of American leaders more harshly than those of more unsavory regimes in nations whose history and ideology have never, in any case, promised better—that is only natural. But it will also judge them more harshly than those of other liberal democratic nations because America from the start made the role of liberal democratic exemplar part of its identity. US foreign policy must somehow accommodate this fact."[41]

The study of America's relationship with genocide cannot and should not substitute for research of the same dynamics elsewhere in the world, particularly in key countries like China and Russia and in sensitive parts of Africa and the Middle East. If Mennecke was right about the weaker traction of the "genocide" label outside the United States, then discovering what other words, stories, or influences can strengthen popular domestic support for prevention efforts in these societies—democratic and not—would be, without a doubt, a worthwhile endeavor.

Making choices on preferred responses to distant atrocities can be contentious and uncertain, for policymakers, but also for journalists and private citizens. Still the approach espoused in this book calls for those who live in countries with better human rights protections to share a more proactive moral commitment to helping those who are less fortunate, even at certain costs. The architects of the Responsibility to Protect doctrine have tried to translate this undertaking into an implementation agenda, thus far with modest success, though, arguably, with long-term potential. In a world beset by rising sectarianism and fears of "others" that is yet to encounter the consequences of global warming, with millions more refugees set to be added to the current levels—the highest since World War II—the threats of violent conflict will continue to occupy our shared future.

As I noted in the preface to this book, one of the aims of this project has been to advance a new research agenda in genocide studies, one that focuses on domestic publics as potentially pivotal actors/factors in policy decision making on atrocity prevention and intervention. One of the areas to explore is the relationship between neglected violent conflicts overseas and internal policy debates in the United States and elsewhere in the West. Arguably, better understanding of the links between mass atrocities perpetrated in the distance and contested domestic topics such as refugee intake and terrorism may one day bring governments—with back-wind from their publics—a step closer to recalibrating cost-benefit calculations on atrocity prevention.[42]

Epilogue

EVEN AFTER 2004, once the Save Darfur Coalition had become the most significant anti-genocide pressure group in American history with notable achievements in congressional advocacy, and in advancing Darfur's visibility, public voices could still not exact sufficient pressure on President Bush to change his essentially noninterventionist policy.[1] The early actions of his successor, Barack Obama, brought initially high hopes for the atrocity prevention community. As a US senator, Obama had professed strong support for a more meaningful American role on Darfur. Soon after taking office, he appointed Samantha Power—an advocate for robust US policies on genocide—as US ambassador to the UN. In August 2011, his White House released a Presidential Study Directive (PSD-10) that designated the prevention of mass atrocities and genocide "a national security interest and a core moral responsibility of the US."[2] However, thereafter the administration's policies on Sudan, Syria, and some other man-made crises were to falter, at times badly.[3] The creation of an Atrocity Prevention Board, a significant step forward, had suffered implementation challenges, which according to observers required but did not receive sufficient support from the commander in chief.[4]

As this book goes to print, a popular uprising in Sudan, supported by the military, has just deposed President Omar al-Bashir (11 April 2019), ending his thirty-year iron grip on the country. As a precarious power struggle ensues between the civilian leaders of the revolt, the Sudanese Army, and the Rapid Support Forces (RSF) - a violent and powerful paramilitary force incorporating among others the notorious Janjaweed, the stakes for Sudan's future could not be higher.[5]

In the days before the uprising however, as in the preceding fifteen years since 2004, Darfur remained in the clutches of violence while the world moved on. The United States was slowly but steadily "normalizing" its relationship with Sudan, a policy embarked on by the Obama administration.[6] President al-Bashir continued to evade a long standing indictment by the International Criminal Court on charges of war crimes, crimes against humanity, and genocide, and was able to travel internationally, including to countries who as parties to the court were legally obliged to arrest and hand him over to the Hague.[7] Eric Reeves continued to report, record, and ring the alarm, but to an even less attentive international community.[8] Syria, Yemen, South Sudan, Myanmar, and other situations involving mass atrocities were occasionally and for short periods capturing global media's attention, but to very modest results. Worse calamities had to befall the people of forgotten conflicts such as Darfur, it seemed, to bring them back to the spotlight and the international agenda.

It is yet to be revealed whether and how President Trump will rise to these and other challenges described in this book.[9] His foreign policy agenda and actions have generated thus far a confused mix of antagonistic and isolationist policies, which oftentimes left America's traditional allies quite frustrated. Firming up constituencies for atrocity prevention will require strong leadership oriented toward inclusiveness, cooperation and good will, not polarization. In the current climate where politics of fear set the official tone and interactions, this kind of leadership is yet to manifest itself. The light from "the city upon the hill" does not shine very brightly these days, it seems. It remains to be seen longer term what approaches will be adopted by upcoming administrations and what impacts shifting power dynamics inside US domestic politics will have on their foreign policy choices.

ACKNOWLEDGMENTS

THIS WORK WAS INSPIRED by two luminaries in my academic journey's skies. First, Eric Reeves, a Sudan expert whose boundless devotion to defending the country's vulnerable peoples has been little short of a marvel. Second is my stepfather and mentor Yehuda Bauer, who even today at the age of ninety-three never ceases to amaze me and so many others with his knowledge, humility, wisdom, and passion. I share any merits from this book with them, together with my wife and children, who had to endure the long and demanding process of researching and writing this book.

My gratitude extends also to all those who have contributed in various ways to the project. First and foremost, to Wendy Lambourne for years of encouragement, commitment, and mentorship. Others to mention are Jake Lynch, Colin Tatz, Aidan Hehir, the late Sheri Rosenberg, Douglas Irvin-Erickson, Dirk Moses, Ben Goldsmith, Joseph Dahm, and Lindsay Jamison. They are all, of course, free of fault for anything wrong or remiss in the text. I was supported also by the academic community around the Centre for Peace and Conflict Studies (today, the Department of Peace and Conflict Studies) at the University of Sydney—most notably Ken Macnab, Stuart Reese, Annie Herro, and my keen students who continue to challenge my thinking every day.

A final group to whom I am indebted are friends and colleagues from the Genocide Prevention Advisory Network (GPANet), which I had the fortune and privilege to learn from over the years. Special thanks are owed to Barbara Harff, Helen Fein, Jennifer Leaning, Liberata Mulamula, Andrea Bartoli, Roy Gutman, Birger Heldt, Tetsushi Ogata, James Smith, and Ekkehard Strauss. I recognize also with great fondness the late Ted Gurr, who had given me first access to this remarkable group.

NOTES

PREFACE

1. This is not to suggest that such research has not been done before; to be sure, a variety of studies have been conducted on the roles and functions of public opinion, the media, and other domestic actors. However, these efforts have come short of an organized, multidisciplinary coordinated research focused on intervention and prevention.

INTRODUCTION

1. George W. Bush, "The 2000 Campaign: 2nd Presidential Debate between Gov. Bush and Vice President Gore" (transcript), *New York Times*, 12 October 2000.
2. Al Gore, "The 2000 Campaign: 2nd Presidential Debate between Gov. Bush and Vice President Gore" (transcript), *New York Times*, 12 October 2000.
3. See the discussion of opinion polls in Chapter 4. Regarding the American elites, see also Stephen Wertheim, "A Solution from Hell: The United States and the Rise of Humanitarian Interventionism, 1991–2003," *Journal of Genocide Research* 12, nos. 3–4 (2010): 158–159.
4. Bill Clinton, *My Life* (New York: Knopf, 2004), 593.
5. Kenneth J. Campbell, *Genocide and the Global Village* (New York: Palgrave, 2001), 49–53.
6. Samantha Power, *"A Problem from Hell": America and the Age of Genocide* (London: Flamingo, 2003), 508–509.
7. John Kerry, "Remarks on Daesh and Genocide," US Department of State, 17 March 2016, https://2009–2017.state.gov/secretary/remarks/2016/03/254782 .htm; US House of Representatives, "H.Con.Res.75, Expressing the Sense of Congress that the Atrocities Perpetrated by ISIL Against Religious and Ethnic Minorities in Iraq and Syria Include War Crimes, Crimes Against Humanity, and Genocide, 14 March 2016," www.congress.gov/bill/114th-congress/house -concurrent-resolution/75.
8. United Nations, "Myanmar Military Leaders Must Face Genocide Charges—UN report," *UN News*, 27 August 2018, https://news.un.org/en/story/2018/08 /1017802.
9. The work itself was published a year later in 1944. Raphael Lemkin, *Axis Rule in Occupied Europe. Laws of Occupation. Analysis of Government. Proposals for Redress* (Washington: Carnegie Endowment for International Peace, Division of International Law, 1944).
10. United Nations, *The Convention on the Prevention and Punishment of the Crime of Genocide, 1948.*
11. In politicides the victim groups are defined not by their communal characteristics (e.g., ethnicity, religion, nationality), as in genocide, but primarily in terms

of their hierarchical position or political opposition to the regime and dominant groups. Barbara Harff and Ted R. Gurr, "Toward Empirical Theory of Genocides and Politicides," *International Studies Quarterly* 37, no. 3 (1988): 360. Controversies over the exact number of cases are due mostly to definitional differences. See the comprehensive list in Barbara Harff, "Genocides and Politicides Events 1955–2002" (Genocide Prevention Advisory Network, 2009), www.gpanet.org/content/genocides-and-politicides-events-1955-2002; Gregory Stanton, "Genocide, Politicides and Other Mass Murder since 1945," www.genocidewatch.org/aboutgenocide/genocidespoliticides.html.

12. On mass violence carried out or supported by the United States, see discussions in Henry C. Theriault, "The Albright-Cohen Report: From Realpolitik Fantasy to Realist Ethics," *Genocide Studies and Prevention* 4, no. 2 (2009): 202–206; Daniel Feierstein, "Getting Things into Perspective (from a Symposium on the Albright-Cohen Report)," *Genocide Studies and Prevention* 4, no. 2 (2009): 156–160.

13. Gerard Prunier, *Darfur: The Ambiguous Genocide* (Ithaca, NY: Cornell University Press, 2005), 156.

14. As discussed in Chapter 4, after Rwanda many believed that if genocide had been declared by the Clinton administration, the United States would have been forced to act much more robustly.

15. As mandated by Article VIII of the Genocide Convention. See comments by US delegate to the UNSC at the Council's 5040th meeting, UN Doc. S/PV.5040 (18 September 2004), 6.

16. Colin Powell, "The Crisis in Darfur: Testimony before the Senate Foreign Relations Committee" (US Department of State, 9 September 2004).

17. Madeleine K. Albright and William S. Cohen, *Preventing Genocide: A Blueprint for U.S. Policymakers* (Washington, DC: US Holocaust Memorial Museum, 2008), xxi.

18. David Scheffer, "Genocide and Atrocity Crimes," *Genocide Studies and Prevention* 1, no. 3 (2006): 229.

19. Ibid., 229.

20. The proposal included the designation of a new field in international law, atrocity law, which would deal with "atrocity crimes." See Scheffer, "Genocide and Atrocity Crimes," 229.

21. David Scheffer, "Atrocity Crimes: Framing the Responsibility to Protect," *Case Western Reserve Journal of International Law* 40, nos. 1–2 (2008): 111.

22. For example, taking action in Iraq in 1991, and again in 2003; in Haiti in 1994; in Goma-Zaire, after the 1994 Rwandan genocide was already over; in Bosnia in 1995 after Srebrenica; and in Kosovo in 1998. Instances of inaction included East Timor in 1975, support for the Khmer Rouge after the Vietnamese occupation of Cambodia in 1979, and inaction over Rwanda in 1994 during the genocide.

23. Power, *"A Problem from Hell,"* xxi. See also quotes from President Clinton in Benjamin A. Valentino, "Still Standing By: Why America and the International Community Fail to Prevent Genocide and Mass Killing" (review essay), *Perspectives on Politics* 1 (2003): 565–566; and also Jimmy Carter, "39th President of the United States, Remarks at the Presentation of the Final Report of the President's Commission on the Holocaust" (White House, 27 September 1979); Ronald Reagan, "40th President of the United States, Remarks at the International Convention of B'nai B'rith," 6 September 1984, in *Public Papers of the Presidents of the United States: Ronald Reagan, 1987* (Washington, DC: GPO, 1994), 479; George H. W. Bush, "Remarks at the Simon Wiesenthal Dinner,

Century Plaza Hotel, Los Angeles, California" (Federal News Service, 16 June 1991).

24. That is, until after the Srebrenica massacres. See Samantha Power, "It's Not Enough to Call It Genocide," *Time*, 4 September 2004.

25. President Truman, who strongly supported the convention, called on the Senate to ratify it, as did Dean Rusk, deputy undersecretary of state. Lawrence J. LeBlanc, *The United States and the Genocide Convention* (Durham, NC: Duke University Press, 1991), 1. See also summary in Power, *A Problem from Hell*, 64–70.

26. A recent example to the importance of domestic politics in the United States was the curtailing of the Obama administration's threat to respond militarily to the use of chemical weapons in Syria in 2013.

27. Surveys that tested the salience of foreign policy goals have ranked altruistic goals considerably lower than self-interest objectives. See the discussion in Chapter 3.

28. Jesse Helms, "American Sovereignty and the UN," *National Interest*, 1 December 2000.

29. On framing, see Robert M. Entman, "Framing: Toward Clarification of a Fractured Paradigm," *Journal of Communication* 43, no. 4 (1993): 51–58; Entman, *Projections of Power: Framing News, Public Opinion, and U.S. Foreign Policy* (Chicago: University of Chicago Press, 2004), 4–6; Doris A. Graber, *Processing the News: How People Tame the Information Tide* (2nd ed.) (New York: Longman, 1988); Daniel Kahneman and Amos Tversky, "Choices, Values, and Frames," *American Psychologist* 39, no. 4 (1984): 341–350.

30. See discussions in John Kane, *Between Virtue and Power: The Persistent Moral Dilemma of US Foreign Policy* (New Haven, CT: Yale University Press, 2008), 3–7; Godfrey Hodgson, *The Myth of American Exceptionalism* (New Haven, CT: Yale University Press, 2009), 9–13; Trevor B. McCrisken, *American Exceptionalism and the Legacy of Vietnam: US Foreign Policy since 1974* (Basingstoke: Palgrave Macmillan, 2003), 1–17.

31. Stanley Hoffmann, "American Exceptionalism: The New Version," in *American Exceptionalism and Human Rights*, ed. Michael Ignatieff (Princeton, NJ: Princeton University Press, 2005), 226.

32. James M. McCormick, *American Foreign Policy and American Values* (Itasca, IL: F. E. Peacock, 1985), 5–21; Roger S. Whitcomb, *The American Approach to Foreign Affairs: An Uncertain Tradition* (Westport, CT: Praeger, 1998), 18–24; Henry W. Brand, *What America Owes the World: The Struggle for the Soul of Foreign Policy* (Cambridge: Cambridge University Press, 1998), preface; McCrisken, *American Exceptionalism*, 11; Henry Kissinger, *American Foreign Policy*, 3rd ed. (New York: Norton, 1977), 91–92; Samuel P. Huntington, *American Politics: The Promise of Disharmony* (Cambridge, MA: Harvard University Press, 1981).

33. McCrisken, *American Exceptionalism,* 2, 17.

34. See the gap between political ideals and political reality in Huntington, *American Politics*, 3–4, 42, 72; between ideals and institutional practices, in Samuel P. Huntington, "American Ideals versus American Institutions," *Political Science Quarterly* 97, no. 1 (1982): 1.

CHAPTER 1 AMERICA'S RELATIONSHIP WITH GENOCIDE

1. Michael P. Scharf and Colin T. McLaughlin, "On Terrorism and Whistleblowing," *Case Western Reserve Journal of International Law* 38, nos. 3–4 (2006–2007): 569.

2. Ibid. See also the story in Michael Scharf, "International Law in Crisis: A Qualitative Empirical Contribution to the Compliance Debate," *Cardozo Law Review* 31 (2009–2010): 78–79.

3. Scharf and McLaughlin, "On Terrorism and Whistleblowing," 570. See also Peter Ronayne, *Never Again? The United States and the Prevention and Punishment of Genocide since the Holocaust* (Lanham, MD: Rowman & Littlefield, 2001), 121.

4. Conrad Harper, "Remarks at a Day-Long Conference," cited in Michael P. Scharf and Paul R. Williams, *Shaping Foreign Policy in Times of Crisis: The Role of International Law and the State Department Legal Adviser* (Cambridge: Cambridge University Press, 2010), 110, emphasis added. For a contrasting view about the genocidal characteristics of the civil war, see William A. Schabas, "Genocide and the International Court of Justice: Finally, a Duty to Prevent the Crime of Crimes," *Genocide Studies and Prevention: An International Journal* 2, no. 2 (2007).

5. Scharf and Williams, *Shaping Foreign Policy,* 147–168.

6. Scharf, "International Law in Crisis," 97.

7. Eugene R. Wittkopf and Christopher M. Jones, with Charles W. Kegley Jr., *American Foreign Policy: Patterns and Processes,* 7th ed. (Belmont, CA: Thomson, 2008), 17. See another broad conceptualization in Kalevi J. Holsti, *International Politics: A Framework for Analysis,* 5th ed. (Englewood Cliffs, NJ: Prentice Hall, 1988), 110–115. A more nuanced (poststructuralist) breakdown of the ideational component, with an emphasis on identities of self and others, is provided in Lene Hansen, *Security as Practice: Discourse Analysis and the Bosnian War* (London: Routledge, 2006), 5–9.

8. Holsti, *International Politics,* 93–94.

9. Ibid., 318–319.

10. Power, *"A Problem from Hell,"* 508. See also Samantha Power, "Never Again: The World's Most Unfulfilled Promise," *Frontline Online,* 1998, www.pbs.org /wgbh/pages/frontline/shows/karadzic/genocide/neveragain.html.

11. Not unlike European powers and neighboring states to countries where genocide was unfolding. Power, *"A Problem from Hell,"* 508.

12. Ibid., 504. The objection to committing US troops, according to Power, was common across the spectrum in the United States, including among the most ardent supporters of interventions.

13. See detailed discussion in ibid., 504–510. See also Brian D. Lepard, *Rethinking Humanitarian Intervention: A Fresh Legal Approach Based on Fundamental Ethical Principles in International Law and World Religions* (University Park: Pennsylvania State University Press, 2002), 375.

14. Power, *"A Problem from Hell,"* 508.

15. Ibid. See also Samantha Power, "Raising the Cost of Genocide," *Dissent* 49, no. 2 (Spring 2002): 85–95.

16. Notably, concerted scholarly attention to these visible cases was for a long time typical of most studies of interventions and noninterventions in the evolving subfield of genocide studies. In recent years, more studies have been published on colonial genocides and other hidden cases of genocide.

17. See the discussion about the American filtered narrative in Alexander Laban Hinton, Thomas La Pointe, and Douglas Irvin-Erickson, "Introduction," in *Hidden Genocides: Power, Knowledge, Memory,* ed. Alexander Laban Hinton, Thomas La Pointe, Douglas Irvin-Erickson (New Brunswick, NJ: Rutgers University Press, 2013), 1–18. See also A. Dirk Moses, "Why the Discipline of 'Genocide Studies' Has Trouble Explaining How Genocides End?" (Social Science Research Council, December 2006), http://howgenocidesend.ssrc.org /Moses/.

18. Ronayne, *Never Again?,* 4–6.

19. Ibid., 3.
20. Ibid., 199–200, 203.
21. Ibid., 3.
22. Ibid., 199.
23. Ibid., 203.
24. Ibid., 3, 9, 198, 203–204.
25. Ibid., 3–4, 204.
26. Campbell, *Genocide and the Global Village*, 4. For critical reviews of Campbell, see H. Hintjens, "Review of Kenneth J. Campbell, Genocide and the Global Village (NY: Palgrave, 2001)," *African Affairs* 102, no. 406 (2003): 162–164; Mia M. Bloom, "Comparative Review Essay of Stuart J. Kaufman, Modern Hatreds: The Symbolic Politics of Ethnic War (Cornell University Press, 2001) and Kenneth J. Campbell, Genocide and the Global Village (NY: Palgrave, 2001)," *Nationalism and Ethnic Politics* 8, no. 3 (Summer 2003): 116–118.
27. Campbell, *Genocide and the Global Village*, 4–5, 100.
28. Ibid., 5.
29. Ibid., 45–51, 99–100.
30. Settling instead on a lesser charge of withholding information that they had about these genocides. Power, *"A Problem from Hell,"* 506.
31. Campbell, *Genocide and the Global Village*, 51–52. See also Philip Everts, "When the Going Gets Rough: Does the Public Support the Use of Military Force?," *World Affairs* 162, no. 3 (Winter 2000): 102–103, 105.
32. Campbell, *Genocide and the Global Village,* 53.
33. Ibid., 50–52. See extended analysis in Chapter 5.
34. Ibid., 102–107.
35. The Global Policy Forum website lists sixty-two incursions of sorts, mainly clandestine military operations, during the second half of the twentieth century alone. Global Policy Forum, "US Interventions: US Military and Clandestine Operations in Foreign Countries—1798–Present" (2005), www.globalpolicy.org/empire/history/interventions.htm.
36. Notably, the same behavior patterns were said to have been present in US responses and nonresponses to genocide. In Thomas G. Weiss, "Halting Genocide: Rhetoric versus Reality," *Genocide Studies and Prevention* 2, no. 1 (2007): 18.
37. Nicholas Wheeler defined selective responses as when agreed moral principles are at stake in two or more crisis situations, but national interests are seen as dictating divergent responses. Wheeler, *Saving Strangers: Humanitarian Intervention in International Society* (Oxford: Oxford University Press, 2000), 31.
38. Mohammed Ayoob, "Third World Perspectives on Humanitarian Interventions and International Administration," *Global Governance* 10 (2004): 101. See also 102–104, and 110–115 on selectivity and double standards in relation to humanitarian interventions. In the context of Darfur, see Alex J. Bellamy, "Responsibility to Protect or Trojan Horse? The Crisis in Darfur and Humanitarian Intervention after Iraq," *Ethics and International Affairs* 19, no. 2 (2005): 38–39.
39. See in Weiss, "Halting Genocide," 19.
40. See detailed discussions in Adam Jones, *Genocide: A Comprehensive Introduction*, 2nd ed. (New York: Taylor & Francis, 2010), chaps. 2 and 12.
41. Jones, *Genocide*, 396; Wheeler, *Saving Strangers*, 309. See also discussion in Taylor B. Seybolt, *Humanitarian Military Intervention: The Conditions for Success and Failure* (Oxford: Oxford University Press, 2007), 20.
42. From a public speech by Clinton in San Francisco, 26 February 1999. Michael T. Klare, "The Clinton Doctrine," *Nation*, 1 April 1999.

43. Power, *"A Problem from Hell,"* 509–510; Campbell, *Genocide and the Global Village*, 49–53; Ronayne, *Never Again?*, 200–202.

44. Kissinger, *American Foreign Policy*, 91–92.

45. McCrisken, *American Exceptionalism*, 2.

46. Ibid, 17.

47. Kane, *Between Virtue and Power*, 3.

48. Ibid., 3.

49. McCrisken, *American Exceptionalism*, 11.

50. Kane, *Between Virtue and Power*, 1.

51. Mainly during the Cold War but also before and after. See the list in Global Policy Forum, "US Interventions."

52. Examples include the 1944 firebombing of Dresden and Tokyo, the dropping of the atomic bombs on Hiroshima and Nagasaki in 1945, the carpet bombing of the countryside in Vietnam, Cambodia, and Laos during the Vietnam War (1969–1973), and other such uses of indiscriminate force. For context on World War II events, see Cathal J. Nolan, "The United States, Moral Norms, and Governing Ideas in World Politics: A Review Essay," *Ethics and International Affairs* 7 (1993): 230; on the Vietnam War, see McCrisken, *American Exceptionalism*, 26, 33.

53. Whitcomb, *American Approach to Foreign Affairs*, 18–24. See discussion of the effects of Vietnam on Americans' sense of "exceptionalism" in McCrisken, *American Exceptionalism*, 4, 26–29, 37, and on the survival of exceptionalism in 36. Notably, Americans were encouraged to see Vietnam as a betrayal by their leaders, not a failure of the nation.

54. Starting with philosophers in ancient Greece, and then Machiavelli, Mazeran, Cromwell, etc.

55. Jacques Semélin, "An International but Especially an American Event," *Genocide Studies and Prevention* 4, no. 2 (2009): 163.

56. In fact, some of the most controversial American policies—the bombing of Hiroshima and Nagasaki in 1945, the war in Vietnam until 1969, and the US policy during the Rwandan genocide—were implemented by Democrat administrations. See discussions in Cathal J. Nolan, "Introduction," in *Ethics and Statecraft: The Moral Dimension of International Affairs*, 2nd ed., ed. Cathal J. Nolan (Westport, CT: Praeger, 2004), 1; Joel H. Rosenthal, "What Constitutes an Ethical Approach to International Affairs?" (Lecture 1; Carnegie Council for Ethics in International Affairs, 2001), www.cceia.org/education/002/course_on_ethics_and_international_affairs/718.html; Joel H. Rosenthal, "The United States: The Moral Nation?" (Lecture 6; Carnegie Council for Ethics in International Affairs, 2001), www.cceia.org/education/002/course_on_ethics_and_international_affairs/723.html.

57. Hans J. Morgenthau, "The Evil of Politics and the Ethics of Evil," *Ethics* 56, no. 1 (1945): 10–18.

58. Robert W. McElroy, *Morality and American Foreign Policy: The Role of Ethics in International Affairs* (Princeton, NJ: Princeton University Press, 1992), 3.

59. Andrew Natsios, "Illusions of Influence: The CNN Effect in Complex Emergencies," in *From Massacres to Genocide: The Media, Public Policy, and Humanitarian Crises*, ed. Robert I. Rotberg and Thomas G. Weiss (Washington, DC: Brookings Institution, 1996), 158; see also Anthony Lake and Roger Morris, "Pentagon Papers (2): The Human Reality of Realpolitik," *Foreign Policy* 4 (1971): 159–160.

60. Cited in Power, *"A Problem from Hell,"* 288.

61. Foreign policy decision making, it was argued, necessarily involves mulling over normative considerations. In Nolan, "Introduction," 1; McElroy, *Morality and American Foreign Policy*, 4.

62. Michael J. Smith, S. Neil MacFarlane, and Thomas Weiss, "Political Interest and Humanitarian Action," *Security Studies* 10, no. 1 (2000): 112–142; Leslie H. Gelb and Justine A. Rosenthal, "The Rise of Ethics in Foreign Policy," *Foreign Affairs* 82, no. 3 (2003): 2; Rosenthal, "United States." On the national interest vs. good international citizenship, see the introduction in Thomas G. Weiss, David P. Forsythe, Roger A. Coates, and Kelly K. Pease, *The United Nations and Changing World Politics*, 6th ed. (Boulder, CO: Westview, 2010), lvi–lviii.

63. Joseph S. Nye, "Redefining the National Interest," *Foreign Affairs* 78, no. 3 (1999): 23. Nye provides as an example the public's opposition to the ethnic cleansing in the Balkans, a salient topic during the Kosovo crisis in 1999.

64. Ibid., 24, 30.

65. Ibid., 24.

66. Rosenthal, "United States."

67. Wheeler, *Saving Strangers*, 202.

68. Power, "Never Again."

69. Andrew S. Natsios, *U.S. Foreign Policy and the Four Horsemen of the Apocalypse: Humanitarian Relief in Complex Emergencies* (Westport, CT: Praeger, 1997), 161.

70. John Shattuck, "Human Rights and Humanitarian Crises: Policy-Making and the Media," in *From Massacres to Genocide: The Media, Public Policy, and Humanitarian Crises*, ed. Robert I. Rotberg and Thomas G. Weiss (Washington, DC: Brookings Institution, 1996), 174.

71. John Mueller, "Public Opinion as a Constraint on US Foreign Policy: Assessing the Perceived Value of American and Foreign Lives" (paper, National Convention of the International Studies Association, Los Angeles, 14–18 March 2000), 7–8.

72. Gray C. Wheeler and David W. Moore, "Clinton's Foreign Policy Ratings Plunge," *Gallup Poll Monthly*, October 1993, 25–28, cited in David T. Burbach, "Presidential Approval and the Use of Force" (Defense and Arms Control Studies working paper, May 1994), 1–2. According to Burbach, Clinton's foreign policy rating dropped even further, from 55 percent in late September to 36 percent after Mogadishu (ibid., 2n5). Notably, however, a decline in Americans' support for the mission is said to have already been robust *before* the firefight. See Eric V. Larson and Bogdan Savych, *American Public Support for U.S. Military Operations from Mogadishu to Baghdad* (Santa Monica, CA: RAND, 2005), 34–35, 39–41, www.rand.org/pubs/monographs/MG231.

73. Mueller, "Public Opinion as a Constraint," 11–12. Mueller argued (14) that even the debacle in Vietnam—a far more important venture—was largely irrelevant to the outcomes of the 1972 presidential election, due to continued majority support for the war and other factors.

74. Steven Kull, "American Public Opinion, the Media, and Genocide Prevention," in "Genocide Prevention, Morality, and the National Interest," by Jerry Fowler, Samantha Power, David Scheffer, Holly Burkhalter, Scott Feil, Roy Gutman, Allen Hertzke, Steven Kull, and Aryeh Neier, *Journal of Human Rights* 1, no. 4 (2002): 459, emphasis added.

75. Ibid., 461. See a more detailed discussion in Chapter 5.

76. Rudolph J. Rummel, *Statistics of Democide: Genocide and Mass Murder since 1990* (Münster: Lit Verlag, 1998), 205. "Democide" is defined by Rummel as "the murder of any person or people by a government, including genocide, politicide, and mass murder." In Rudolph J. Rummel, *Death by Government* (New Brunswick, NJ: Transaction, 1994), 31.

77. Lake and Morris, "Pentagon Papers (2)," 157–162. In the commentary, the two authors responded to the shock felt by many Americans following the public release of the Pentagon Papers (which effectively exposed offenses and misdeeds by successive US presidents and their administrations in relation to the "crisis" and then war in Vietnam).
78. Lake and Morris, "Pentagon Papers (2)," 157–158.
79. That is, the assumption in government was that these tough choices rarely needed to be formally posed, if at all, "until domestic political opposition (and public opinion, informed by media coverage of the human tragedies involved) is stimulated to hinder or stop a particular policy." Ibid., 161.
80. Ibid., 158.
81. Ibid., 158–159.
82. Ibid., 159–160.
83. Ibid., 160.
84. Ibid., 161.
85. Power, *"A Problem from Hell,"* 286.
86. Ibid., 287.
87. Ibid., 315.
88. Ibid., 311–312.
89. On 4 August 1993, Marshall Harris (Michael Gordon, "A State Dept. Aide on Bosnia Resigns on Partition Issue," *New York Times*, 5 August 1993, A1, A11); on 6 August 1993, Jon Western (Power, *"A Problem from Hell,"* 314); on 23 August 1993, Steven Walker (Daniel Williams, "A Third State Dept. Official Resigns over Balkan Policy," *Washington Post*, 24 August 1993). See also Scharf and McLaughlin, "On Terrorism and Whistleblowing," 570.
90. In Feierstein, "Getting Things into Perspective," 156. See also Hinton, La Pointe, and Irvin-Erickson, "Introduction," 1–4; and, more generally, Jeffrey S. Bachman, *The United States and Genocide: (Re)Defining the Relationship* (New York: Routledge, 2018).
91. Daniel Feierstein, "Human Rights? What a Good Idea! From Universal Jurisdiction to Preventive Criminology" (paper, annual conference of the International Association of Genocide Scholars, University of Queensland, July 2017).

CHAPTER 2 A POLICY-OPINION NEXUS

1. See Chapter 1.
2. On internal and external legitimacy, see Allen Buchanan, "The Internal Legitimacy of Humanitarian Intervention," *Journal of Political Philosophy* 7, no. 1 (1999): 72; Richard Vernon, "Humanitarian Intervention and the Internal Legitimacy Problem," *Journal of Global Ethics* 4, no. 1 (2008): 37–49. On international legitimacy, see Thomas M. Franck, *The Power of Legitimacy among Nations* (New York: Oxford University Press, 1990); Ian Clark, *Legitimacy in International Society* (Oxford: Oxford University Press, 2005); Ian Clark, *International Legitimacy and World Society* (Oxford: Oxford University Press, 2007); Christian Reus-Smit, "The Politics of International Law," in *The Politics of International Law*, ed. Christian Reus-Smit (Cambridge: Cambridge University Press, 2004), 14–44; Jutta Brunnée and Stephen J. Toope, *Legitimacy and Legality in International Law: An Interactional Account* (Cambridge: Cambridge University Press, 2010).
3. Clark, *Legitimacy in International Society*, 2. While the original Roman word *legitimus* meant "lawful; according to the law," in medieval times its meaning transmuted into "what conforms to ancient custom and to customary procedure."

See Dolf Sternberg, "Legitimacy," in *International Encyclopaedia of the Social Sciences*, ed. D. Stills (New York: Macmillan, 1968), 245.

4. Clark, *Legitimacy in International Society*, 185.

5. Ibid.

6. Philip J. Powlick, "The Sources of Public Opinion for American Foreign Policy Officials," *International Study Quarterly* 39, no. 4 (1995): 428.

7. Clark, *Legitimacy in International Society*, 185.

8. Helms, "American Sovereignty and the UN."

9. Thomas B. Trout, "Rhetoric Revisited: Political Legitimation and the Cold War," *International Studies Quarterly* 19, no. 3 (1975): 253, emphasis added.

10. Ibid., 254.

11. Ibid., 257.

12. Ibid., 258–259.

13. Ibid., 259.

14. Richard Melanson, *American Foreign Policy since the Vietnam War: The Search for Consensus from Richard Nixon to George W. Bush*, 4th ed. (Armonk, NY: M.E. Sharpe, 2005).

15. Melanson, *American Foreign Policy*, 37. Melanson cites here an unpublished study: Thomas B. Trout, "Legitimating Containment and Détente: A Comparative Analysis" (paper, Mid-West Political Science Association, Chicago, April 1979), 2–4.

16. Trout, "Legitimating Containment and Détente," 4, cited in Melanson, *American Foreign Policy*, 38.

17. Melanson, *American Foreign Policy*, 38.

18. McCrisken, *American Exceptionalism*, 180–187.

19. Ibid., 187.

20. Daniel J. Whelan, "Beyond the Black Heart: The United States and Human Rights," *Human Rights & Human Welfare* 3, no. 1 (2003): 25–56.

21. McCrisken, *American Exceptionalism*, 185–187.

22. Madeleine K. Albright and William S. Cohen, *Preventing Genocide: A Blueprint for US Policymakers* (Washington, DC: Holocaust Memorial Museum, 2008), 1. Prevention here includes responses to ongoing mass atrocities.

23. Lawrence Woocher, "A Reflection from the United States: Advancing Genocide Prevention through a High-Level Task Force," *Politorbis* 47, no. 2 (2009): 139.

24. Ibid., 139.

25. Ibid.

26. Natsios, "Illusions of Influence," 166.

27. Ibid., 166.

28. Ibid.

29. Shattuck, "Human Rights and Humanitarian Crises," 174.

30. Robert C. DiPrizio, *Armed Humanitarians: U.S. Interventions from Northern Iraq to Kosovo* (Baltimore: Johns Hopkins University Press, 2002), 164.

31. See extended discussion in Donald M. Snow, *United States Foreign Policy: Politics Beyond the Water's Edge*, 3rd ed. (Boston: Thomson Wadsworth, 2005), 89–118.

32. Ibid., 90–95. Notably, these prerogatives have been constrained by America's Founding Fathers, who, fearing concentration of too much power in the hands of one actor, created a system of checks and balances among the different components of government: the legislative, the executive, and the judicial.

33. The 1973 War Powers Act/Resolution, which was meant to check this power and subject it to congressional oversight, has had only partial success, and US

presents have continued since to use Authorizations for Use of Military Force to circumvent the constitutional congressional prerogative of declaring war.

34. Snow, *United States Foreign Policy*, 90–92, 95–96.
35. Murray Edelman, *Political Language: Words That Succeed and Policies That Fail* (New York: Academic Press, 1977), 142. Hansen also argued (*Security as Practice*, 23) that the internal/external foreign policy communications of states have been so pervasive that they left very little room for entirely "nonverbal" actions.
36. Poststructuralists have gone further than others ontologically to engage a foreign policy that they say is constructed mostly through "discourse." On poststructuralist theory, see Hansen, *Security as Practice*, 18, 21. On the origins of structuralist thought, see, e.g., Ferdinand de Saussure, *Writings in General Linguistics* (Oxford: Oxford University Press, 2006). Hansen, *Security as Practice*, 2–4.
37. McCrisken, *American Exceptionalism*, 18.
38. Ferdinand Tesón, *Humanitarian Intervention: An Inquiry into Law and Morality* (Dobbs Ferry, NY: Transnational, 1988), cited in Wheeler, *Saving Strangers*, 286.
39. Michael Hunt, *Ideology and US Foreign Policy* (New Haven, CT: Yale University Press, 1987), 15. Hunt also claimed that a failure by a public speaker to disclose genuine views on fundamental issues runs the risk over time of creating false public expectations and potentially politically dangerous misunderstandings. Indulgence in blatantly inconsistent rhetoric, he wrote, leads eventually to a diminished force and credibility. It is only when the rules expounded above are violated or the audience is left unconvinced that cultural insights could be misleading.
40. Hansen, *Security as Practice*, 7. See similarly Rosenthal, "United States."
41. Entman, *Projections of Power*, 5; Steven Livingston and David Stephen, "American Network Coverage of Rwanda in the Context of General Trends in International News," in *Early Warning and Early Response*, ed. Susanne Schmeidl and Howard Adelman (New York: Columbia International Affairs Online, 1998).
42. This type of coverage tends to produce what is known as "horse race" framing, often criticized for substituting emphasis on policy and substance with a focus on actors, their characteristics, and their successes or failures. Entman emphasizes actors' technique, success, and representativeness as the criteria used to measure this legitimacy. See Entman, *Projections of Power*, 6; Shanto Iyengar and Jennifer McGrady, *Media Politics: A Citizen's Guide* (New York: Norton, 2007), 223.
43. Entman, *Projections of Power*, 5. See also, from a poststructuralist perspective, Hansen's discussion in *Security as Practice*, xvi–xvii.
44. Entman, *Projections of Power*, 6. Note here the direct similarity between at least three of the four functions pointed to by Entman and the aspects of discourse with which this study is concerned. The attention paid in framing analysis to problem definition, moral evaluation, and proposed remedies closely parallels this study's focus on problem representation (mainly in relation to genocide), normative imperatives (e.g., "never again"), and the discussion of policy options.
45. Amy Mitchell et al., "How Americans Get Their News" (Pew Research Center, 7 July 2016). For more about the process of attitude formation in a discussion of the purposive belief systems model, see Benjamin I. Page with Marshall M. Bouton, *The Foreign Policy Disconnect: What Americans Want from Our Leaders but Don't Get* (Chicago: University of Chicago Press, 2006), 104–105.
46. Entman, *Projections of Power*, 123. Entman argued that in foreign policy there are few if any cases where a pure, unmediated public opinion emerges directly from reality and not from the media. Ibid., 124.
47. Ibid., 12.

48. Even those who do not follow the media may be indirectly influenced by it through family members, friends, or colleagues who do. See Iyengar and McGrady, *Media Politics.*

49. For example, hegemonic theorizing could argue that the stronger the influence of political elites through partisan cues, agenda setting, and other types of framing on the public, the more likely it is that the same constraints on moral concerns that affect political elites will also indirectly affect public opinion through these framing effects. It is also possible, however (as discussed later in the book), that the frame will be controlled by journalists or other elites who hold different attitudes.

50. Iyengar and McGrady, *Media Politics.* See also Stuart Oskamp, *Attitudes and Opinions* (Englewood Cliffs, NJ.: Prentice Hall, 1977), 17.

51. Thomas E. Patterson, "The News as a Reflection of Public Opinion," in *The Sage Book of Public Opinion Research,* ed. Wolfgang Donsbach and Michael W. Traugott (Thousand Oaks, CA: Sage, 2008), 8.

52. In relation to the United States, see Lawrence R. Jacobs and Benjamin I. Page, "Who Influences U.S. Foreign Policy?," *American Political Science Review* 99, no. 1 (2005): 107–123. Salience may be defined as "the relative significance of an issue to an actor . . . relative to all other issues." See discussion in Stuart N. Soroka, "Media, Public Opinion, and Foreign Policy," *Press/Politics* 8, no. 1 (2003): 29.

53. See Maxwell McCombs, "Building Consensus: The News Media's Agenda-Setting Roles," *Political Communication* 14 (1997): 435–436, http://blog.roodo .com/research_information/7496232b.pdf. Agenda setting is defined by McCombs as the ability of the mass media to transfer the salience of items on their agendas to the public agenda. Ibid., 433.

54. See, e.g., Peter Viggo Jakobsen, "Focus on the CNN Effect Misses the Point: The Real Media Impact on Conflict Management Is Invisible and Indirect," *Journal of Peace Research* 37, no. 2 (2000): 133.

55. Valentino, "Still Standing By," 566.

56. Eyal Mayroz, "'Ever Again?' The United States, Genocide Suppression, and the Crisis in Darfur," *Journal of Genocide Research* 10, no. 3 (2008): 379.

57. In Steven Livingston, "Clarifying the CNN Effect: An Examination of Media Effects According to Type of Military Intervention" (Research Paper R-18, Joan Shorenstein Center on Media, Politics and Public Policy, Harvard University, John F. Kennedy School of Government, June 1997), 10.

58. Based on the indexing model theory, the media would "index,'" or closely reflect elite debates only. Critical analysis of executive policies and decisions would appear on the news only if actors inside the government (administration or Congress) have done so first. Critical views expressed outside of Washington will not be reported. It is therefore only when elites disagree about foreign policy that the media will reflect their debates in ways which may affect foreign policy. See Lance W. Bennett, "Toward a Theory of Press-State Relations in the United States," *Journal of Communication* 40, no. 2, 1990: 103–125; Jonathan Mermin. *Debating War and Peace: Media Coverage of US Intervention in the Post-Vietnam Era* (Princeton, NJ: Princeton University Press, 1999), 7, 26, 143, 151–152; Iyengar and McGrady, *Media Politics,* 7.

59. The list includes World War II; certain Cold War crises before 1963; the Korea War; the Vietnam War; fleetingly, the Soviet invasion of Afghanistan in late 1979 presumably embellished by the Iran hostage crisis of 1979–1981; the apparently heightened prospect in the mid-1980s of nuclear war; the Gulf crisis and war; the terrorist attacks of 2001 within the United States and the ensuing war in Afghanistan; and the war against Iraq. Mueller, "Public Opinion as a Constraint," 4.

60. Page, *Foreign Policy Disconnect*, 43. The more "altruistic" goals were defined in such terms as "promoting and defending human rights in other countries" or "helping to improve the standard of living of less developed nations."

61. Of respondents, 39 percent considered it a very important foreign policy goal. Notably, Page had cautioned against taking these results as clear indications of weak altruistic tendencies within American society, pointing out that when adding together the "very important" and "somewhat important" categories, public support in these surveys would have risen to 90 percent. This high figure demonstrated to Page the readiness of most Americans to support this altruistic goal. Still, the way the questions were phrased would have indicated a principled support more than an actual commitment to the protection of human rights.

62. See also the definition in Oskamp, *Attitudes and Opinions*, 16. Another well-cited definition is Valdimer Orlando Key's from 1964: "those opinions held by private persons which governments find it prudent to heed" (cited in Powlick, "Sources of Public Opinion," 429).

63. Anthony Oberschall, "The Historical Roots of Public Opinion Research," in *The Sage Book of Public Opinion Research*, ed. Wolfgang Donsbach and Michael W. Traugott (Thousand Oaks, CA: Sage, 2008), 83.

64. Ibid.

65. Ole Holsti, "Foreword," in Richard Sobel, *The Impact of Public Opinion on U.S. Foreign Policy since Vietnam: Constraining the Colossus* (Oxford: Oxford University Press, 2001). See also discussion in Powlick, "Sources of Public Opinion," 430, on challenges to the importance attributed by American presidents to polls' results.

66. In relation to the use of public opinion by interest groups, see Mayling Birney, Ian Shapiro, and Michael J. Graetz, "The Political Uses of Public Opinion. Lessons from the Estate Tax Repeal" (unpublished paper, 2007), 2.

67. Valdimer Orlando Key Jr., *Public Opinion and American Democracy* (New York: Knopf, 1961), 263. About factoring anticipated latent reactions of the public into policy decisions, see Jane Mansbridge, "Rethinking Representation," *American Political Science Review* 97, no. 4 (November 2003): 516–520.

68. Powlick, "Sources of Public Opinion," 429.

69. Iyengar and McGrady, *Media Politics*, 11.

70. Ibid.

71. Richard A. Brody, *Assessing the President: The Media, Elite Opinion and Public Support* (Stanford, CA: Stanford University Press, 1991), 3.

72. Iyengar and McGrady, *Media Politics*, 11.

73. See summary in Thomas Knecht, "Public Opinion and Foreign Policy: The Stages of Presidential Decision Making," *International Studies Quarterly* 50 (2006): 708.

74. A detailed review of the historical evolution of the debate falls outside the scope of this book. See examples in Walter Lippmann, *Public Opinion* (New York: Harcourt, Brace, 1922); Walter Lippmann, *The Phantom Public* (New York: Harcourt, Brace, 1925); Gabriel A. Almond, *The American People and Foreign Policy* (New York: Harcourt Brace, 1950); George F. Kennan, *American Diplomacy, 1900–1950* (Chicago: University of Chicago Press, 1950); Hans J. Morgenthau, *Politics among Nations: The Struggle for Power and Peace*, 5th ed. (New York: Knopf, 1954); Walter Lippmann, *Essays in the Public Philosophy* (Boston: Little Brown, 1955); James N. Rosenau, *Public Opinion and Foreign Policy* (New York: Random House, 1961); Philip E. Converse, "The Nature of Belief Systems in Mass Publics," in *Ideology and Discontent*, ed. David Apter (New York: Free Press, 1964).

75. Eugene Wittkopf, *Faces of Internationalism: Public Opinion and American Foreign Policy* (Durham, NC: Duke University Press, 1990); Benjamin I. Page and Robert Y. Shapiro, *The Rational Public: Fifty Years of Trends in Americans' Policy Preferences* (Chicago: University of Chicago Press, 1992); Bruce W. Jentleson, "The Pretty Prudent Public: Post Post-Vietnam American Opinion and the Use of Military Force," *International Studies Quarterly* 36 (1992): 49–74; Ole R. Holsti, *Public Opinion and American Foreign Policy* (Ann Arbor: University of Michigan Press, 1996); Page, *Foreign Policy Disconnect*; Soroka, "Media, Public Opinion, and Foreign Policy," 27.

76. Page, *Foreign Policy Disconnect*, 228. See earlier contradicting reports in Powlick, "Sources of Public Opinion," 428.

77. Page, *Foreign Policy Disconnect*, 243.

78. For a detailed discussion, see ibid., 219–220.

79. Ibid., 243.

80. See the full argument, data, and analysis in Steven Kull and Mac I. Destler, *Misreading the Public: The Myth of a New Isolationism* (Washington, DC: Brookings Institution, 1999).

81. For example, Ken Kollman, *Outside Lobbying: Public Opinion and Interest Group Strategies* (Princeton, NJ: Princeton University Press, 1998), 9. On agenda setting in general, see Maxwell McCombs, "The Agenda-Setting Role of the Mass Media in the Shaping of Public Opinion" (manuscript, University of Texas at Austin, 2003); on agenda setting and media effects, see Iyengar and McGrady, *Media Politics*, chap. 8.

82. On framing, see Entman, "Framing," 51–58; Entman, *Projections of Power*, 4–6; Graber, *Processing the News*; Kahneman and Tversky, "Choices, Values, and Frames." On framing and agenda setting, see Jim A. Kuypers, Stephen D. Cooper, and Matthew T. Althouse, "The President and the Press: The Framing of George W. Bush's Speech to the United Nations on November 10, 2001," *American Communication Journal* 10, no. 3 (2008): 1–22.

83. Entman, *Projections of Power*, 10, 123–124.

84. See, e.g., Soroka, "Media, Public Opinion, and Foreign Policy," 28.

85. "Elites" here include the White House or other administration officials, members of Congress and their staffs, "think tankers," political/military/academic experts, interest groups, journalists, and even celebrities.

86. On persuasion and propaganda, see Teun A. Van Dijk, "Discourse and Manipulation," *Discourse & Society* 17, no. 3 (2006): 356–383.

87. Entman, *Projections of Power,* 123.

88. Ibid., 124.

89. As political communication scholars point out, the media may also impact national polls as survey questions and responses are both informed and shaped by media cues. Ibid., 21. Bernard Cohen, *The Public's Impact on Foreign Policy* (Boston: Little, Brown, 1973), 111–113; Entman, *Projections of Power*, 12–16; Kull and Destler, *Misreading the Public*, 219–221; Powlick, "Sources of Public Opinion," 434–437, 446–447. See also Steven Kull and Clay Ramsay, "US Public Opinion on Intervention in Bosnia," in *International Public Opinion and the Bosnia Crisis*, ed. Richard Sobel and Eric Shiraev (New York: Lexington Books, 2003), 105; Entman, *Projections of Power*, 19–20, 68–69.

90. Entman, *Projections of Power*, 122–143. Of course, congressional discourses and behavior are studied by policymakers not only as indicators of public opinion but also as representations of one of the most dominant players in American domestic politics.

91. A couple of methodological concerns need to be addressed. First, Entman has noted that policymakers rarely have the time to study in detail the information

they receive (*Projections of Power*, 12). This shortcoming may reduce their ability to construct a detailed image of what the public wants and thus the accuracy of the method proposed here. Likely variances in how different policymakers prioritize and/or interpret public opinion indicators increase also the difficulty to recreate such a picture. To address the challenges, the analysis explores multiple potential choices that administration officials could have faced at key decision junctions.

CHAPTER 3 WORDS VERSUS DEEDS IN AMERICA'S RELATIONSHIP WITH GENOCIDE

1. Power, *"A Problem from Hell,"* xxi.
2. The archives are considered the most extensive online resources of presidential public communications. See www.presidency.ucsb.edu.
3. The three instances included a scathing attack on China in relation to Tibet by presidential candidate Richard Nixon (1960); requests to the Senate to ratify the Genocide Convention by Nixon (1970); and in the context of a visit to Auschwitz by President Ford (1976). No uses of the term were found in the archived public communications of Eisenhower, Kennedy, or Johnson. Before 1951, Truman had invoked "genocide" mostly in his (failed) attempt to get the Genocide Convention through the Senate.
4. Carter, "39th President of the United States."
5. Notably, Carter took office in January 1977, well into the atrocities.
6. Ronayne, *Never Again?*, 68–69.
7. Richard Holbrooke, "Testimony at US House of Representatives, Subcommittee on International Organization" (House Hearing on Cambodia, 26 July 1977), cited in Ronayne, *Never Again?*, 68. See also Keith Pomakoy, *Helping Humanity: American Policy and Genocide Rescue* (Lanham, MD: Lexington Books, 2011).
8. Warren Christopher, "Human Rights: Cambodia," *Department of State Bulletin*, February 1978, 32, cited in Ronayne, *Never Again?*, 69.
9. Carter invoked it on 21 April 1978. Kia Guarino, "American Presidents and Humanitarian Crises: The Rhetorical Marginalization of Genocide in Cambodia, Bosnia and Rwanda" (honors thesis, Boston College, December 2008), 31; Ronayne, *Never Again?*, 71.
10. Jimmy Carter, "Human Rights Violations in Cambodia Statement by the President" (American Presidency Project, 21 April 1978).
11. Not once during this time did he mention the Holocaust in this context.
12. Jimmy Carter, "Aid for Kampucheans Remarks Announcing Additional Relief Efforts" (American Presidency Project, 24 October 1979). Jimmy Carter, "Interview with the President Remarks and a Question-and-Answer Session with Editors and Broadcasters from Minnesota" (American Presidency Project, 26 October 1979). See discussion of the Carter administration's avoidance of calling Cambodia "genocide" in Power, *"A Problem from Hell,"* 124.
13. Carter was said to have supported the Khmer Rouge for two main reasons: they had the support of America's new ally China and were considered the only feasible alternative to America's nemesis Vietnam as rulers of Cambodia. In Power, *"A Problem from Hell,"* 146–147.
14. Content analysis of the American Presidency Project archives.
15. The US failure to act had contrasted with its partial responsibility for the country's takeover by the Khmer Rouge. During the Vietnam War, Cambodian civilians were massacred by the tens of thousands by American bombings, "collateral damage" in the futile US attempts to eradicate North Vietnamese

insurgents hiding in the Cambodian countryside. This increased markedly the support for the then unpopular Khmer Rouge revolutionaries.

16. Reagan, "40th President of the United States," 479.
17. Power, *"A Problem from Hell,"* 160.
18. The president had committed himself to laying a wreath at a West German cemetery where, as it turned out, forty-nine Waffen-SS officials were also buried. Unable to wriggle out of the commitment and facing a media frenzy and vocal public criticism, Reagan decided to control the damage by throwing his weight behind the ratification of the Genocide Convention. Power, *"A Problem from Hell,"* 161–163.
19. Ronald Reagan, "Remarks at the National Legislative Conference of the Building and Construction Trades Department, AFL-CIO" (American Presidency Project, 5 April 1982).
20. Public statements by Reagan on 22 April 1981; 5 April 1982; 24 May, 6 June 1985; 5 March 1986; respectively.
21. Reagan, "Remarks at the National Legislative Conference of the Building and Construction Trades Department, AFL-CIO," emphasis added.
22. Based on a search of the American Presidency Project archives, conducted 30 May 2012. Notably, in at least nine instances, the word "holocaust" was used in the combination "nuclear holocaust," a term popular in discourses of American Cold War presidents.
23. See genocides/politicides during Reagan's presidency in Barbara Harff's list at www.gpanet.org/content/genocides-and-politicides-events-1955-2002.
24. For example, the ratification of the Genocide Convention.
25. Except presidential candidate Nixon's mentioning of Tibet in 1960.
26. George H. W. Bush, "Remarks on the Situation in Bosnia and an Exchange with Reporters in Colorado Springs" (American Presidency Project, 6 August 1992); George H. W. Bush, "The President's News Conference" (American Presidency Project, 7 August 1992).
27. George H. W. Bush, "Remarks to the Conference on Security and Cooperation in Europe in Helsinki, Finland" (American Presidency Project, 9 July 1992); Bush, "Remarks on the Situation in Bosnia"; George H. W. Bush, "Presidential Debate in St. Louis" (American Presidency Project, 11 October 1992).
28. Notably, the word "genocide" was not used on this occasion. Bush, "Remarks at the Simon Wiesenthal Dinner."
29. Ronayne, *Never Again?*, 119; Jon Western, "Sources of Humanitarian Intervention: Beliefs, Information, and Advocacy in U.S. Decisions on Somalia and Bosnia," in *The Domestic Sources of American Foreign Policy: Insights and Evidence*, 5th ed., ed. Eugene R. Wittkopf and James M. McCormick (Lanham, MD: Rowman & Littlefield, 2008), 357.
30. Ronayne, *Never Again?*, 118.
31. George H. W. Bush, "Remarks at the Community Welcome for Returning Troops in Sumter, South Carolina" (American Presidency Project, 17 March 1991); George H. W. Bush, "Remarks and a Question-and-Answer Session at a Rotary Club Dinner in Portsmouth, New Hampshire" (American Presidency Project, 15 January 1992); Bush, "Presidential Debate in St. Louis."
32. Bush, "Presidential Debate in St. Louis."
33. Dissenters within the State Department, some of whom ended up resigning in protest of the US failure to act. Power, *"A Problem from Hell,"* 288–293; Ronayne, *Never Again?*, 116–120.
34. Guarino, "American Presidents," 77. See also commentary by Bush in response to questions: Bush, "Remarks on the Situation in Bosnia"; Bush, "President's News Conference," 7 August 1992. Notably, the ICJ's confinement of its

genocide determination in Bosnia to the 1995 Srebrenica massacres (International Court of Justice, *Case Concerning the Application of the Convention on the Prevention and Punishment of the Crime of Genocide (Bosnia and Herzegovina vs. Serbia and Montenegro)*, 26 February 2007, para. 297) could be seen in hindsight as vindication of this rhetorical policy.

35. United Nations, *General Assembly Resolution A/47/92* (17 December 1992). The wording was "abhorrent policy of 'ethnic cleansing,' which is a form of genocide." According to Power (*"A Problem from Hell,"* 292), this was the closest Bush ever got to acknowledging "genocide" in Bosnia.

36. Power, *"A Problem from Hell,"* 292–293.

37. Piers Robinson, "The CNN Effect Revisited," *Critical Studies in Media Communication* 22, no. 4 (2005): 344–349., 344.

38. Sam Fulwood III, "Clinton Steps Up His Support for Military Action in Bosnia," *Los Angeles Times*, 6 August 1992.

39. Clifford Krauss, "U.S. Backs Away from Charge of Atrocities in Bosnia Camps," *New York Times*, 5 August 1992, emphasis added.

40. Hansen, *Security as Practice*, 116, 214; Ronayne, *Never Again?*, 121. See analyses of Clinton's rhetoric on Bosnia in Guarino, "American Presidents," 69–80; Hansen, *Security as Practice*, 111–115, 132–144, 181–184. Early enthusiasm inside the administration to the idea of "lift and strike"—lifting the arms embargo unilaterally from Bosnia's Muslims and offering them a protective aerial NATO shield against Bosnian-Serb aggression—had dwindled, reportedly due to strong European resistance and the apparent difficulty to transport weapons to the Muslims without ground force support. Ronayne, *Never Again?*, 122–125.

41. Guarino, "American Presidents," 77; Hansen, *Security as Practice*, 6. In relation to "ethnic cleansing," see Rony Blum, Gregory H. Stanton, Shira Sagi, and Elihu D. Richter, "'Ethnic Cleansing' Bleaches the Atrocities of Genocide," *European Journal of Public Health* 18, no. 2 (2008): 204–209.

42. Hansen, *Security as Practice*, 106–111, 164–179 (on the "Balkan" discourse), 111–115, 181–184 (on the "genocide" discourse). See also Guarino, "American Presidents," 71–73. Notably, according to Hansen (*Security as Practice*, 13, 132–144), even those who employed a "genocide discourse" in Congress and in other places to advocate strong action did not support the use of American ground troops to try to stop the atrocities.

43. William Clinton, "Remarks of President Bill Clinton at the Dedication Ceremonies for the United States Holocaust Memorial Museum" (ushmm.org, 22 April 1993).

44. William J. Clinton, "The President's News Conference" (American Presidency Project, 23 April 1993). For similar language two days before the inauguration, see William J. Clinton, "Exchange with Reporters Prior to Discussions with President Vaclav Havel of the Czech Republic" (American Presidency Project, 20 April 1993).

45. Clinton, "President's News Conference," 23 April 1993.

46. Clinton, *My Life*, 593.

47. Andrew Davidson, Kas Roussy, Mark Gollom, and Jessica Wong, "Bush, Clinton Get Standing Ovation after Toronto 'Conversation,'" *CBC News*, 29 May 2009, www.cbc.ca/news/canada/toronto/story/2009/05/29/clinton-bush -conversation-toronto.html.

48. For example, not once during the genocide did Clinton assemble his top advisors to discuss the US response. Power, *"A Problem from Hell,"* 366.

49. Ibid., 367.

50. Ibid., 334–336, 369–370, 372–273.

51. Ibid., 366, 371–377.

52. Guarino, "American Presidents," 89. See also Douglas Jehl, "Officials Told to Avoid Calling Rwanda Killings 'Genocide,'" *New York Times*, 10 June 1994.

53. Guarino, "American Presidents," 94–96.

54. Ibid., 88.

55. In relation to Bosnia, see ibid., 71–73. For analysis of Clinton's discourse, see ibid., 92–93.

56. Ibid., 93–94.

57. William J. Clinton, "Interview on CNN's 'Global Forum with President Clinton'" (American Presidency Project, 3 May 1994); William J. Clinton, "Interview with the French Media in Paris" (American Presidency Project, 7 June 1994).

58. Power, *"A Problem from Hell,"* 378; Anthony Lake and Wesley Clark, "Press Briefing by National Security Advisor Tony Lake and Director for Strategic Plans and Policy General Wesley Clark" (American Presidency Project, 5 May 1994).

59. In comparison, the already protracted crisis in Bosnia had attracted during the same period 133 separate references, but not a single reference to genocide, except an indirect reference by Clinton in William J. Clinton, "Memorandum on Assistance to the International Tribunal for the Former Yugoslavia" (American Presidency Project, 16 May 1994) (based on a search of the American Presidency Project archives, conducted 30 May 2012).

60. William J. Clinton, "Remarks to the White House Conference on Africa" (American Presidency Project, 27 June 1994), emphasis added.

61. Power, *"A Problem from Hell,"* 359–364. UNSC Resolution 918 of 17 May 1994 carefully acknowledged that "acts of genocide may have been committed."

62. William J. Clinton, "Statement on the Closing of the Embassy of Rwanda" (American Presidency Project, 15 July 1994), emphasis added.

63. Anthony Lake, "Press Briefing by National Security Advisor Tony Lake, Chairman of the Joint Chiefs of Staff General John Shalikashvili and Acting Secretary of Defense John Deutch" (American Presidency Project, 29 July 1994); William J. Clinton, "Letter to Congressional Leaders on Humanitarian Assistance for Rwandan Refugees" (American Presidency Project, 1 August 1994).

64. More senior officials who agitated for a bombing solution from inside the administration included Richard Holbrooke, Madeleine Albright, Al Gore, John Shattuck, David Scheffer, and Ambassador Peter Galbraith. At a cabinet meeting with Clinton on 18 July, Gore argued that Srebrenica was a case of genocide and that the United States therefore could not keep quiet. Power, *"A Problem from Hell,"* 412–413. See also Ibid., 392–393, 422, 435–437.

65. William J. Clinton, "Letter to Congressional Leaders Reporting on the Deployment of United States Aircraft to Bosnia-Herzegovina" (American Presidency Project, 1 September 1995).

66. Power, *"A Problem from Hell,"* 439–440.

67. The United Nations was portrayed by Clinton as a separate entity over which the United States had very little influence. William J. Clinton, "The President's News Conference with President Kim Yong-sam of South Korea" (American Presidency Project, 27 July 1995); William J. Clinton, "Remarks on Signing Emergency Supplemental Appropriations and Rescissions Legislation and an Exchange with Reporters" (American Presidency Project, 27 July 1995); William J. Clinton, "The President's News Conference" (American Presidency Project, 10 August 1995); William J. Clinton, "Interview with Tabitha Soren of MTV" (American Presidency Project, 11 August 1995). William J. Clinton, "Remarks on Welfare Reform and an Exchange with Reporters" (American Presidency Project, 13 July 1995); Clinton, "Remarks on Signing Emergency

Supplemental Appropriations"; Clinton, "President's News Conference with President Kim Yong-sam." When pushed to the sidelines, Clinton used this line of defense even after the attack. See Clinton, "President's News Conference," 10 August 1995; William J. Clinton, "Remarks in a Question-and-Answer Session at the Godfrey Sperling Luncheon" (American Presidency Project, 25 September 1995). See, on the tense relationship with NATO, Power, *"A Problem from Hell,"* 423, 429, 435–436.

68. Clinton, "President's News Conference with President Kim Yong-sam."
69. Clinton, "Letter to Congressional Leaders Reporting on the Deployment."
70. Ibid. An even shorter message (without the legal justifications) was delivered to the media during a visit to Honolulu, in which Clinton "reiterated" the rationale for the campaign. The bombing of Sarajevo, he said, was an "outrageous act in a terrible war" that contravened commitments by NATO and US leadership. NATO's objective was to make clear to the Bosnian Serbs that they had nothing to gain and everything to lose by continuing to attack safe areas and slaughter innocent civilians. In William J. Clinton, "Remarks on Arrival in Honolulu, Hawaii" (American Presidency Project, 31 August 1995).
71. See details in Chapter 5.
72. The ten public references to Srebrenica were made on 11, 13, 27 July; 10, 11 August; 1, 25 September; 31 October; and 25 November 1995. Based on a search of the American Presidency Project archives, conducted 30 May 2012. During the same period Clinton had used the term "genocide" in three different speeches, but none directly in relation to Bosnia. At a press briefing on 11 August 1995, the White House speaker indirectly referred to genocide but not in a direct way or to make a meaningful point. Mike McCurry, "Press Briefing by Michael McCurry" (American Presidency Project, 11 August 1995). In his letter to Congress that announced the commencement of the campaign (1 September 1995), Clinton did invoke the Bosnian Serb capture of the safe area to justify his decision but mentioned only the displacement of forty thousand civilians, not the massacres. The NATO bombing, Clinton also wrote, was in response to the "tragic and inexcusable" Serb attack on Sarajevo, aimed to stop the threat to other UN-declared safe areas, and was authorized by various UNSC resolutions and NATO decisions. In Clinton, "Letter to Congressional Leaders Reporting on the Deployment."
73. In an emotive speech that turned out to be a rehearsal for his address to the nation the following day, Clinton outlined the case for a military action against the Serbs in Kosovo and spoke of the "genocide" that took place during 1995 "in the heart of Europe." This was a clear, even if implicit, reference to the massacres in Srebrenica. See William J. Clinton, "Remarks at the Legislative Convention of the American Federation of State, County, and Municipal Employees" (American Presidency Project, 23 March 1999). Notably, an earlier indirect reference took place in December 1998, when Clinton announced financial support for genocide survivors in Bosnia, Rwanda, and Cambodia. In William J. Clinton, "Remarks on Presenting the Eleanor Roosevelt Awards for Human Rights" (American Presidency Project, 10 December 1998).
74. Ruling of the International Court of Justice on the Application of the Genocide Convention, para 297.
75. William J. Clinton, "Remarks by the President to Genocide Survivors, Assistance Workers, and US and Rwanda Government Officials" (White House, Office of the Press Secretary, 25 March 1998).
76. Ibid.
77. Power argued that American policymakers were no longer delusional about their ability to reason with the Milosevic regime (in Power, *"A Problem from*

Hell," 447–8). For counterviews, see, e.g., Noam Chomsky, *The New Military Humanism: Lessons from Kosovo* (London: Pluto Press, 1999), 106–114.

78. Instead of one to two weeks, as forecasted by the allies based on misapplication of the quick Serb capitulation in Bosnia in 1995.

79. Over fifteen thousand feet.

80. On 23, 24, 30, 31 March; 1 April; 7, 11, 12, 13, 19 May (notably, in five other results, the use of the term "genocide" was either not instigated by White House officials or not related to the events in Kosovo). The strongest reference to genocide in relation to Kosovo was in Clinton's statement: "We must not allow, if we have the ability to stop it, ethnic cleansing or *genocide* anywhere we can stop it, *particularly at the edge of Europe*." William J. Clinton, "Remarks at the Electronic Industries Alliance Dinner" (American Presidency Project, 30 March 1999).

81. William J. Clinton, "Interview with Yevgeniy Kiselev of Russia's NTV in Cologne" (American Presidency Project, 20 June 1999); William J. Clinton, "Remarks Following Discussions with European Union Leaders and an Exchange with Reporters in Bonn" (American Presidency Project, 21 June 1999). See also William J. Clinton, "The President's News Conference" (American Presidency Project, 25 June 1999).

82. Even though spikes in the use of the term corresponded chronologically to the interventions in Bosnia and Kosovo (see Figure 3.2).

83. No references to "genocide" in the context of the Bosnian crisis during 1993, 1994, and 1995 before Srebrenica; one reference in 1995 after Srebrenica (McCurry, "Press Briefing by Michael McCurry"), and no references in 1996. Notably, the actual number of references to the keyword search of "genocide AND Bosnia" was sixteen; but in all instances but one, the references to "genocide" were either not made by the White House or not related to Bosnia.

84. See earlier in this chapter.

85. Notably, the actual number of references to the keyword search of "genocide AND Kosovo" was twenty-four; but in all instances but one, the references to "genocide" were not made by the White House or not related to Kosovo.

86. About the term, see Blum et al., "'Ethnic Cleansing' Bleaches the Atrocities of Genocide."

87. Three references to "ethnic cleansing AND Bosnia" in 1992; thirty-seven references in 1993; eight references in 1994; one reference in 1995 before Srebrenica; ten references in 1995 after Srebrenica; three references in 1996. A keyword search for the terms "ethnic cleansing AND Bosnia" in the American Presidency Project archives (conducted 30 May 2012).

88. Notably, attempts to broaden the interpretation of "destroy" to cover also "ethnic cleansing" were rejected in 2007 by the ICJ in the Bosnia versus Serbia case. The deportation or displacement of members of a group that constitute "ethnic cleansing," wrote the judges, was not necessarily equivalent to its destruction, even when effected by force. See the Application of the Genocide Convention, para. 190, and William A. Schabas, "What is Genocide? What are the Gaps in the Convention? How to Prevent Genocide?" *Politorbis* 47, no. 2 (2009): 37, 39.

89. While Clinton and other American presidents did not often apply Holocaust analogies to contemporary crises, they still used the frame more extensively than "genocide" analogies.

90. For example, not once in relation to Rwanda (based on a search of the American Presidency Project archives, conducted 30 May 2012). Of course without the European context and concentration camps, the analogy would have been found difficult to embrace.

91. For example, in Clinton, "Exchange with Reporters Prior to Discussions"; Clinton, "President's News Conference," 23 April 1993.

92. Compared to zero references to "the Holocaust," "concentration camps," "death camps," or "barb-wire," between January and late October 1995. See later references in William J. Clinton, "Remarks on the Balkan Peace Process and an Exchange With Reporters" (American Presidency Project, 31 October 1995) (". . . the worst atrocities in Europe since World War II: mass executions, ethnic cleansing, concentration camps . . ."); Mike McCurry, "Press Briefing by Mike McCurry" (American Presidency Project, 22 November 1995); William J. Clinton, "Address to the Nation on Implementation of the Peace Agreement in Bosnia-Herzegovina" (American Presidency Project, 27 November 1995) (". . . skeletal prisoners caged behind barbed-wire fences . . . defenceless men and boys shot down into mass graves, evoking visions of World War II concentration camps . . ."); William J. Clinton, "Remarks to the Parliament of the United Kingdom in London" (American Presidency Project, 29 November 1995); William J. Clinton, "The President's Radio Address" (American Presidency Project, 2 December 1995); William J. Clinton, "Proclamation 6855—Human Rights Day, Bill of Rights Day, and Human Rights Week" (American Presidency Project, 5 December 1995); William J. Clinton, "Remarks on the Balkan Peace Process Following a Meeting with Elie Wiesel and an Exchange with Reporters" (American Presidency Project, 13 December 1995) (". . . skeletal prisoners behind barbed wire fences in what can only be called concentration camps . . .").

93. William J. Clinton, "Address to the Nation on Airstrikes Against Serbian Targets in the Federal Republic of Yugoslavia (Serbia and Montenegro)" (American Presidency Project, 24 March 1999); William J. Clinton, "Remarks to the Military Community at Norfolk Naval Station" (American Presidency Project, 1 April 1999); William J. Clinton, "Remarks at the Seventh Millennium Evening at the White House" (American Presidency Project, 12 April 1999); William J. Clinton, "Remarks Following a Meeting with Congressional Leaders and an Exchange with Reporters" (American Presidency Project, 13 April 1999); William J. Clinton, "Remarks and a Question-and-Answer Session with the American Society of Newspaper Editors in San Francisco, California" (American Presidency Project, 15 April 1999); William J. Clinton, "Remarks to the Community at Spangdahlem Air Base, Germany" (American Presidency Project, 5 May 1999); William J. Clinton, "Remarks to the Veterans of Foreign Wars of the United States at Fort McNair, Maryland" (American Presidency Project, 13 May 1999); William J. Clinton, "Commencement Address at the United States Air Force Academy in Colorado Springs" (American Presidency Project, 2 June 1999); William J. Clinton, "Remarks on Presenting the President's Award for Furthering Employment of People with Disabilities" (American Presidency Project, 4 June 1999); William J. Clinton, "Remarks at Whiteman Air Force Base in Knob Noster, Missouri" (American Presidency Project, 11 June 1999); William J. Clinton, "Interview with Wolf Blitzer of Cable News Network's 'Late Edition' in Cologne" (American Presidency Project, 20 June 1999); Clinton, "President's News Conference," 25 June 1999.

94. Clinton, "Remarks to the Veterans of Foreign Wars."

95. Clinton was described as a "glib rhetorician, capable of drawing on any and every traditional source of persuasion as it suited his immediate purposes." In Kane, *Between Virtue and Power*, 310.

96. See, on "defending the defenseless" in William J. Clinton, "Interview with Dan Rather of CBS News" (American Presidency Project, 31 March 1999); on "advancing the cause of peace" in Clinton, "Address to the Nation on Airstrikes."

97. Selective and conditional American leadership in McCrisken, *American Exceptionalism,* 147; pursuit of global freedoms and world peace in Clinton, "Remarks on the Balkan Peace Process"; Clinton, "Address to the Nation on Implementation"; cited also in McCrisken, *American Exceptionalism,* 174–175.

98. Trout, "Legitimating Containment and Détente," 4, cited in Melanson, *American Foreign Policy,* 38.

99. Based on a search of the American Presidency Project archives, conducted 30 May 2012.

100. For example, Clinton, "Address to the Nation on Implementation"; William J. Clinton, "Remarks to American Troops at Tuzla Airfield, Bosnia-Herzegovina" (American Presidency Project, 13 January 1996); William J. Clinton, "Remarks to the Community at Fort Polk, Louisiana" (American Presidency Project, 18 March 1996); William J. Clinton, "Remarks at a Veterans Day Ceremony in Arlington, Virginia" (American Presidency Project, 11 November 1998).

101. Clinton, "Interview on CNN's 'Global Forum with President Clinton.'"

102. Ibid. In terms of action, the United States was not going to be the world's policeman but to join other states in relieving suffering and restoring peace. Still, it would not hesitate to act unilaterally in cases where its core national interests could be affected. Clinton acknowledged that the three pillars of his foreign policy—security, prosperity, and the advancement of democracy—did not provide satisfactory answers to the epidemic of post–Cold War crises, such as in Bosnia and Rwanda. Although the American interest in Rwanda was not as direct as in Bosnia, said Clinton, the former still merited American concern and assistance. However, despite acknowledging the military and political aspects of the genocide in Rwanda, Clinton's rhetoric remained focused on the task of heading off starvation.

103. William J. Clinton, "Remarks Announcing Participation in Missions in Bosnia and Zaire and an Exchange with Reporters" (American Presidency Project, 15 November 1996), emphasis added.

104. William J. Clinton, "Commencement Address at the United States Military Academy in West Point, New York" (American Presidency Project, 31 May 1997).

105. William J. Clinton, "Remarks on United States Foreign Policy in San Francisco" (American Presidency Project, 26 February 1999), emphasis added. See Klare, "Clinton Doctrine." To some, this was the essence of the "Clinton Doctrine."

106. William J. Clinton, "Crisis in the Balkans: Clinton's Remarks in Defense of Military Intervention in Balkans," *New York Times,* 14 May 1999, www.nytimes.com/1999/05/14/world/crisis-balkans-clinton-s-remarks-defense-military-intervention-balkans.html. There were also fears in the United States that war in Kosovo could bring about a regional war (Power, *"A Problem from Hell,"* 446). Interestingly, Clinton argued also that the confrontation should not be understood as "the inevitable result . . . of centuries-old animosities." Admitting to his own failure of understanding, and hence of rhetoric, during the earlier Bosnia crisis, he now pointed to the systematic and organized nature of the perpetrated atrocities and to their political (rather than "tribal" or emotive) nature.

107. William J. Clinton, "Remarks by President Clinton to the KFOR Troops at Skopje, Macedonia" (22 June 1999).

108. David Jablonsky, "Army Transformation: A Tale of Two Doctrines," in *Transforming Defense,* ed. Conrad C. Crane (Carlisle, PA: Strategic Studies Institute, December 2001), 60–61.

109. Clinton, "Interview with Wolf Blitzer," emphasis added.

110. The intervention in Haiti was supported by Gore and rejected by Bush; Lebanon (which took place during Reagan's presidency) was supported by Bush and rejected by Gore.
111. Bush, "2000 Campaign."
112. George W. Bush, *This Week*, 23 January 2000.
113. Ibid.
114. Bush, "2000 Campaign."
115. In an interview on ABC's *This Week* (23 January 2000), Bush said that instead of committing troops to Rwanda he would have pressed the United Nations and other world organizations to take action.
116. Gore, "2000 Campaign."
117. See the same point in a fact sheet released by Gore's campaign a few months earlier in Gore 2000, "Fact Sheet on George W. Bush's Foreign Policy," *US Newswire*, 30 April 2000, www.fas.org/nuke/control/abmt/news/0430-103.htm.
118. Ibid.
119. Clinton, "Interview on CNN's 'Global Forum with President Clinton.'"
120. The 2000 debate roughly coincided with the release of Kull and Destler's study, *Misreading the Public*, which revealed significant discrepancies between foreign policy attitudes of American publics and policymakers' perceptions of these attitudes on a variety of policy issues. Thus, Gore and Bush's support for Clinton's Rwanda policy could have also been a case of misreading the public.
121. The Holocaust was used to justify the intervention in Kosovo and mobilize domestic support for sending American peacekeepers to Bosnia.
122. For some commentators, the intervention in Haiti was proof to the contrary, as Clinton needed to overcome strong opposition in Congress and elsewhere. However, others believe that Clinton was pushed into the intervention against his will. See, e.g., Kane, *Between Virtue and Power*, 302, and in general, 306, 310.
123. Support for action in the polls.
124. As mentioned, after the NATO bombing, Clinton and his staff did make a few references to "genocide and ethnic cleansing." But before and during the campaign, the most that the administration could offer as an official policy was David Scheffer's narrative of "indicators of genocide unfolding." David Scheffer, "Foreign Press Center Briefing" (Federal News Service, 5 April 1999), cited in Power, *"A Problem from Hell,"* 468.
125. Clinton, "Interview with Dan Rather," emphases added.
126. William J. Clinton, "Remarks at the Veterans of Foreign Wars of the United States 100th National Convention in Kansas City, Missouri" (American Presidency Project, 16 August 1999); William J. Clinton, "Remarks to the 54th Session of the United Nations General Assembly in New York City" (American Presidency Project, 21 September 1999); William J. Clinton, "Proclamation 7258—Human Rights Day, Bill of Rights Day, and Human Rights Week" (American Presidency Project, 6 December 1999); William J. Clinton, "Remarks to the Conference on the Progressive Tradition in Princeton, New Jersey" (American Presidency Project, 5 October 2000); William J. Clinton, "Remarks at a Reception for Representative Maurice D. Hinchey in Kingston, New York" (American Presidency Project, 23 October 2000).
127. Barack H. Obama, "Presidential Study Directive on Mass Atrocities" (White House, Office of the Press Secretary, 4 August 2011), www.whitehouse.gov/the-press-office/2011/08/04/presidential-study-directive-mass-atrocities.
128. Often indicative not only of policy positions but also of politicians' perceptions of public attitudes.

CHAPTER 4 DOMESTIC RESPONSES TO GENOCIDE

1. Power, *"A Problem from Hell,"* 508.
2. See in relation to media coverage and Congress in Cohen, *Public's Impact on Foreign Policy*, 111–113; Entman, *Projections of Power*, 12–16; Kull and Destler, *Misreading the Public*, 219–221; Powlick, "Sources of Public Opinion," 434–437, 446–447. On opinion polls, see Cohen, *Public's Impact on Foreign Policy*, 115–117; Kull and Destler, *Misreading the Public*, 208–213; Powlick, "Sources of Public Opinion," 434–435, 438–439, 446–447. Notably, among policymakers the distrust of opinion polls' findings was allegedly higher than the other two indicators.
3. See Sam McFarland and Melissa Mathews, "Do Americans Care about Human Rights?," *Journal of Human Rights* 4 (2005): 309–310.
4. Norbert Schwarz and Gerd Bohner, "The Construction of Attitudes," in *Blackwell Handbook of Social Psychology: Intraindividual Processes*, ed. Abraham Tesser and Norbert Schwarz (Oxford: Blackwell, 2001), 438.
5. Mueller, "Public Opinion as a Constraint," 8–9; Kull, "American Public Opinion," 459–460.
6. Kull was director of the Program on International Policy Attitudes (PIPA) at the University of Maryland. Kull and Destler, *Misreading the Public*; Steven Kull and Clay Ramsay, "Elite Misperceptions of U.S. Public Opinion and Foreign Policy," in *Decision Making in a Glass House: Mass Media, Public Opinion, and American and European Foreign Policy in the 21st Century*, ed. Brigitte L. Nacos, Robert Shapiro, and Pierangelo Isernia (New York: Rowman & Littlefield, 2000), 95–110; Kull, "American Public Opinion"; Kull and Ramsay, "US Public Opinion."
7. Kull, "American Public Opinion," 459–460.
8. Ibid., 463.
9. Kull and Ramsay, "US Public Opinion," 72–73. See contradictory evidence and divergent conclusions (discussed later) in Andrew Kohut, "Post–Cold War Attitudes toward the Use of Force," in *The Use of Force after the Cold War*, ed. H. W. Brands, Darren J. Pierson, and Reynolds S. Kiefer (College Station: Texas A&M University Press, 2003), 173–174.
10. Kull and Ramsay, "US Public Opinion," 71–72; for example, 69 percent in April 1994 and 58 percent in *Los Angeles Times* in January 1993.
11. Kull, "American Public Opinion," 461.
12. Ibid., 460.
13. Cited in Steven Kull et al., "Americans on the Crisis in Sudan" (PIPA/Knowledge Networks Poll, 20 July 2004), 6.
14. Ibid.
15. Kull, "American Public Opinion," 460.
16. Wertheim, "Solution from Hell," 158.
17. Kull, "American Public Opinion," 460.
18. Cited in Kull and Destler, *Misreading the Public*, 52–53. The context was the debate about whether to extend US participation in the UN peacekeeping mission to Bosnia.
19. Kull, "American Public Opinion," 463.
20. Ibid., 462.
21. Andrew Kohut and Robert C. Toth, "Arms and the People," *Foreign Affairs* 73, no. 6 (1994): 53–59. See also in Campbell, *Genocide and the Global Village*, 50.
22. Kohut, "Post–Cold War Attitudes," 172–173. See also Kohut and Toth, "Arms and the People," 54. Notably, these results are not presented here because they did not include questions related to our topic of genocide.

23. Kull and Ramsay, "US Public Opinion," 70. The divergent depictions of burden sharing regarded multilateral rather than unilateral US actions.
24. Ibid., 75.
25. Campbell, *Genocide and the Global Village*, 51. Notably, the theoretical coherence of the argument may have been lacking. That is, Campbell used a broader definition of "genocide" than the problematic but legally recognized 1948 definition. He pointed to Kosovo as "genocide" and described "ethnic cleansing" as a euphemism for genocide (ibid., 81).
26. Ibid., 81.
27. Kohut, "Post–Cold War Attitudes," 176.
28. Wertheim, "Solution from Hell," 151–152. The third righteous motive in the statement "to protect innocent lives" might have been inhibited by the term "civil war," a much less emotive situation than genocide.
29. The statement read, "If a government is committing atrocities against its people so that a significant number of people are being killed, at some point the countries of the world, including the U.S., should intervene with force if necessary to stop the killing" (cited in Kull, "American Public Opinion," 462).
30. Power, *"A Problem from Hell,"* 374.
31. Kull, "American Public Opinion," 460.
32. Power, *"A Problem from Hell,"* 356.
33. Steven Livingston, "Limited Vision: How Both the American Media and Government Failed Rwanda," in *The Media and the Rwanda Genocide*, ed. Allan Thompson (London: Pluto Press, 2007), 191–194.
34. Ibid. See also Livingston and Stephen, "American Network Coverage," 1–18.
35. Linda Melvern, "Missing the Story: The Media and the Rwandan Genocide," in Thompson, *Media and the Rwanda Genocide*, 198. See a US-focused analysis in Melissa Wall, "An Analysis of News Magazine Coverage of the Rwanda Crisis in the United States," in Thompson, *Media and the Rwanda Genocide*, 265–266, 268–269; Ronayne, *Never Again?*, 160–161; Power, *"A Problem from Hell,"* 355–356.
36. Robinson, "CNN Effect Revisited," 345.
37. Allan J. Kuperman, "How the Media Missed Rwanda Genocide," in Thompson, *Media and the Rwanda Genocide*, 256.
38. Ibid., 258.
39. Ibid., 256–257.
40. Power, *"A Problem from Hell,"* 374. See, e.g., *Washington Post*, "Horror in Rwanda, Shame in the U.N.," 3 May 1994. See exception in Herman Cohen, "Getting Rwanda Wrong," *Washington Post*, 3 June 1994.
41. Ibid.
42. Wertheim, "Solution from Hell," 157.
43. Ibid., 157.
44. Piers Robinson, *The CNN Effect: The Myth of News, Foreign Policy and Intervention* (London: Routledge, 2002), 115.
45. Ibid.
46. Power, *"A Problem from Hell,"* 377.
47. See the exception to congressional inaction, a letter to President Clinton from Senators Paul Simon and Jim Jeffords, dated 13 May 1994 (*Congressional Record* 140, no. 72 [June 10, 1994]).
48. Power, *"A Problem from Hell,"* 352.
49. Ibid., 375–377.
50. Operation "Support Hope." On the US motivation, see Tony Marley, "The Triumph of Evil" (interview), *Frontline-PBS*, 26 January 1999.

51. An exception was Herman Cohen, who commented in an op-ed (*Washington Post*, 3 June 1994) that despite an earlier pledge by President Clinton that he would not allow another Holocaust, "Another Holocaust may have just slipped by, hardly noticed." Cohen, "Getting Rwanda Wrong." In an analysis of a CNN effect on the crisis, Robinson also emphasized the strong impact of fear of casualties after Somalia on the elite consensus against intervention. Robinson, *CNN Effect*, 115.

52. Wertheim, "Solution from Hell," 152.

53. Ibid., 153. He cites (153) the Pentagon's assistant for regional humanitarian affairs as blaming in hindsight the little political attention to Rwanda among other things on absence of predetermined foreign policy goal of halting genocide when feasible. In Yael S. Aronoff, "An Apology Is Not Enough: What Will Happen in the Next Case of Genocide?," *Washington Post*, 9 April 1998, A25.

54. Power, *"A Problem from Hell,"* 373–374.

55. Power, *"A Problem from Hell,"* 334–335, 361, 367–369; Melvern, "Missing the Story," 208–209. Rwanda's embassy to the United States was shut down in mid-July, eleven days *after* the capital Kigali was taken over by the Tutsi rebels' forces. Clinton, "Statement on the Closing of the Embassy of Rwanda."

56. The argument made by the British delegate was that to call the events "genocide" and not to act would make the council a laughing stock. Melvern, "Missing the Story," 204–205.

57. Ibid., 208.

58. Or by compromising operational security.

59. Livingston, "Limited Vision," 189–191.

60. Robinson, *CNN Effect*, 116.

61. Western, "Sources of Humanitarian Intervention," 357–358, 360.

62. Ibid., 358.

63. Power, *"A Problem from Hell,"* 269–293.

64. Western, "Sources of Humanitarian Intervention," 362.

65. Power, *"A Problem from Hell,"* 276. See a dissenting analysis in Kohut and Toth, "Arms and the People," 53–54, 59.

66. See discussion in Western, "Sources of Humanitarian Intervention," 362–366.

67. Warren P. Strobel, *Late-Breaking Foreign Policy: The News Media's Influence on Peace Operations* (Washington, DC: US Institute of Peace Press, 1997), 138–139; Power, *"A Problem from Hell,"* 285.

68. Power, *"A Problem from Hell,"* 286.

69. Western, "Sources of Humanitarian Intervention," 366; Power, *"A Problem from Hell,"* 285–286; Roy Gutman, "American Public Opinion, the Media and Genocide Prevention," in Fowler et al., "Genocide Prevention, Morality, and the National Interest," 454.

70. Robinson counted forty-eight articles related to the crisis in the *New York Times* and twenty-one in the *Washington Post* during the first four days after the massacre (front-page articles almost every day). In the mass media, CNN filed 132 reports during the same period, and the three major networks featured Bosnia in prominent places in their evening editions. In Robinson, *CNN Effect*, 90.

71. Power, *"A Problem from Hell,"* 392, 397–399.

72. The Dutch force was widely accused of not standing up to the Bosnian Serb forces, and the findings of an official enquiry led to the resignation of the entire Dutch government seven years later. See Andrew Osborn and Paul Brown, "Dutch Cabinet Resigns over Srebrenica Massacre," *Guardian*, 17 April 2002.

73. Power, *"A Problem from Hell,"* 422, 430–431.

74. Ibid., 432.

75. Human Rights Watch concluded that a case of genocide should make the group put aside its mistrust of military power and recommend armed intervention. Others, like Scott Simon on National Public Radio, warned about the risks of using Holocaust terminology, pointing out that the Holocaust, Rwanda, and Cambodia had raised the bar for American concern or action too high.
76. Robinson, *CNN Effect*, 83–84.
77. Power, *"A Problem from Hell,"* 421–422.
78. Ibid., 422–423, 425–429, 437. Almost half the Democrats in the Senate broke ranks to support the lifting of the embargo.
79. Ibid., 423.
80. Clinton, "Letter to Congressional Leaders Reporting on the Deployment."
81. Using American troops to stop genocide: 77 percent (2002 CCFR/GMF public survey combined data). Page, *Foreign Policy Disconnect*, 104–105.
82. See manifestations of mass opinion behavior in Powlick, "Sources of Public Opinion," 429.
83. A seasoned African American guide at the Holocaust Museum in Washington told this author that African American visitors identify more with European Jews of the 1940s than with the black Darfuri victims of Darfur.
84. As measured by both opinion and behavior.
85. The elites owe at least part of their perceived influence to their image as mass opinion setters.
86. Paul Slovic, "'If I look at the Mass I Will Never Act': Psychic Numbing and Genocide," *Judgment and Decision Making* 2, no. 2 (2007): 79–95; also more broadly Hanna Zagefka and Trevor James, "Psychology of Charitable Donations to Disaster Victims and Beyond," *Social Issues and Policy Review* 9, no. 1 (2015): 155–192.
87. Ibid.
88. See Paul Bloom, *Against Empathy: The Case for Rational Compassion* (London: Bodley Head, 2017), as well as various studies by Paul Slovic. See, more broadly, Johanna R. Vollhardt, "The Role of Social Psychology in Preventing Group-Selective Mass Atrocities," in *Reconstructing Atrocity Prevention*, ed. Sheri P. Rosenberg, Tibi Galis, and Alex Zucker (Cambridge: Cambridge University Press, 2015).
89. Slovic, "'If I look.'"
90. Paul Slovic and Daniel Västfjäll, "The More Who Die, the Less We Care: Psychic Numbing and Genocide," in *Behavioural Public Policy*, ed. Adam Oliver (Cambridge: Cambridge University Press, 2013), 100–101.
91. See Susan D. Moeller, *Compassion Fatigue: How the Media Sell Disease, Famine, War, and Death*. New York: Routledge, 1999.

CHAPTER 5 AMERICA AND THE FIRST GENOCIDE
OF THE TWENTY-FIRST CENTURY

1. Independent International Commission on Kosovo, *The Kosovo Report* (Oxford: Oxford University Press, 2000), 4.
2. Andrew S. Natsios, *Sudan, South Sudan, and Darfur: What Everyone Needs to Know* (Oxford: Oxford University Press, 2012), 138–139.
3. Tactics already used with devastating but effective results in the Nuba Mountains of Sudan. See Prunier, *Darfur*, 104–105.
4. Even the Sudanese national press was said not to have picked up the story until the middle of 2003. Prunier, *Darfur*, 125.

5. Amnesty International, *Sudan: Looming Crisis in Darfur* (London: Amnesty International, 2003).

6. Eric Reeves, "The Face of War in Darfur (Sudan): Many Tens of Thousands Flee Khartoum's Campaign of Aerial Bombardment, Militia Attacks," sudan-reeves.org, 8 October 2003.

7. Eric Reeves, "The Accelerating Catastrophe in Darfur (Sudan): Khartoum Fixes Upon a Policy of War and Civilian Destruction," sudanreeves.org, 24 November 2003; Eric Reeves, "Human Destruction and Displacement in Darfur: War, Humanitarian Access, and 'Ethnic Cleansing,'" sudanreeves.org, 12 December 2003.

8. Jan Egeland, "The World" (interview), *BBC/Public Radio International*, 18 December 2003.

9. Eric Reeves, "'Ethnic Cleansing' in Darfur: Systematic, Ethnically-Based Denial of Humanitarian Aid Is No Context for a Sustainable Peace Agreement in Sudan," sudanreeves.org, 30 December 2003.

10. Eric Reeves, "Genocide in Darfur: The End of Agnosticism," sudanreeves.org, 1 February 2004.

11. Eric Reeves, "New Attacks on Civilians Far to the North in Darfur; More Than 1,000 Human Beings Now Dying Weekly in Darfur: What is the Threshold for an Emergency Humanitarian Intervention?," sudanreeves.org, 8 February 2004. Also, Eric Reeves, "No Further Evasion of the Essential Question: What Will We Do in Darfur?," sudanreeves.org, 4 April 2004.

12. Eric Reeves, "Sudan Peace Talks Face the Threat of a Month-Long Break: Darfur Will Pay the Terrible Price for Adjournment," sudanreeves .org, 21 January 2004. Also, Eric Reeves, "The Beginning of the End for Sudan's Peace Process? Khartoum Engineers a Disastrous Suspension of the Naivasha Talks," *Sudan Tribune*, 22 January 2004; Eric Reeves, "Darfur and the Diplomatic Logic of Appeasement: Concluding Peace Talks at Naivasha Must Not, and Cannot, Entail Expediency," sudanreeves.org, 26 January 2004.

13. Eric Reeves, "Catastrophe in Darfur Exploding: UN Now Estimates That Millions Are Affected by War; Aerial Attacks on Civilians Accelerate Dramatically," sudanreeves.org, 27 January 2004. Also, Reeves, "Beginning of the End for Sudan's Peace Process?"; Reeves, "Darfur and the Diplomatic Logic of Appeasement"; Reeves, "Emergency Humanitarian Intervention for Darfur."

14. Reeves, "Genocide in Darfur."

15. In August 2003, the US Agency for International Development (USAID) allocated US$40 million to IDPs in Darfur through UNICEF (in Natsios, *Sudan, South Sudan, and Darfur*, 156). Both Andrew Natsios, head of USAID, and his assistant, Roger Winter, have made multiple trips to Sudan since late 2003. See Andrew Natsios, "Remarks to the Press en Route Khartoum" (US Department of State, 29 June 2004). See also Stephen A. Kostas, "Making the Determination of Genocide in Darfur," in *Genocide in Darfur: Investigating the Atrocities in the Sudan*, ed. Samuel Totten and Eric Markusen (New York: Routledge, 2006), 112.

16. It also emphasized that the crisis in Darfur should not be linked to the ongoing peace talks between North and South Sudan in Kenya. US Department of State, "Sudan: Situation in Darfur" (16 December 2003).

17. Kostas, "Making the Determination of Genocide in Darfur," 112. See also Colin L. Powell, "Opening Remarks before the House Appropriations Subcommittee on Commerce, Justice, State, The Judiciary and Related Agencies" (US Department of State Archives, 3 March 2004).

18. USAID, "Statement by Andrew S. Natsios USAID Administrator and Special Humanitarian Coordinator for Sudan," *ReliefWeb*, 3 February 2004, emphasis added.

19. Charles Snyder, "Sudan: Peace Agreement Around the Corner?" (Testimony before the Subcommittee on Africa of the House International Relations Committee; US Department of State, 11 March 2004). In truth, evidence of Khartoum's participation in atrocities against Darfuri noncombatants was available for a while. Relying on various sources, Reeves wrote in 27 January 2004 about the free rein that the Sudanese government was giving to "the now heavily armed Janjaweed" (Reeves, "Sudan Peace Talks Face the Threat of a Month-Long Break"). In early February Reeves concluded, based on publicly available evidence, "All bombing attacks, all helicopter gunship attacks, are . . . incontrovertibly ordered by Khartoum." Reeves, "Genocide in Darfur."

20. Reeves, "Genocide in Darfur." The US warning to Sudan was reported by Julie Flint in the *Daily Star* already in February. Julie Flint, "Peace in South Sudan Hinges on End to War in Darfur," *Daily Star*, 19 February 2004. See more details in a press briefing conducted by Snyder five months later: US State Department, "Signing of the Naivasha Protocols" (press briefing by Assistant Secretary Snyder; 27 May 2004).

21. Kostas, "Making the Determination of Genocide in Darfur," 116. Heinze argued also that a true sense of international urgency became apparent only in April 2004, after Annan (at the UN Human Rights Commission on the 10th Anniversary) compared the situation in Darfur to Rwanda. Annan spoke about taking action, in the sense of a continuum of steps that could include military action. Eric A. Heinze, "The Rhetoric of Genocide in U.S. Foreign Policy: Rwanda and Darfur Compared," *Political Science Quarterly* 122, no. 3 (2007): 367.

22. Agence France-Presse, "West Sudan's Darfur Conflict 'World's Greatest Humanitarian Crisis,'" *Sudan Tribune*, 19 March 2004.

23. *BBC News*, "Mass Rape Atrocity in West Sudan," 19 March 2004.

24. Ibid.

25. USAID, "Statement of Roger Winter, USAID Assistant Administrator for the Democracy, Conflict and Humanitarian Assistance Bureau" (31 March 2004).

26. United Nations, "Press Briefing on Humanitarian Crisis in Darfur, Sudan" (2 April 2004). Months earlier, in 18 December, Egeland already warned that Darfur was "probably the world's greatest humanitarian catastrophe." Egeland, "The World."

27. Human Rights Watch, "Sudan: Massive Atrocities in Darfur" (3 April 2004).

28. Kofi Annan, "Action Plan to Prevent Genocide, Speech Delivered to the UN Human Rights Commission, 7 April 2004" (UN press release, SG/SM/9197 AFR/893 HR/CN/1077).

29. George W. Bush, "President Condemns Atrocities in Sudan: Statement by the President" (White House, 7 April 2004). Notably, his statement the same day about the Rwandan anniversary did not mention Darfur or any other ongoing crisis. See George W. Bush, "Statement on the 10th Anniversary of the 1994 Rwanda Genocide" (American Presidency Project, 7 April 2004).

30. US Department of State, "Signing of the Darfur Humanitarian Cease-Fire" (press statement, 9 April 2004).

31. Stephanie Nebehay, "US Likens West Sudan 'Ethnic Cleansing' to Rwanda," *Sudan Tribune*, 22 April 2004. Earlier Williamson wrote in the *Chicago Sun-Times*, "African countries and the entire world must decide if we will act to try to stop the genocide in Darfur or if we will respond with silence and inaction as

we did in Rwanda 10 years ago." Richard S. Williamson, "National Voices—Stop the Genocide in Sudan," *Chicago Sun-Times*, 11 April 2004.

32. The first draft failed to win sufficient support among the African and Arab delegations.

33. Notably, this was a repeat of much earlier warnings from the UN. Colin L. Powell, "The InterAction 2004 Annual Forum Luncheon" (US Department of State, 18 May 2004).

34. Ibid.

35. On 26 May, a public statement in honor of the new North-South peace agreement, though more subtly worded, was not as constraining (Colin L. Powell, "Signing of the Naivasha Protocols" [US Department of State, 26 May 2004]). The text read, "We look forward to embarking on a new relationship with a peaceful Sudan, including beginning the process of normalization of bilateral relations once the problems of Darfur are also resolved." On 11 June, and 30 June, commentaries (during *New York Times* and NPR interviews) were clear and explicit (in Colin L. Powell, "Interview by Marc Lacey of the New York Times" [US Department of State, 11 June 2004]; Colin L. Powell, "Interview on National Public Radio with Michele Norris" [US Department of State, 30 June 2004]). See also Colin L. Powell, "Remarks to the Africa Policy Advisory Panel Conference at the Center for Strategic and International Studies" (US Department of State, 8 July 2004).

36. George Gedda, "Sudan Is Removed from a US Terror List," *Boston Globe*, 19 May 2004. For a critique of the timing, see Eric Reeves, "US Congress Calls on Khartoum 'to Grant Full, Unconditional, and Immediate [Humanitarian] Access to Darfur,' Even as the Regime Deliberately Blocks US Aid Efforts and Officials: The Genocide Accelerates," sudanreeves.org, 19 May 2004.

37. International Crisis Group, "ICG Africa Report N°80: Sudan: Now or Never in Darfur" (23 May 2004), i, emphases added. Notably, while the ethnic nature of the crisis was acknowledged much earlier by the NGO, this was the first time it explicitly termed it "ethnic cleansing."

38. US Department of State, "Signing of the Naivasha Protocols." Previously, high-level officials had tended to skirt terminology debates. Notably, in his statement from 7 April President Bush did use the word "atrocities"; but the most commonly used euphemisms were less risky: "catastrophe," "situation," "tragedy," and "disaster." Now official rhetoric was hardening. See Bush, "President Condemns Atrocities in Sudan"; Powell, "Opening Remarks before the House Appropriations Subcommittee"; Colin L. Powell, "Remarks with Georgian Prime Minister Zurab Zhvania after their Meeting" (US Department of State, 3 March 2004); Colin L. Powell, "Remarks with Bulgarian Foreign Minister Solomon Passy after Their Meeting" (US Department of State, 5 May 2004).

39. Condoleezza Rice: "Press Briefing by National Security Advisor, Dr. Condoleezza Rice on the G8 Summit" (American Presidency Project, 7 June 2004).

40. White House, "G-8 Statement on Sudan" (American Presidency Project, 10 June 2004). The declaration also pledged members' support (referring explicitly only to humanitarian aid) and called on the UN to lead the international efforts to avert the disaster. US Department of State, "G-8 Statement on Sudan" (11 June 2004), emphasis added.

41. United Nations, *Security Council Resolution 1547* (11 June 2004). On the lead-up, see discussion in Alex J. Bellamy and Paul D. Williams, "The UN Security Council and the Question of Humanitarian Intervention in Darfur," *Journal of Military Ethics* 5, no. 2 (2006): 149–150. Prior to that, the UN Security Council

released a mild press statement on 2 April (United Nations, "Press Statement on Darfur, Sudan by Security Council President" (UN Document SC/8050 AFR/883, 2 April 2004), and a presidential statement in 25 May, allegedly, on US insistence. See US Department of State, "Daily Press Briefing—25 May 2004" (9 April 2004). See text of presidential statement in United Nations, "Statement by the President of the Security Council" (25 May 2004).

42. Powell, "Interview by Marc Lacey." Pressed again about the issue, Powell added that even without having a full intelligence report in front of him, he was still confident in saying that in the US belief, the government of Sudan did provide support to these militias.

43. Ibid.

44. Ibid.

45. Roger Winter, "Sudan: Statement of Roger Winter, Assistant Administrator USAID, Before the Committee on Foreign Relations Subcommittee on Africa" (USAID, 15 June 2004). In fact, back in February 2004, Winter told journalists, "The question arises: Is this an ethnic cleansing in motion that is taking place there [Darfur]? I don't have the answer for that—I'm not a human rights lawyer, [but] it sure looks like that." In Jim Fisher-Thompson, "US Official Cites Possible 'Ethnic Cleansing' in Sudan," *Sudan Tribune*, 26 February 2004.

46. Eric Reeves, "Kofi Annan Declares He Has Seen No Reports to Suggest 'Ethnic Cleansing' or Genocide," sudanreeves.org, 18 June 2004.

47. Ibid. According to Samantha Power, Renaud Muselier, the French secretary of state for foreign affairs, used similar comments by Annan to support his claims that Darfur was not "genocide" or "ethnic cleansing," but a civil war. In Samantha Power, "Dying in Darfur: Can the Ethnic Cleansing in Sudan Be Stopped?," *New Yorker*, 23 August 2004, 11.

48. Pierre-Richard Prosper, "Ambassador-at-Large for War Crimes Testifies in Congress" (US Department of State, 24 June 2004).

49. US Department of State, "Daily Press Briefing by Spokesman Richard Boucher" (US Department of State, 24 June 2004).

50. Ibid.

51. White House, "Statement of Administration Policy: H.R. 4613—Department of Defense Appropriations Bill, FY 2005" (American Presidency Project, 22 June 2004); White House, "Text of U.S.-EU Declaration on Sudan" (American Presidency Project, 26 June 2004). For before the trip, see White House, "Statement by the Press Secretary: President Directs Secretary Powell to Travel to Sudan" (American Presidency Project, 29 June 2004); Colin L. Powell, "Remarks Following Meeting with Haitian Interim President Boniface Alexandre" (US Department of State, 24 June 2004). For during the trip, see Colin L. Powell, "Remarks with Foreign Minister Ismail of the Republic of Sudan" (US Department of State, 29 June 2004); Colin L. Powell, "Remarks en Route Khartoum from Darfur" (US Department of State, 30 June 2004); Colin L. Powell, "Remarks with Foreign Minister Mustafa Osman Ismail of the Republic of Sudan after Their Meetings at the Airport" (US Department of State, 30 June 2004); Colin L. Powell, "Remarks after the Secretary's Tour of the Abu Shouk Camp" (US Department of State, 30 June 2004).

52. Powell, "Remarks to the Press en Route Khartoum."

53. Colin L. Powell, "Interview on PBS's Charlie Rose" (US Department of State, 16 July 2004).

54. Powell, "Remarks with Foreign Minister Ismail"; Powell, "Remarks en Route Khartoum from Darfur"; Powell, "Remarks after the Secretary's Tour"; Colin L. Powell, "Interview on CNN with Jeff Koinange" (US Department of State, 30 June 2004); Powell, "Interview on National Public Radio."

55. Powell, "Interview on National Public Radio." See also Powell's op-ed, "Darfur," *Wall Street Journal*, 5 August 2004.

56. Powell, "Remarks en Route Khartoum from Darfur."

57. Colin L. Powell, "Remarks with UN Secretary General Kofi Annan after Meeting" (US Department of State, 22 July 2004). See also Colin L. Powell, "Remarks at UNITY 2004: Journalists of Color Convention" (US Department of State, 5 August 2004).

58. Powell, "Remarks to the Africa Policy Advisory Panel Conference"; Colin L. Powell, "Remarks en Route to Cairo" (US Department of State, 27 July 2004). About lifting of restrictions on Sudan, see also Colin L. Powell, "Interview on Al Arabiya with Lukman Ahmed" (US Department of State, 15 September 2004).

59. Colin L. Powell, "Remarks to the Press in Kuwait" (US Department of State, 29 July 2004); Powell, "Remarks at UNITY 2004"; Colin L. Powell, "Interview by Cincinnati Enquirer Editorial Board" (US Department of State, 16 August 2004).

60. Powell, "Remarks en Route Khartoum from Darfur."

61. Powell, "Remarks with UN Secretary General."

62. Powell, "Interview on PBS's Charlie Rose"; Powell, "Remarks with UN Secretary General"; Colin L. Powell, "Interview on ABC's This Week with George Stephanopoulos" (US Department of State, 12 September 2004).

63. Andrew Natsios, "United States Policy in Sudan" (press conference; US Department of State, 27 April 2004), http://2001-2009.state.gov/p/af/rls/rm/31856 .htm.

64. Susan E. Rice and Gayle E. Smith, "The Darfur Catastrophe," *Washington Post*, 30 May 2004.

65. See arguments against military intervention in David Rieff, "Moral Blindness: The Case Against Troops for Darfur," *New Republic* 234, no. 21/22 (2006): 13–16; see also J. Stephen Morrison and Chester A. Crocker, "Time to Focus on the Real Choices in Darfur," *Washington Post*, 7 November 2006.

66. Helen Fessenden, "Lawmakers Seek Viable Solution to Sudan's Humanitarian Crisis," *CQ Weekly* 62 (3 July 2004): 1638.

67. Powell, "Interview by Cincinnati Enquirer Editorial Board."

68. The logistical challenges were posed by Darfur's geographical size and distance from suitable supply sources, including the lack of roads and railways, no modern air bases, no guaranteed supply of fuel, etc.

69. Ibid.; Powell, "Interview on CNN with Jeff Koinange"; Powell, "Interview on National Public Radio"; Powell, "Interview on PBS's Charlie Rose"; Colin L. Powell, "Remarks with Serbian President Boris Tadic after Their Meeting" (US Department of State, 20 July 2004); Colin L. Powell, "Remarks with Bulgarian Foreign Minister Solomon Passy after Their Meeting" (US Department of State, 22 July 2004); Powell, "Remarks with UN Secretary General"; Powell, "Remarks at UNITY 2004."

70. Powell, "Remarks en Route Khartoum from Darfur."

71. Powell, "Interview on National Public Radio."

72. Powell, "Interview on PBS's Charlie Rose."

73. Powell, "Interview on National Public Radio," emphases added. On 5 August, Powell again said, "Declaring [Darfur] a genocide does not require or cause any action that we are not now taking or could not take right now without a declaration of genocide" (in Powell, "Remarks at UNITY 2004").

74. In G. Jeffrey MacDonald, "In Sudan Crisis, a Duty to Intervene?," *Christian Science Monitor*, 21 July 2004.

75. John F. Kerry, "Remarks to the 95th Annual NAACP Convention in Philadelphia" (American Presidency Project, 15 July 2004), emphases added.

76. White House, "Press Gaggle by Scott McClellan" (American Presidency Project, 16 July 2004).

77. US House of Representatives, "House of Representatives Resolution 467: 'Declaring Genocide in Darfur, Sudan'" (Library of U.S. Congress, 22 July 2004) (see also Senate Resolution 133).

78. Heinze, "Rhetoric of Genocide," 369–371.

79. US Department of State, "Congress Set to Declare Darfur Region a Zone of Genocide" (13 July 2004).

80. Frank Wolf, "Stop the Killing in Darfur" (remarks of Frank R. Wolf in the U.S. House of Representatives, 108th Cong., 2nd Sess.), *Congressional Record* 150 (2 April 2004): E-518. According to Helen Fessenden ("Lawmakers Seek Viable Solution," 1639), other members of Congress to invoke the term frequently were Mike De Wine (R-OH), John McCain (R-AZ), and Jon Corzine (D-NJ) (cited in Heinze, "Rhetoric of Genocide," 369).

81. US House of Representatives, "H.Con.Res.403, 'Condemning the Government of the Republic of the Sudan for Its Attacks against Innocent Civilians in the Impoverished Darfur Region of Western Sudan'" (17 May 2004). The resolution was triggered by a testimony of John Prendergast in one of the House committees.

82. According to Fessenden ("Lawmakers Seek Viable Solution," 1639), these efforts ultimately led Bush to dispatch Powell to Darfur to investigate the killing.

83. House of Representatives, "Resolution 467," articles 6, 10. The *Financial Times* cited Senators Brownback and Corzine in saying that the purpose of the resolution was not to oblige the United States to intervene in Darfur but to "add moral weight to efforts to pass a United Nations resolution" (Alex Barker, "Bush Faces Pressures to Call Sudan 'Genocide,'" *Financial Times*, 14 July 2004).

84. United Nations, *Security Council Resolution 1556* (30 July 2004), passed with abstentions from China and Algeria.

85. Ibid. By using the term "measures" instead of "sanctions," explained Powell, the drafters of the resolution made it easier for some UNSC members to support the draft. In Colin L. Powell, "Interview with Brit Hume of Fox News Channel's 'Special Report with Brit Hume'" (US Department of State, 4 August 2004).

86. On the discussion at the UNSC, see Bellamy and Williams, "UN Security Council," 150–151.

87. Powell, "Interview with Brit Hume."

88. Colin L. Powell, "Remarks with Egyptian Foreign Minister Ahmed Aboul Gheit" (US Department of State, 28 July 2004); Colin L. Powell, "Interview with Nihal Saad of Egyptian Television" (US Department of State, 28 July 2004); Colin L. Powell, "Interview with Kamal Abdel Raouf of Al Akhbar Newspaper" (US Department of State, 28 July 2004); Colin L. Powell, "Interview with Rima Hamed Al Shamikh of Al Ikhbariya TV" (US Department of State, 29 July 2004); Colin L. Powell, "Interview with Hassan Moawad of Al Arabiya TV" (US Department of State, 29 July 2004).

89. US Department of State, "Daily Press Briefing by Deputy Spokesman Adam Ereli" (30 July 2004).

90. Bellamy and Williams, "UN Security Council," 151–152.

91. Based on a search of the US Department of State Archives, 18 November 2012.

92. George W. Bush, "Remarks on Signing the Department of Defense Appropriations Act, 2005" (American Presidency Project, 5 August 2004).

93. Powell, "Darfur."

94. George W. Bush, "Statement by the Press Secretary: President Welcomes Political Talks to Bring Lasting Solution to Darfur" (American Presidency Project, 26 August 2004).

95. The ADT was established with the help of the NGO Coalition for International Justice. For a detailed account, see Samuel Totten and Eric Markusen, "Research Note: The U.S. Government Darfur Genocide Investigation," *Journal of Genocide Research* 7, no. 2 (2005): 279–290. A report summary, "Documenting Atrocities in Darfur," was released on 9 September 2004 by the Bureau of Democracy, Human Rights, and Labor and the Bureau of Intelligence and Research at the State Department.

96. Powell, "Interview by Cincinnati Enquirer Editorial Board."

97. Ibid.

98. Powell, "Crisis in Darfur," emphases added.

99. Ibid., all emphases added.

100. Ibid.

101. George W. Bush, "Statement on the Situation in Sudan" (American Presidency Project, 9 September 2004), emphases added.

102. George W. Bush, "President Speaks to the United Nations General Assembly" (White House press release, 21 September 2004), emphasis added.

103. John F. Kerry, "Remarks to the 124th Annual Session of the National Baptist Convention in New Orleans" (American Presidency Project, 9 September 2004), emphasis added.

104. Powell, "Remarks at UNITY 2004"; Powell, "Darfur"; Colin L. Powell, "Remarks to the Press en Route Washington" (US Department of State, 1 September 2004); Powell, "Crisis in Darfur."

105. John F. Kerry, "Remarks to the Congressional Black Caucus Foundation's 34th Annual Legislative Conference in Washington, DC" (American Presidency Project, 11 September 2004).

106. See journalists' questions in Colin L. Powell, "Remarks at the 2004 Herbert Quandt Distinguished Lecture" (US Department of State, 10 September 2004); Colin L. Powell, "Interview on NBC's Meet the Press with Tim Russert" (US Department of State, 12 September 2004); Colin L. Powell, "Interview on Fox News Sunday with Chris Wallace" (US Department of State, 12 September 2004); Powell, "Interview on ABC's This Week"; Colin L. Powell, "Interview on the Michael Reagan Show" (US Department of State, 28 September 2004).

107. The week after the genocide determination, Powell, by his own account, was spending half of his day on Sudan. In Colin L. Powell, "Remarks at Teach Africa Youth Forum" (US Department of State, 17 September 2004).

108. Powell, "Remarks at the 2004 Herbert Quandt Distinguished Lecture"; Powell, "Interview on NBC's Meet the Press."

109. Ibid.; Powell, "Interview on the Michael Reagan Show."

110. Powell, "Interview on NBC's Meet the Press." See also Colin L. Powell, "Remarks at the Southern Center for International Studies" (US Department of State, 1 October 2004).

111. Powell, "Interview on the Michael Reagan Show."

112. Powell, "Interview on ABC's This Week." See also Powell, "Crisis in Darfur"; Colin L. Powell, "Interview by Arshad Mohammed and Saul Hudson of Reuters" (US Department of State, 12 September 2004).

113. Colin L. Powell, "Interview by Matt Lee and Christophe de Roquefeuil of Agence France Presse" (US Department of State, 29 September 2004). See also Powell, "Crisis in Darfur"; Powell, "Interview by Arshad Mohammed and Saul Hudson of Reuters."

114. Powell, "Interview on Fox News."
115. Powell, "Interview on the Michael Reagan Show."
116. Ibid. When not pointing elsewhere, Powell continued to dodge hard questions, such as if it was time for stronger action. Colin L. Powell, "The Africare Bishop T. Walker Memorial Dinner" (US Department of State, 1 October 2004).
117. Powell was often asked if he was not frustrated with the lack of international support for his genocide determination. See, e.g., Colin L. Powell, "Interview with Russ Spence of WAGA/Fox 5" (US Department of State, 1 October 2004).
118. John F. Kerry, "Presidential Debate in Coral Gables, Florida" (American Presidency Project, 30 September 2004), emphases added.
119. George W. Bush, "Presidential Debate in Coral Gables, Florida" (American Presidency Project, 30 September 2004).
120. United Nations, *Security Council Resolution 1564* (18 September 2004).
121. Michael G. MacKinnon, "The United Nations Security Council," in *The International Politics of Mass Atrocities: The Case of Darfur*, ed. David R. Black and Paul D. Williams (London: Routledge, 2010), 75. See also Bellamy and Williams, "UN Security Council," 152.
122. Bellamy and Williams, "UN Security Council," 153–154.
123. Colin L. Powell, "Interview by Clarence Page of the Chicago Tribune" (US Department of State, 14 October 2004).
124. Colin L. Powell, "Interview with Barry Schweid, George Gedda, and Anne Gearan of Associated Press" (US Department of State, 17 December 2004). See a general discussion of the "moral hazard" in Chapter 1.
125. Based on a search of the US Department of State Archives, 18 November 2012. Notably, part of this was said to be renewed prioritization of the North-South Naivasha peace talks. See *Washington Post*, "US Shift on Darfur Policy," 27 December 2004.
126. Powell, "Interview on PBS's Charlie Rose"; Colin L. Powell, "Interview by Hany El-Konayyesi of Abu Dhabi TV" (US Department of State, 21 October 2004). See also Colin L. Powell, "Interview with Regis Le Sommier of Paris Match" (US Department of State, 13 December 2004).
127. Colin L. Powell, "Interview with the USA Today Editorial Board" (US Department of State, 18 October 2004).
128. Issuing but a few short, inconsequential references, mostly in the context of the financial and small logistical US support for the now slightly expanded AU mission. George W. Bush, "Statement by the Press Secretary on the Expanded African Union (AU) Mission in Sudan" (American Presidency Project, 18 October 2004); George W. Bush, "Statement by the Press Secretary: Humanitarian Assistance for the People of Darfur" (American Presidency Project, 21 October 2004); George W. Bush, "Press Briefing by Scott McClellan" (American Presidency Project, 16 November 2004).
129. For more details, see Karen DeYoung, "Falling on His Sword," *Washington Post*, 1 October 2006.
130. See on escalation of the violence, *Washington Post*, "US Shift on Darfur Policy"; on Darfur dropping off the radar, in Prunier, *Darfur*, 128; Scott Straus, "Rwanda and Darfur: A Comparative Analysis," *Genocide Studies and Prevention* 1, no. 1 (2006): 52. A small spike in media attention did take place in mid-January 2005, in the context of the signing of the North-South Sudan peace agreement (Comprehensive Peace Agreement). After the handover in late January, Rice, the new secretary of state, referred to Darfur only in passing (February 2005), in

contexts of the International Criminal Court (ICC), Egypt's role, and administration budgetary requests for 2005.

131. United Nations, *Security Council Resolution 1574* (19 November 2004).
132. Bush, "Statement by the Press Secretary on the Expanded African Union."
133. Kerry did so in a televised debate in late September 2004.
134. The analysis of President Bush's rhetoric in relation to Darfur suggests that his reported "anger" and "sadness" over the events were not reflected in a significant way in either their frequency or force.
135. Stedjan and Thomas-Jensen have argued that despite its strong rhetoric on Darfur, the Bush administration did not take any meaningful steps to create costs for the Sudanese officials most responsible. In Scott Stedjan and Colin Thomas-Jensen, "The United States," in *The International Politics of Mass Atrocities: The Case of Darfur*, ed. David R. Black and Paul D. Williams (London: Routledge, 2010), 157–176, 166.
136. As recalled, nonintervention in Rwanda was justified by some politicians on grounds of "no US interests"; the interventions in Kosovo and in Bosnia in 1995 were claimed to be essential to regional stability and for the interests of important US allies.
137. Powell did promise already in May 2004 that the North-South negotiations would not affect the US response to Darfur, so staying on the moral side of the crisis was not limited to the "genocide" label.

CHAPTER 6 DETERMINING FACTORS IN THE MAKING OF THE US DARFUR POLICY

1. Stedjan and Thomas-Jensen, "United States," 158.
2. See Power, "Dying in Darfur," 2; Paul D. Williams and Alex J. Bellamy, "The Responsibility to Protect and the Crisis in Darfur," *Security Dialogue* 36, no. 1 (March 2005): 35.
3. John Prendergast, "So How Come We Haven't Stopped It?," *Washington Post*, 19 November 2006. See also Prunier, *Darfur*, 139–140. For summaries of US-Sudan relationships since the early 1990s, see Williams and Bellamy, "Responsibility to Protect," 34–35; Gerald Caplan, "From Rwanda to Darfur: Lessons Learned?," *Pambazuka News: Weekly Forum for Social Justice in Africa*, 12 January 2006; Stedjan and Thomas-Jensen, "United States," 164–165.
4. President Bush's war on terror was a central foreign policy issue in the 2004 election. Stedjan and Thomas-Jensen, "United States," 159.
5. Prendergast, "So How Come We Haven't Stopped It?" About the American-Sudanese Intelligence officials' relationships, see Caplan, "From Rwanda to Darfur"; Jonathan Steele, "Darfur Wasn't Genocide and Sudan Is Not a Terrorist State," *Guardian*, 7 October 2005.
6. Martin W. Daly, *Darfur's Sorrow: A History of Destruction and Genocide* (Oxford: Oxford University Press, 2007), 293.
7. See Stedjan and Thomas-Jensen, "United States," 166–167, 171.
8. Kostas, "Making the Determination of Genocide in Darfur," 119 (interview with Lorne Craner); Williams and Bellamy, "Responsibility to Protect," 38.
9. Prendergast, "So How Come We Haven't Stopped It?"; Julie Flint and Alex de Waal, *Darfur: A Short History of a Long War* (New York: Zed Books, 2006), 128–129; Williams and Bellamy, "Responsibility to Protect," 35, 38–40; Heinze, "Rhetoric of Genocide," 370–372.
10. Reeves, "Sudan Peace Talks Face the Threat of a Month-Long Break." See also Reeves, "Beginning of the End for Sudan's Peace Process?"; Reeves, "Darfur

and the Diplomatic Logic of Appeasement"; Reeves, "Emergency Humanitarian Intervention for Darfur."

11. Cited in Reeves, "Emergency Humanitarian Intervention for Darfur."

12. United Nations, "Sudan: More Pressure on Parties Urged in Prelude to Talks Resumption" (UN Integrated Regional Information Networks [IRIN], 5 February 2004). Heinze argued that had a more robust US policy (such as pushing hard for economic sanctions at the Security Council, or even going militarily) upset the North–South agreement, this would have hurt the administration domestically more than the failure to act in Darfur. Heinze, "Rhetoric of Genocide," 380. A report to the UN by Francis Deng in 27 September 2004 also warned of the negative effects of military action on the North–South agreement. In Francis M. Deng, "Specific Groups and Individuals: Mass Exoduses and Displaced Persons" (Report of the Representative of the Secretary-General on Internally Displaced Persons, United Nations Economic and Social Council, E/CN.4/2005/8, 27 September 2004). Thus, both American and UN officials preferred an "African solution."

13. See *Washington Post*, "US Shift on Darfur Policy"; Stedjan and Thomas-Jensen, "United States," 165–166, 171.

14. See analyses of the impact of the war in Iraq on humanitarian intervention in Darfur and in general in James Kurth, "Humanitarian Intervention after Iraq: Legal Ideals vs. Military Realities," *Orbis* 50, no. 1 (Winter 2006): 87–101; Bellamy, "Responsibility to Protect," 31–54; David Clark, "Iraq Has Wrecked Our Case for Humanitarian Wars: The US Neo-cons Have Broken the Kosovo Liberal Intervention Consensus," *Guardian*, 12 August 2003; Stedjan and Thomas-Jensen, "United States," 164.

15. Stedjan and Thomas-Jensen, "United States," 167–169. Notably, the invasion of Iraq took place one month after the crisis in Darfur broke out in early 2003.

16. See Power, "Dying in Darfur"; Bellamy, "Responsibility to Protect," 33.

17. Samuel Totten, "The U.S. Investigation into the Darfur Crisis and Its Determination of Genocide: A Critical Analysis," in Totten and Markusen, *Genocide in Darfur*, 208.

18. The WMD rationale for the war included also allegations of Saddam–al-Qaeda links. See in relation to the loss of legitimacy in Bellamy, "Responsibility to Protect," 51; Straus, "Rwanda and Darfur," 52; Kurth, "Humanitarian Intervention after Iraq," 88–89; Heinze, "Rhetoric of Genocide," 377–378.

19. Don Cheadle and John Prendergast, *"Not on Our Watch": The Mission to End Genocide in Darfur and Beyond* (New York: Hyperion, 2007), 99.

20. Both China and Russia have been staunch objectors to attempts to override state sovereignty based on humanitarian pretexts. Their motives are often regarded in the West as a mixture of ideological beliefs and fear of being targeted themselves for their poor human rights records in Tibet, Xinjiang (China), and Chechnya (Russia). Their economic interests in Sudan are discussed in this chapter.

21. China: oil and arms sales; Russia: arms deals; the United States: the North–South negotiations and collaboration in the war on terror.

22. Daly, *Darfur's Sorrow*, 295; Eric Reeves, "Impending Failure in Abuja, UN Security Council Inaction, Humanitarian Deterioration: The Darfur Crisis out of Control," sudanreeves.org, 24 August 2004.

23. Prunier, *Darfur*, 152; Daly, *Darfur's Sorrow*, 285.

24. Daly, *Darfur's Sorrow*, 285. Notably, de Waal argued that complex relationships between competing elites in Khartoum and local powers on the periphery, such as in Darfur, resulted in a dysfunctional Sudanese leadership, largely incapable of negotiating effective peace agreements. See Alex de Waal, "Sudan: The

Turbulent State," in *War in Darfur and the Search for Peace*, ed. Alex de Waal (Cambridge, MA: Global Equity Initiative, Harvard University, 2007), 23–24.

25. Eric Reeves, "Halting Genocide in Darfur, Preserving the North-South Peace Agreement: Both Require Removal of Khartoum's National Islamic Front from Power," sudanreeves.org, 9 August 2004; Daly, *Darfur's Sorrow*, 285.

26. Baba G. Kingibe, "African Union Briefing" (interview; Voices on Genocide Prevention, 9 March 2006).

27. This has indeed decreased international attention to the region, leading to easing of public pressure on governments to act. See Eric Reeves, "A Comprehensive Approach to Sudan" (interview; Voices on Genocide Prevention, 26 January 2006); Sally Chin, "No Power to Protect: The African Union Mission in Darfur" (interview; Voices on Genocide Prevention, 5 January 2006). See also Flint and de Waal, *Darfur*, 115–116. Power, in *"A Problem from Hell,"* also describes efforts to seal off leakage of information on atrocities, or their denial, by perpetrators in Turkey (Armenian genocide), Nazi Germany, Cambodia, and Iraq (Kurdish genocide).

28. The Sudanese may have learned from scare tactics used by the Serbs against the American threat of military intervention in Bosnia, of invoking publicly sensitive memories from Vietnam. See Power, *"A Problem from Hell,"* 284–285.

29. John Prendergast, "Civilian Protection, Accountability and Root Causes in Darfur" (interview; Voices on Genocide Prevention, 23 March 2006).

30. Daly, *Darfur's Sorrow*, 286; Eric Reeves, "Holding Khartoum accountable in Darfur," *Boston Globe,* 6 September 2007.

31. Totten and Markusen, *Genocide in Darfur*, xxviii.

32. Daly, *Darfur's Sorrow*, 294; Prendergast, "Civilian Protection, Accountability and Root Causes in Darfur"; Eric Reeves, "All Quiet: America's Sudan Strategy Has Changed for the Worse," *New Republic Online*, 27 October 2005.

33. Totten, "U.S. Investigation," 210. See also Piiparinen's inexplicably emphatic analysis in Touko Piiparinen, "Reconsidering the Silence over the Ultimate Crime: A Functional Shift in Crisis Management from the Rwandan Genocide to Darfur," *Journal of Genocide Research* 9, no. 1 (March 2007): 78–79, 86.

34. See, e.g., Cheadle and Prendergast, *"Not on Our Watch,"* 90–91, 96.

35. Richard Holbrooke, "How Did 'Never Again' Become Just Words?," *Washington Post*, 4 April 2004.

36. UN Doc. E/CN.4/2005/7 para. 36.

37. Martin Mennecke, "What's in a Name? Reflections on Using, Not Using, and Overusing the 'G-Word,'" *Genocide Studies and Prevention* 2, no. 1 (2007): 62, 66; Gareth Evans, "Genocide or Crime? Actions Speak Louder Than Words in Darfur," *European Voice*, 18 February 2005; Prunier, *Darfur*, 129, 156; Straus, "Rwanda and Darfur," 51; Juan E. Mendez, "United Nations Report from the Special Advisor on Genocide Prevention" (interview; Voices on Genocide Prevention, 16 February 2006); Power, "Dying in Darfur."

38. Ibid., 37–38.

39. Martha Minow, "Naming Horror: Legal and Political Words for Mass Atrocities," *Genocide Studies and Prevention* 2, no. 1 (2007): 37–42. The efforts, according to Minow, should have focused consequently on "pursuing better leadership, better media and educational efforts to mobilize sustained public responsiveness, and the development of a richer spectrum of available responses to join national and international efforts to halt mass and dehumanizing violence."

40. Scheffer, "Genocide and Atrocity Crimes," 230.

41. Ibid., 230.

42. Ibid., 230–231.

43. Ibid., 231.

44. David Bosco, "Crime of Crimes," *Washington Post*, 6 March 2005. David Bosco was at the time of writing a senior editor at *Foreign Policy Magazine*.

45. Ibid. Bosco suggested stirring away altogether from the "genocide debate" and the legal requirements to prove intent or establish the status of the victims as a recognized group. A widespread slaughter can demand intervention even if it falls outside of the "genocide" standard, he argued. He supported the idea to use "crimes against humanity" as the criterion for intervention, saying, "Do we really care . . . whether the victims of atrocities are members of a distinct tribe or simply political opponents of the regime?"

46. Ibid.

47. Notably, no policymakers or observers had come out to propose before the US determination on Darfur was issued that a no-genocide verdict on the part of the State Department would *reduce* America's moral responsibility to respond. Thus, if a determination of genocide had suggested for some a stronger US obligation to act, the inverse logic did not manifest itself in public discussions.

48. United Nations, "Report of the International Commission of Inquiry on Darfur to the United Nations Secretary-General" (25 January 2005), 518–519, 522.

49. See, e.g., Jerry Fowler, "A New Chapter of Irony: The Legal Definition of Genocide and the Implications of Powell's Determination," in Totten and Markusen, *Genocide in Darfur*, 135, and William A. Schabas, "Genocide, Crimes against Humanity and Darfur: The Commission of Inquiry's Findings on Genocide," *Cardozo Law Review* 27, no. 2 (2006): 1710–1711.

50. David Luban, "Calling Genocide by Its Rightful Name: Lemkin's Word, Darfur, and the UN Report," *Chicago Journal of International Law* 7, no. 1 (2006): 306.

51. Ibid., 306.

52. Ibid., 304. Note that this assertion was problematic, since under responsibility to protect (incorporated by the 2005 World Summit), both "genocide" and "crimes against humanity" constituted situations in which the international community had an obligation to take a similar action.

53. Ibid., 306, 308.

54. It has been argued, in fact, that it was the first time a sovereign state officially accused another state of committing genocide while it was still unfolding. Totten and Markusen, "Research Note," 279; Eric Reeves, "Watching Genocide, Doing Nothing: The Final Betrayal of Darfur," *Dissent*, Fall 2006.

55. Power, "It's Not Enough to Call It Genocide."

56. Luban, "Calling Genocide by Its Rightful Name," 304–305; Straus, "Rwanda and Darfur," 49; Samantha Power, "Bystanders to Genocide," *Atlantic Monthly*, September 2001, 1–24.

57. Ramesh Thakur, *The United Nations, Peace and Security: From Collective Security to the Responsibility to Protect* (Cambridge: Cambridge University Press, 2006), 57–58. Not only did the United States assist in thwarting the expansion of the UN peacekeeping mission in Rwanda, but it also played a key role in orchestrating the almost complete withdrawal of the force, allowing the genocide to continue unabated. Campbell, *Genocide and the Global Village*, 78; Power, *"A Problem from Hell,"* 366–368.

58. Genocide Convention, Article VIII. For other opinions on this issue, see Power, *"A Problem from Hell,"* 58; Flint and de Waal, *Darfur*, 131; Straus, "Rwanda and Darfur," 51.

59. This coverage lasted until the December 2004 tsunami disaster caused Darfur to largely disappear from the headlines. See Prunier, *Darfur*, 128; Straus, "Rwanda and Darfur," 52. Notably, Prunier (*Darfur*, 140) argues, citing a confidential interview he conducted in October 2004 with a "high ranking member of the

US Administration," that Powell was "practically ordered to use the term 'genocide' in his high-profile speech."

60. Straus, "Rwanda and Darfur," 50; Rebecca Hamilton and Chad Hazlett, "'Not on Our Watch': The Emergence of the American Movement for Darfur," in de Waal, *War in Darfur and the Search for Peace*, 342–343.

61. See in relation to France in Power, "Dying in Darfur," 11; Prunier, *Darfur*, 157; Karen E. Smith, *Genocide and the Europeans* (Cambridge: Cambridge University Press, 2010), 229; See also Prunier, *Darfur*, 157. The European Union called it "tantamount to genocide." It has been argued that the referral of the case by the United States to the UNSC and the subsequent establishment of the International Commission of Inquiry on Darfur allowed the European governments to defer to the council difficult decisions about genocide and about intervention. See extended discussion in Smith, *Genocide and the Europeans*, 228–232.

62. The same was noted by Pierre-Richard Prosper, former US ambassador-at-large for war crimes issues. Kostas, "Making the Determination of Genocide in Darfur," 123–124.

63. See International Development Committee, British House of Commons, "Darfur, Sudan: The Responsibility to Protect, Fifth Report of Session 2004–2005" (2005), 51.

64. Heinze, "Rhetoric of Genocide," 383.

65. See, e.g., Alex J. Bellamy, "Whither the Responsibility to Protect: Humanitarian Intervention and the 2005 World Summit," *Ethics and International Affairs* 20, no. 2 (2006): 159–160; Bellamy and Williams, "UN Security Council," 149–154.

66. Najib al-Khayr Abd-al-Wahab, "Sudan Prefers AU Mediation in Darfur Crisis, Says US Stance Isolated" (interview), *Global Newswire—Asia Africa Intelligence Wire*, 12 September 2004; Ramesh Thakur, "Western Medicine Is No Cure for Darfur's Ills," *Financial Review*, 31 August 2004; Michael Clough, "Darfur: Whose Responsibility to Protect" (New York: Human Rights Watch, 2005); Heinze, "Rhetoric of Genocide," 369–371; Peter Beaumont, "US 'Hyping' Darfur Genocide Fear," *Observer*, 21 October 2004; Stedjan and Thomas-Jensen, "United States," 168. See extended study of international responses to Darfur in *The International Politics of Mass Atrocities: The Case of Darfur*, edited by David R. Black and Paul D. Williams. London: Routledge, 2010.

67. Human Rights Watch, "UN: Darfur Resolution a Historic Failure" (2004); Eric Reeves, "Failure to Mount a Humanitarian Intervention in Darfur: Historical Context for Dramatically Escalating Insecurity," sudanreeves.org, 29 November 2004.

68. Eric Reeves, "Current Proposals for Responding to Genocide in Darfur: A Compendium and Critique of Suggestions from the International Community," sudanreeves.org, 23 September 2004.

69. Prunier, *Darfur*, 139–140. See also, for a more critical view, Schabas, "Genocide, Crimes against Humanity, and Darfur," 1717–1718.

70. *BBC News*, "'Never Again': John Danforth Interview Transcript," 3 July 2005, http://news.bbc.co.uk/1/hi/programmes/panorama/4647211.stm. Notably, before his post at the UN, Danforth served as a special envoy to Sudan for President Bush.

71. Heinze, "Rhetoric of Genocide," 376, 381.

72. Heinze, "Rhetoric of Genocide," 376, 381. Objections to using the term were voiced by Amnesty, Human Rights Watch, and Médecins Sans Frontières.

73. Alex de Waal, "What Does Adding the 'Genocide' Label to the Darfur Crisis Really Mean?," *Index on Censorship*, 2 February 2005. Notably, Rwanda's impact on the US State Department's policy in Darfur was corroborated by Lorne

Craner, former assistant secretary of state for democracy, human rights and labor in 2004. Its precise effects, though, were said to be unclear. See Kostas, "Making the Determination of Genocide in Darfur," 114, 124.

74. Pointed to by Craner, in Kostas, "Making the Determination of Genocide in Darfur," 114.

75. Heinze, "Rhetoric of Genocide," 380.

76. To allow US oil companies barred from operating in Sudan by an executive order from 1997 to compete for Sudanese oil leases after the war. See Power, "Dying in Darfur," 2; Williams and Bellamy, "Responsibility to Protect," 35.

77. Kostas, "Making the Determination of Genocide in Darfur," 115.

78. Ibid., 115.

79. Kostas wrote, "The United States was exasperated by the international inertia, and Craner believed that if the United States could *authoritatively* call it 'genocide' it might mobilize European governments to take a more aggressive approach" (116). He also wrote, "For, Prosper, investigating for genocide permitted an answer to a difficult legal question and would allow the use of a mechanism to refer the matter to the United Nations Security Council" (117).

80. Ibid., 119–120. Arguably, as it would have been difficult for the administration to ignore or thwart the conclusions of the investigation once reached, Prosper's claim that top State Department officials were willing to accept any verdict is plausible.

81. See Eyal Mayroz, "The Legal Duty to 'Prevent': After the Onset of Genocide," *Journal of Genocide Research* 14, no. 1 (2012): 79–98; Eyal Mayroz, "Genocide: To Prevent and Punish 'Radical Evil,'" in *International Criminal Law in Context*, ed. Philipp Kastner (Oxon: Routledge, 2018), 71–90.

82. See Chapter 1.

83. See Powell's testimony to the Foreign Relations Committee quoted in Chapter 5.

84. As seen in the complications in the International Criminal Court (ICC) case against Sudanese president Omar al-Bashir.

85. Cohen, The *Public's Impact on Foreign Policy*, 111–113; Entman, *Projections of Power*, 12–16; Kull and Destler, *Misreading the Public*, 219–221; Powlick, "Sources of Public Opinion," 434–437, 446–447; Cohen, *Public's Impact on Foreign Policy*, 115–117; Kull and Destler, *Misreading the Public*, 208–213; Powlick, "Sources of Public Opinion," 434–435, 438–439, 446–447. Notably, policymakers were found to distrust opinion polls more than the other two indicators.

86. Melvern described the print media coverage as "sparse" and "intermittent." Linda Melvern, "Rwanda and Darfur: The Media and the Security Council," *International Relations* 20, no. 1 (March 2006): 100. See also Jerry Fowler, "Voices on Genocide Prevention" (US Holocaust Memorial Museum, 6 November 2006), and results from a survey conducted by Ricchiardi for the *American Journalism Review* among print and broadcast media editors and producers. In Sherry Ricchiardi, "Déjà Vu," *American Journalism Review*, February/March 2005, 38–39. Based on the survey, Nicholas Kristof for the *New York Times* and Emily Wax for the *Washington Post* were among the few journalists who took risks to cover the conflict from within Darfur. Notably, an editorial in the *Oregonian* (Portland) went so far as to argue that by motivating the world press, politicians, and diplomats to take action, Kristof's stories have saved "tens of thousands" or even "hundreds of thousands" of lives in Darfur (ibid., 37). See also on the coverage of the two papers in Antal Wozniak, "Genocide in the News: Media Attention and Media Framing of the Darfur Conflict" (paper, International Communication Association, San Francisco, 2007); Power,

"Dying in Darfur." Ricchiardi highlighted also the coverage on National Public Radio.

87. Ricchiardi, "Déjà Vu," 38, 40; Carrol Bogert, "Another Africa Calamity—Will Media Slumber On?," *Los Angeles Times*, 28 April 2004.

88. Ricchiardi, "Déjà Vu," 39.

89. Where a local slant was found (as in the case of the *Kansas City Star*—with two local senators active on Darfur), the coverage began earlier and was more substantial. See ibid., 37–40.

90. Ibid., 36.

91. Bogert, "Another Africa Calamity"; Ricchiardi, "Déjà Vu," 39.

92. Ricchiardi, "Déjà Vu," 38–40. Glen Ruga, director of the Center for Balkan Development, interviewed by Ricchiardi, argued that it is a vicious cycle where the public may not be interested in a story until the media start covering it. So, the media must take the first step (39).

93. Ibid., 37.

94. Ibid., 35. On the Sudanese effort to seal off media access to Darfur, see Reeves, "Comprehensive Approach to Sudan"; Chin, "No Power to Protect." See also Flint and de Waal, *Darfur*, 115–116. Power, in *"A Problem from Hell,"* also describes efforts to seal off leakage of information on atrocities, and their denial by perpetrators in Turkey (Armenian genocide), Nazi Germany, Cambodia, and Iraq (Kurdish genocide).

95. A claim supported by contrasting the limited coverage of Rwanda with that of Bosnia. Bogert, "Another Africa Calamity"; Ricchiardi, "Déjà Vu," 38–39.

96. Ricchiardi, "Déjà Vu," 39. The news media cannot afford to linger for too long on one story without risking losing rating competitions due to audiences' boredom or compassion fatigue.

97. American Progress Action Fund, americanactionprogress.org (2005).

98. According to the 2005 study of the American Progress Action Fund, the gap between infotainment stories and the coverage of Darfur was even larger in June 2005, with CNN, Fox News, NBC/MSNBC, ABC, and CBS running fifty times as many stories about Michael Jackson and twelve times as many stories about Tom Cruise as they did about the crisis. These tendencies bring to memory how the events in Rwanda ten years earlier were overshadowed in the United States by the media coverage of the O. J. Simpson trial.

99. Harry C. Blaney III, "Speaking Out: The Lessons of Darfur," *Foreign Service Journal* 81, no. 12 (December 2004): 8; Prunier, *Darfur*, 151.

100. Blaney, "Speaking Out." Lynch and McGoldrick explain that lack of context in news reports leaves the reader to speculate on the reasons for the violence and thus to infer causes such as "ancient hatreds," "religious fanaticism," or "tribal anarchy." Jake Lynch and Annabel McGoldrick, *Peace Journalism* (Gloucestershire: Hawthorn Press, 2005), 63.

101. In Melvern, "Rwanda and Darfur," 100.

102. Bogert, "Another Africa Calamity." The piece was published soon after the 10 Year Commemoration of the Rwandan genocide.

103. Melvern, "Rwanda and Darfur."

104. Caplan, "From Rwanda to Darfur."

105. Deborah Murphy, "Narrating Darfur: Darfur in the U.S. Press, March–September 2004," in de Waal, *War in Darfur and the Search for Peace*, 315.

106. Including a call for US military action if the UN failed to act. US House of Representatives, "House of Representatives Resolution H. Con. Res. 467: 'Declaring Genocide in Darfur, Sudan'" (22 July 2004) (see also Senate Resolution 133).

107. Chicago Council on Foreign Relations, *Global Views 2004: American Public Opinion and Foreign Policy* (Chicago: Chicago Council on Foreign Relations, 2004), 24. The poll was conducted between 6 and 12 July. See description of surveyed elites also in Kull and Destler, *Misreading the Public*, 25.

108. Ibid., 29.

109. Steven Kull, et al. "Americans on the Crisis in Sudan." PIPA/Knowledge Networks Poll, 20 July 2004.

110. Ibid.

111. As discussed in Chapter 5, a hypothetical genocide determination by the UN in a 1995 poll in relation to Rwanda and Bosnia elicited 80 percent support for a military intervention.

112. International Crisis Group and Zogbi International, "Africa Briefing No. 26: Do Americans Care about Darfur?" (1 June 2005), 4. Notably, while the word "genocide" was omitted from the question in favor of the less emotive word "killings," a link to the term was used in an earlier question in the survey that assessed its applicability to the situation in Darfur. Respondents' support for describing Darfur as either genocide or a crime against humanity was still high at 80 percent (10 percent objected) three months after Powell's genocide determination had been challenged by the UN's Commission on Darfur.

113. PIPA, "The Darfur Crisis: African and American Public Opinion" (June 2005).

114. Nonetheless, given the conditions in Iraq, the willingness by many Americans to continue to support a military operation in Darfur was quite remarkable.

115. Cheadle and Prendergast, *"Not on Our Watch,"* 91.

116. See also Heinze, "Rhetoric of Genocide," 381–382.

117. See also Eric Reeves, "Secretary of State Colin Powell's Genocide Determination: What It Does, and Doesn't, Mean for Darfur," sudanreeves.org, 10 September 2004; Taylor B. Seybolt, "The Darfur Atrocities Documentation Project: A Precedent for the Future? A Perspective from Washington D.C.," in Totten and Markusen, *Genocide in Darfur*, 168.

118. See, e.g., Totten, "U.S. Investigation," 214, 219.

119. Human Rights Watch, "Darfur Destroyed: Ethnic Cleansing by Government and Militia Forces in Western Sudan" (6 May 2004), 58.

120. International Development Committee, British House of Commons, "Darfur, Sudan," 51. Dr. Mukesh Kapila was UN resident and humanitarian coordinator in the Sudan during 2003–2004.

121. See analysis of the US stand in Human Rights Watch, "Too Little, Too Late: Sudanese and International Response 2004," http://hrw.org/reports/2004/sudan0504/8.htm. Interestingly, the first time, according to Power (*"A Problem from Hell,"* 362), that the United States officially used the word "genocide" on Rwanda was in the UN Commission on Human Rights.

122. See Kostas, "Making the Determination of Genocide in Darfur," 116–117.

123. Cambodia, Northern Iraq during the Anfal campaign, Bosnia until NATO's bombing, Rwanda, etc.

124. Kull et al., "Americans on the Crisis in Sudan," 6. While these numbers reflected public awareness of the crisis *before* the genocide determination and were to grow significantly by June 2005, the public discussion in the United States was already going on for some time by mid-2004. Also, network coverage did not increase by much even after the determinations.

125. *Washington Post*, "US Shift on Darfur Policy."

126. For a list of organizations that have declared genocide in Darfur, see Eric Reeves, "Darfur 101," *New Republic Online*, 5 May 2006. See also Yehuda Bauer, "Remembrance and Beyond" (keynote address, United Nations Holocaust Memorial Day, 27 January 2006); Mika Vehnämäki, "Darfur Scorched:

Looming Genocide in Western Sudan," *Journal of Genocide Research* 8, no. 1 (March 2006): 78; Prunier, *Darfur,* 156; Luban, "Calling Genocide by Its Rightful Name," 315; Prendergast, "So How Come We Haven't Stopped It?"; Totten and Markusen, "Research Note," 285; Gregory H. Stanton, "Genocide Emergency: Darfur, Sudan" (Genocide Watch, 2004); Straus, "Rwanda and Darfur," 50.

127. Reeves, "Darfur 101." According to Reeves, while Amnesty International did not officially use the term "genocide" on Darfur, Amnesty USA director William Schultz has been explicit with his own personal view that Darfur was indeed genocide. For evidence in support of the existence of intent of Sudanese officials to perpetrate genocide in Darfur, see Flint and de Waal, *Darfur,* 106.

128. See Michael Clough, "It's Hell in Darfur, but Is It Genocide? The Sudanese Government Has Targeted Villagers, but Not a Whole Race," *Los Angeles Times,* 14 May 2006; Nelson Kasfir, "Sudan's Darfur: Is It Genocide?' *Current History* 104, no. 682 (May 2005): 99–102.

129. See Evans, "Genocide or Crime?" See also Prunier, *Darfur,* 129, 156; Straus, "Rwanda and Darfur," 51; Mendez, "United Nations Report"; Power, "Dying in Darfur."

130. Seybolt, "Darfur Atrocities Documentation Project," 168.

131. Ibid., 163, 167; Totten, "U.S. Investigation," 218.

132. Cheadle and Prendergast, *"Not on Our Watch,"* 96.

CONCLUSION

1. Later CEO of the NGO International Crisis Group.

2. See Kishore Mahbubani, "The Permanent and Elected Council Members," in *The UN Security Council: From the Cold War to the 21st Century,* ed. David M. Malone (Boulder, CO: Lynne Rienner, 2004), 263, and Kishore Mahbubani, "The UN Security Council: From the Cold War to the 21st Century" (transcript of presentation, Carnegie Council on Ethics in International Affairs, 4 March 2004).

3. Mahbubani, "Permanent and Elected Council Members," 263.

4. Cara Vanayan, "Humanitarian Intervention and the Failure to Protect: Sham Compliance and the Limitations of the Norm Life Cycle Model" (master's thesis, University of Ottawa), 2008, 111; Mueller, "Public Opinion as a Constraint," 10.

5. Robert J. Art and Patrick M. Cronin, *The United States and Coercive Diplomacy* (Washington, DC: US Institute for Peace Press, 2003).

6. Nicholas Wheeler wrote about a similar clash between charges of interference in the internal affairs of another state when trying to do "something" and accusations of moral indifference when doing nothing. See Wheeler, *Saving Strangers,* 1.

7. Iyengar and McGrady, *Media Politics,* 11; Kull and Destler, *Misreading the Public,* 233.

8. Eyal Mayroz, "Between Empathy and Fear: Recalibrating Incentives for Atrocity Prevention," in *"Last Lectures": The Prevention/Intervention of Genocide,* ed. Samuel Totten (London: Routledge, 2018), 34–39.

9. Power, *"A Problem from Hell,"* 510.

10. On the effects of public opinion, particularly among the Christian right, see Heinze, "Rhetoric of Genocide," 379.

11. Wheeler, *Saving Strangers,* 287.

12. Notably, at times the problem could be of incorrect analysis rather than of deficient or inaccurate communication of data.

13. See Power, *"A Problem from Hell,"* 505–506. Power argues that those officials who "didn't know" chose not to. At times, though, the information may have failed to reach high-level decision makers, especially during the early stages of crises.

14. The term "inaction" suggests the absence of any type of response, whereas these days it is more about governments engaging in ineffective or insufficient action or rhetoric than about ignoring a genocidal crisis altogether.

15. Vanayan, "Humanitarian Intervention," 11–12.

16. At the time of writing 137 states. See lists of states parties, understandings, and reservations on the Prevent Genocide website, http://preventgenocide.org/law /convention.

17. About President Bush's "not on my watch," see Power, *"A Problem from Hell,"* 511.

18. Hamilton and Hazlett, "'Not on Our Watch,'" 366.

19. See Chapters 5 and 6.

20. Nor confer additional legal obligations on the United States and the international community.

21. Inter Press Service (Stockholm), 30 January 2004, emphases added.

22. See extended discussions in Mayroz, "Legal Duty to 'Prevent,'" 79–98, and Mayroz, "Genocide," 71–90.

23. See interventions in Somalia (1992–1993), Haiti (1994), East Timor (1999), and Sierra Leone (2001) versus the noninterventions in Cambodia, Rwanda, Darfur, and elsewhere.

24. Kurt Mills, *International Responses to Mass Atrocities in Africa: Responsibility to Protect, Prosecute, and Palliate* (Philadelphia: University of Pennsylvania Press, 2015), 206; Rebecca Hamilton, *Fighting for Darfur: Public Action and the Struggle to Stop Genocide* (Basingstoke: Palgrave Macmillan, 2011), 110; Mennecke, "What's in a Name?," 64; Medina Haeri, "Saving Darfur: Does Advocacy Help or Hinder Conflict Resolution?," *Praxis: The Fletcher Journal of Human Security*, no. 23 (2008): 43. Of course, the genocide label would not have been the only factor, as protractedness of conflicts goes a long way to reducing their media visibility.

25. Albright and Cohen, *A Blueprint for US Policymakers*, xxi.

26. Even the "no-genocide" determination by the independent Commission of Inquiry on Darfur was alleged to have been influenced by political directives from UN officials.

27. See, e.g., David Morse, "Appeasement Driven by Oil: The Bush Administration and Darfur," TomDispatch.com, 2006, www.tomdispatch.com/index.mhtml ?pid=124232; Blaney, "Speaking Out"; Caplan, "From Rwanda to Darfur"; Eric Reeves, "As the International Community Postures, Sudan's Many Crises Deepen", sudanreeves.com, 14 February 2006; Nicholas D. Kristof, "A Wimp on Genocide," *New York Times*, 18 September 2005.

28. Famous examples included the 1996 expulsion of Osama bin Laden from his base in Sudan and the withdrawal of Sudanese support from terrorist organizations about the same time. Cheadle and Prendergast, *"Not on Our Watch,"* 64; Murphy, "Narrating Darfur," 322. See also Prendergast, "So How Come We Haven't Stopped It?"; Susan E. Rice, Anthony Lake, and Donald M. Payne, "We Saved Europeans. Why Not Africans?," *Washington Post*, 2 October 2006; Nick Grono and John Prendergast, "To Halt Sudan's Atrocities, Follow the Money," *International Herald Tribune*, 22 August 2006; Stedjan and Thomas-Jensen, "United States," 164.

29. Stedjan and Thomas-Jensen, "United States," 171, 174.

30. See, e.g., Andrea Bartoli and Tetsushi Ogata, "Supporting Regional Approaches to Genocide Prevention: The International Conference on the Great Lakes

Region (ICGLR)" (paper, Genocide Prevention Advisory Network, 2010), www.gpanet.org/content/supporting-regional-approaches-genocide -prevention-international-conference-great-lakes-regi.

31. Huntington, "American Ideals versus American Institutions," 1.
32. See reflections and critiques of the *Mass Atrocity Response Operations Handbook*, produced by Harvard's Kennedy School and the US Army Peacekeeping and Stability Operations, in the special edition of *Genocide Studies and Prevention: An International Journal* 6, no. 1 (2011).
33. Power, *"A Problem from Hell,"* 84.
34. J. William Fulbright, *The Arrogance of Power* (New York: Random House, 1966), 20.
35. Kane, *Between Virtue and Power*, 3–7.
36. See, e.g., Theriault, "Albright-Cohen Report," 202–206.
37. See more on US defense of its sovereignty in Edward Luck, *Mixed Messages: American Politics and International Organization, 1919–1999* (Washington, DC: Brookings Institution, 1999); Richard N. Haass, *The Opportunity: America's Moment to Alter History's Course* (New York: Public Affairs, 2005), 41.
38. See detailed discussion in chap. 3 of Josef Joffe, *Uberpower: The Imperial Temptation of America* (New York: Norton, 2006), 67–94.
39. For example State Failure (now Political Instability) Task Force, led originally by Ted Gurr with Barbara Harff, first Atrocities Prevention Interagency Working Group, established in 1998. See in James P. Finkel, "Atrocity Prevention at the Crossroads: Assessing the President's Atrocity Prevention Board after Two Years" (Center for the Prevention of Genocide Series of Occasional Papers no. 2, September 2014), 7. See also US-based NGO Genocide Watch, founded by Gregory Stanton, http://www.genocidewatch.org.
40. Mennecke, "What's in a Name?," 60.
41. Kane, *Between Virtue and Power*, 333–334. Motivations behind condemnations of the United States could be attributed to one or more of the following factors: political self-interest, contradictory interpretations of events, anger over misbehavior by a world power, concerns over negative side effects of interventions (e.g., repercussions on local civilian populations, fears of jeopardizing peace negotiations, distrust of the readiness of the powers to follow up interventions with long-term peacebuilding efforts), empathy for the target of an intervention (the "underdog"), cultural or political affiliations, perceived personal or national grievances toward the United States, and outright anti-Americanism.
42. See discussion in Mayroz, "Between Empathy and Fear," 34–40.

Epilogue

1. The Save Darfur Coalition was a grassroots movement of religious organizations, "interested legislators," NGOs, students, and a small number of committed journalists. See Hamilton and Hazlett, "'Not on Our Watch,'" 361, 364, 366; Daly, *Darfur's Sorrow*, 292–293; Scott Straus, "'Atrocity Statistics' and Other Lessons from Darfur," in Totten and Markusen, *Genocide in Darfur*, 193. Civil society efforts are covered in detail in other literature. See, e.g., Hamilton, *Fighting for Darfur*. As noted by Stedjan and Thomas-Jensen, "The [Save Darfur] movement created a small political cost and the administration responded with rhetoric and some diplomacy." Stedjan and Thomas-Jensen, "United States," 161.
2. Obama, "Presidential Study Directive on Mass Atrocities."
3. See numerous critiques of the administration's policies on Sudan by Eric Reeves at sudanreeves.org. See also analysis of President Obama's discourses on the

crises in Libya, Syria, and Iraq by Matthew Levinger, "A Core National Security Interest: Framing Atrocities Prevention," *Politics and Governance* 3, no. 4 (2015): 26–43; Martin Levinger, "Why the U.S. Government Failed to Anticipate the Rwandan Genocide of 1994: Lessons for Early Warning and Prevention," *Genocide Studies and Prevention* 9, no. 3 (2016): 53–55.

4. Finkel, "Atrocity Prevention at the Crossroads," 27 (see the rest of the article for a detailed review). See also Levinger, "Core National Security Interest," 26–27; James P. Finkel, "Moving Beyond the Crossroads: Strengthening the Atrocity Prevention Board," *Genocide Studies and Prevention* 9, no. 2 (2015): 138–149.

5. Jérôme Tubiana. "The Man Who Terrorized Darfur Is Leading Sudan's Supposed Transition." *Foreign Policy.* 14 May 2019. www.foreignpolicy.com/2019 /05/14/man-who-terrorized-darfur-is-leading-sudans-supposed-transition -hemeti-rsf-janjaweed-bashir-khartoum/.

6. Jehanne Henry, "US Considers Lifting Sudan's 'Terror State' Designation: Move Ignores Sudan's Abuses Against Its Own People" (Human Rights Watch, 7 November 2018), www.hrw.org/news/2018/11/07/us-considers-lifting-sudans -terror-state-designation.

7. United Nations, "International Criminal Court Prosecutor Presses for More Active Security Council Role in Supporting Arrest, Transfer of Indicted Fugitives" (20 June 2018), www.un.org/press/en/2018/sc13388.doc.htm.

8. See sudanreeves.org.

9. According to James Finkel, the bureaucratic approach to atrocity prevention has not changed much since the 2017 handover. James P. Finkel, "Global Approaches to Atrocity Prevention: Introduction to the Special Issue," *Genocide Studies and Prevention* 11, no. 3 (2018): 3.

BIBLIOGRAPHY

PRIMARY SOURCES

Bush, George H. W. "Presidential Debate in St. Louis." American Presidency Project, 11 October 1992.

———. "The President's News Conference." American Presidency Project, 7 August 1992.

———. "Remarks and a Question-and-Answer Session at a Rotary Club Dinner in Portsmouth, New Hampshire." American Presidency Project, 15 January 1992.

———. "Remarks at the Community Welcome for Returning Troops in Sumter, South Carolina." American Presidency Project, 17 March 1991.

———. "Remarks at the Simon Wiesenthal Dinner, Century Plaza Hotel, Los Angeles, California." Federal News Service, 16 June 1991.

———. "Remarks on the Situation in Bosnia and an Exchange with Reporters in Colorado Springs." American Presidency Project, 6 August 1992.

———. "Remarks to the Conference on Security and Cooperation in Europe in Helsinki, Finland." American Presidency Project, 9 July 1992.

Bush, George W. "President Condemns Atrocities in Sudan: Statement by the President." White House, 7 April 2004.

———. "Presidential Debate in Coral Gables, Florida." American Presidency Project, 30 September 2004.

———. "President Speaks to the United Nations General Assembly." White House press release, 21 September 2004.

———. "Press Briefing by Scott McClellan." American Presidency Project, 16 November 2004.

———. "Remarks on Signing the Department of Defense Appropriations Act, 2005." American Presidency Project, 5 August 2004.

———. "Statement by the Press Secretary: Humanitarian Assistance for the People of Darfur." American Presidency Project, 21 October 2004.

———. "Statement by the Press Secretary on the Expanded African Union (AU) Mission in Sudan." American Presidency Project, 18 October 2004.

———. "Statement by the Press Secretary: President Welcomes Political Talks to Bring Lasting Solution to Darfur." American Presidency Project, 26 August 2004.

———. "Statement on the Situation in Sudan." American Presidency Project, 9 September 2004.

———. "Statement on the 10th Anniversary of the 1994 Rwanda Genocide." American Presidency Project, 7 April 2004.

———. This Week, 23 January 2000.

———. "The 2000 Campaign: 2nd Presidential Debate between Gov. Bush and Vice President Gore" (transcript). New York Times, 12 October 2000. www.nytimes.com/2000/10/12/us/2000-campaign-2nd-presidential-debate-between-gov-bush-vice-president-gore.html?pagewanted=all&src=pm.

Carter, Jimmy. "Aid for Kampucheans Remarks Announcing Additional Relief Efforts." American Presidency Project, 24 October 1979.

———. "Human Rights Violations in Cambodia Statement by the President." American Presidency Project, 21 April 1978.

———. "Interview with the President Remarks and a Question-and-Answer Session with Editors and Broadcasters from Minnesota." American Presidency Project, 26 October 1979.

———. "39th President of the United States, Remarks at the Presentation of the Final Report of the President's Commission on the Holocaust." White House, 27 September 1979.

Clinton, William J. "Address to the Nation on Airstrikes Against Serbian Targets in the Federal Republic of Yugoslavia (Serbia and Montenegro)." American Presidency Project, 24 March 1999.

———. "Address to the Nation on Implementation of the Peace Agreement in Bosnia-Herzegovina." American Presidency Project, 27 November 1995.

———. "Commencement Address at the United States Air Force Academy in Colorado Springs." American Presidency Project, 2 June 1999.

———. "Commencement Address at the United States Military Academy in West Point, New York." American Presidency Project, 31 May 1997.

———. "Crisis in the Balkans: Clinton's Remarks in Defense of Military Intervention in Balkans." *New York Times*, 14 May 1999. www.nytimes.com/1999/05/14/world/crisis-balkans-clinton-s-remarks-defense-military-intervention-balkans.html.

———. "Exchange with Reporters Prior to Discussions with President Vaclav Havel of the Czech Republic." American Presidency Project, 20 April 1993.

———. "Interview on CNN's 'Global Forum with President Clinton.'" American Presidency Project, 3 May 1994.

———. "Interview with Dan Rather of CBS News." American Presidency Project, 31 March 1999.

———. "Interview with the French Media in Paris." American Presidency Project, 7 June 1994.

———. "Interview with Tabitha Soren of MTV." American Presidency Project, 11 August 1995.

———. "Interview with Wolf Blitzer of Cable News Network's 'Late Edition' in Cologne." American Presidency Project, 20 June 1999.

———. "Interview with Yevgeniy Kiselev of Russia's NTV in Cologne." American Presidency Project, 20 June 1999.

———. "Letter to Congressional Leaders on Humanitarian Assistance for Rwandan Refugees." American Presidency Project, 1 August 1994.

———. "Letter to Congressional Leaders Reporting on the Deployment of United States Aircraft to Bosnia-Herzegovina." American Presidency Project, 1 September 1995.

———. "Memorandum on Assistance to the International Tribunal for the Former Yugoslavia." American Presidency Project, 16 May 1994.

———. *My Life*. New York: Knopf, 2004.

———. "The President's News Conference." American Presidency Project, 23 April 1993.

———. "The President's News Conference." American Presidency Project, 10 August 1995.

———. "The President's News Conference." American Presidency Project, 25 June 1999.

———. "The President's News Conference with President Kim Yong-sam of South Korea." American Presidency Project, 27 July 1995.

———. "The President's Radio Address." American Presidency Project, 2 December 1995.

———. "Proclamation 6855—Human Rights Day, Bill of Rights Day, and Human Rights Week." American Presidency Project, 5 December 1995.

———. "Proclamation 7258—Human Rights Day, Bill of Rights Day, and Human Rights Week." American Presidency Project, 6 December 1999.

———. "Remarks Announcing Participation in Missions in Bosnia and Zaire and an Exchange with Reporters." American Presidency Project, 15 November 1996.

———. "Remarks at the Electronic Industries Alliance Dinner." American Presidency Project, 30 March 1999.

———. "Remarks at the Legislative Convention of the American Federation of State, County, and Municipal Employees." American Presidency Project, 23 March 1999.

———. "Remarks at a Reception for Representative Maurice D. Hinchey in Kingston, New York." American Presidency Project, 23 October 2000.

———. "Remarks at the Seventh Millennium Evening at the White House." American Presidency Project, 12 April 1999.

———. "Remarks at a Veterans Day Ceremony in Arlington, Virginia." American Presidency Project, 11 November 1998.

———. "Remarks at the Veterans of Foreign Wars of the United States 100th National Convention in Kansas City, Missouri." American Presidency Project, 16 August 1999.

———. "Remarks at Whiteman Air Force Base in Knob Noster, Missouri." American Presidency Project, 11 June 1999.

———. "Remarks by President Clinton to the KFOR Troops at Skopje, Macedonia." American Presidency Project, 22 June 1999.

———. "Remarks by the President to Genocide Survivors, Assistance Workers, and US and Rwanda Government Officials." White House, Office of the Press Secretary, 25 March 1998.

———. "Remarks Following Discussions with European Union Leaders and an Exchange with Reporters in Bonn." American Presidency Project, 21 June 1999.

———. "Remarks Following a Meeting with Congressional Leaders and an Exchange with Reporters." American Presidency Project, 13 April 1999.

———. "Remarks in a Question-and-Answer Session at the Godfrey Sperling Luncheon." American Presidency Project, 25 September 1995.

———. "Remarks of President Bill Clinton at the Dedication Ceremonies for the United States Holocaust Memorial Museum." ushmm.org, 22 April 1993.

———. "Remarks on Arrival in Honolulu, Hawaii." American Presidency Project, 31 August 1995.

———. "Remarks on the Balkan Peace Process and an Exchange with Reporters." American Presidency Project, 31 October 1995.

———. "Remarks on the Balkan Peace Process Following a Meeting with Elie Wiesel and an Exchange with Reporters." American Presidency Project, 13 December 1995.

———. "Remarks on Presenting the Eleanor Roosevelt Awards for Human Rights." American Presidency Project, 10 December 1998.

———. "Remarks on Presenting the President's Award for Furthering Employment of People with Disabilities." American Presidency Project, 4 June 1999.

———. "Remarks on Signing Emergency Supplemental Appropriations and Rescisions Legislation and an Exchange with Reporters." American Presidency Project, 27 July 1995.

———. "Remarks on United States Foreign Policy in San Francisco." American Presidency Project, 26 February 1999.

———. "Remarks on Welfare Reform and an Exchange with Reporters." American Presidency Project, 13 July 1995.

———. "Remarks and a Question-and-Answer Session with the American Society of Newspaper Editors in San Francisco, California." American Presidency Project, 15 April 1999.

———. "Remarks to American Troops at Tuzla Airfield, Bosnia-Herzegovina." American Presidency Project, 13 January 1996.

———. "Remarks to the Community at Fort Polk, Louisiana." American Presidency Project, 18 March 1996.

———. "Remarks to the Community at Spangdahlem Air Base, Germany." American Presidency Project, 5 May 1999.

———. "Remarks to the Conference on the Progressive Tradition in Princeton, New Jersey." American Presidency Project, 5 October 2000.

———. "Remarks to the 54th Session of the United Nations General Assembly in New York City." American Presidency Project, 21 September 1999.

———. "Remarks to the Military Community at Norfolk Naval Station." American Presidency Project, 1 April 1999.

———. "Remarks to the Parliament of the United Kingdom in London." American Presidency Project, 29 November 1995.

———. "Remarks to the Veterans of Foreign Wars of the United States at Fort McNair, Maryland." American Presidency Project, 13 May 1999.

———. "Remarks to the White House Conference on Africa." American Presidency Project, 27 June 1994.

———. "Statement on the Closing of the Embassy of Rwanda." American Presidency Project, 15 July 1994.

Fisher-Thompson, Jim. "US Official Cites Possible 'Ethnic Cleansing' in Sudan." *Sudan Tribune*, 26 February 2004. http://sudantribune.com/spip.php?article1921.

Gore, Al. "The 2000 Campaign: 2nd Presidential Debate between Gov. Bush and Vice President Gore" (transcript). *New York Times*, 12 October 2000. www .nytimes.com/2000/10/12/us/2000-campaign-2nd-presidential-debate-between -gov-bush-vice-president-gore.html?pagewanted=all&src=pm.

Gore 2000. "Fact Sheet on George W. Bush's Foreign Policy." *US Newswire*, 30 April 2000. www.fas.org/nuke/control/abmt/news/0430-103.htm.

Holbrooke, Richard. "Testimony at US House of Representatives, Subcommittee on International Organization." House Hearing on Cambodia, 26 July 1977.

Kerry, John F. "Presidential Debate in Coral Gables, Florida." American Presidency Project, 30 September 2004.

———. "Remarks on Daesh and Genocide." US Department of State, 17 March 2016. https://2009-2017.state.gov/secretary/remarks/2016/03/254782.htm.

———. "Remarks to the Congressional Black Caucus Foundation's 34th Legislative Conference in Washington, DC." American Presidency Project, 11 September 2004.

———. "Remarks to the 95th Annual NAACP Convention in Philadelphia." American Presidency Project, 15 July 2004.

———. "Remarks to the 124th Annual Session of the National Baptist Convention in New Orleans." American Presidency Project, 9 September 2004.

Lake, Anthony. "Press Briefing by National Security Advisor Tony Lake, Chairman of the Joint Chiefs of Staff General John Shalikashvili and Acting Secretary of Defense John Deutch." American Presidency Project, 29 July 1994.

Lake, Anthony, and Wesley Clark. "Press Briefing by National Security Advisor Tony Lake and Director for Strategic Plans and Policy General Wesley Clark." American Presidency Project, 5 May 1994.

McCurry, Mike. "Press Briefing by Michael McCurry." American Presidency Project, 11 August 1995.

————. "Press Briefing by Mike McCurry." American Presidency Project, 22 November 1995.

Natsios, Andrew S. "United States Policy in Sudan" (press conference). US Department of State, 27 April 2004. http://2001-2009.state.gov/p/af/rls/rm/31856.htm.

Obama, Barack H. "Presidential Study Directive on Mass Atrocities." White House, Office of the Press Secretary, 4 August 2011. www.whitehouse.gov/the-press-office/2011/08/04/presidential-study-directive-mass-atrocities.

Powell, Colin L. "The Africare Bishop T. Walker Memorial Dinner." US Department of State, 1 October 2004. http://2001-2009.state.gov/secretary/former/powell/remarks/37900.htm.

————. "The Crisis in Darfur: Testimony before the Senate Foreign Relations Committee." US Department of State, 9 September 2004.

————. "Darfur." *Wall Street Journal*, 5 August 2004.

————. "The InterAction 2004 Annual Forum Luncheon." US Department of State, 18 May 2004. http://2001-2009.state.gov/secretary/former/powell/remarks/32580.htm.

————. "Interview by Arshad Mohammed and Saul Hudson of Reuters." US Department of State, 12 September 2004. http://2001-2009.state.gov/secretary/former/powell/remarks/36177.htm.

————. "Interview by Cincinnati Enquirer Editorial Board." US Department of State, 16 August 2004. http://2001-2009.state.gov/secretary/former/powell/remarks/35290.htm.

————. "Interview by Clarence Page of the Chicago Tribune." US Department of State, 14 October 2004. http://2001-2009.state.gov/secretary/former/powell/remarks/37155.htm.

————. "Interview by Hany El-Konayyesi of Abu Dhabi TV." US Department of State, 21 October 2004. http://2001-2009.state.gov/secretary/former/powell/remarks/39935.htm.

————. "Interview by Marc Lacey of the New York Times." US Department of State, 11 June 2004. http://2001-2009.state.gov/secretary/former/powell/remarks/33472.htm.

————. "Interview by Matt Lee and Christophe de Roquefeuil of Agence France Presse." US Department of State, 29 September 2004. http://2001-2009.state.gov/secretary/former/powell/remarks/36614.htm.

————. "Interview on ABC's This Week with George Stephanopoulos." US Department of State, 12 September 2004. http://2001-2009.state.gov/secretary/former/powell/remarks/36099.htm.

————. "Interview on Al Arabiya with Lukman Ahmed." US Department of State, 15 September 2004. http://2001-2009.state.gov/secretary/former/powell/remarks/36226.htm.

————. "Remarks to the Press en Route Khartoum." US Department of State, 29 June 2004. http://2001-2009.state.gov/secretary/former/powell/remarks/34033.htm.

————. "Interview on CNN with Jeff Koinange." US Department of State, 30 June 2004. http://2001-2009.state.gov/secretary/former/powell/remarks/34061.htm.

————. "Interview on Fox News Sunday with Chris Wallace." US Department of State, 12 September 2004. http://2001-2009.state.gov/secretary/former/powell/remarks/36097.htm.

————. "Interview on the Michael Reagan Show." US Department of State, 28 September 2004. http://2001-2009.state.gov/secretary/former/powell/remarks/36572.htm.

————. "Interview on National Public Radio with Michele Norris." US Department of State, 30 June 2004. http://2001-2009.state.gov/secretary/former/powell/remarks/34053.htm.

———. "Interview on NBC's Meet the Press with Tim Russert." US Department of State, 12 September 2004. http://2001-2009.state.gov/secretary/former/powell/remarks/36100.htm.

———. "Interview on PBS's Charlie Rose." US Department of State, 16 July 2004. http://2001-2009.state.gov/secretary/former/powell/remarks/34445.htm.

———. "Interview with Barry Schweid, George Gedda, and Anne Gearan of Associated Press." US Department of State, 17 December 2004. http://2001-2009.state.gov/secretary/former/powell/remarks/37155.htm.

———. "Interview with Brit Hume of Fox News Channel's 'Special Report with Brit Hume.'" US Department of State, 4 August 2004. http://2001-2009.state.gov/secretary/former/powell/remarks/34948.htm.

———. "Interview with Hassan Moawad of Al Arabiya TV." US Department of State, 29 July 2004. http://2001-2009.state.gov/secretary/former/powell/remarks/34798.htm.

———. "Interview with Kamal Abdel Raouf of Al Akhbar Newspaper." US Department of State, 28 July 2004. http://2001-2009.state.gov/secretary/former/powell/remarks/34731.htm.

———. "Interview with Nihal Saad of Egyptian Television." US Department of State, 28 July 2004. http://2001-2009.state.gov/secretary/former/powell/remarks/34730.htm.

———. "Interview with Regis Le Sommier of Paris Match." US Department of State, 13 December 2004. http://2001-2009.state.gov/secretary/former/powell/remarks/40008.htm.

———. "Interview with Rima Hamed Al Shamikh of Al Ikhbariya TV." US Department of State, 29 July 2004. http://2001-2009.state.gov/secretary/former/powell/remarks/34789.htm.

———. "Interview with Russ Spence of WAGA/Fox 5." US Department of State, 1 October 2004. http://2001-2009.state.gov/secretary/former/powell/remarks/36688.htm.

———. "Interview with the USA Today Editorial Board." US Department of State, 18 October 2004. http://2001-2009.state.gov/secretary/former/powell/remarks/37184.htm.

———. "Opening Remarks before the House Appropriations Subcommittee on Commerce, Justice, State, the Judiciary and Related Agencies." US Department of State Archives, 3 March 2004. http://2001-2009.state.gov/secretary/former/powell/remarks/30142.htm.

———. "Remarks after the Secretary's Tour of the Abu Shouk Camp." US Department of State, 30 June 2004. http://2001-2009.state.gov/secretary/former/powell/remarks/34067.htm.

———. "Remarks at the Southern Center for International Studies." US Department of State, 1 October 2004. http://2001-2009.state.gov/secretary/former/powell/remarks/36694.htm.

———. "Remarks at Teach Africa Youth Forum." US Department of State, 17 September 2004. http://2001-2009.state.gov/secretary/former/powell/remarks/36276.htm.

———. "Remarks at the 2004 Herbert Quandt Distinguished Lecture." US Department of State, 10 September 2004. http://2001-2009.state.gov/secretary/former/powell/remarks/36095.htm.

———. "Remarks at UNITY 2004: Journalists of Color Convention." US Department of State, 5 August 2004. http://2001-2009.state.gov/secretary/former/powell/remarks/34986.htm.

———. "Remarks en Route Khartoum from Darfur." US Department of State, 30 June 2004. http://2001-2009.state.gov/secretary/former/powell/remarks/34066.htm.

————. "Remarks en Route to Cairo." US Department of State, 27 July 2004. http://2001-2009.state.gov/secretary/former/powell/remarks/34722.htm.

————. "Remarks Following Meeting with Haitian Interim President Boniface Alexandre." US Department of State, 24 June 2004. http://2001-2009.state.gov /secretary/former/powell/remarks/33892.htm.

————. "Remarks to the Africa Policy Advisory Panel Conference at the Center for Strategic and International Studies." US Department of State, 8 July 2004. http://2001-2009.state.gov/secretary/former/powell/remarks/34251.htm.

————. "Remarks to the Press en Route Washington." US Department of State, 1 September 2004. http://2001-2009.state.gov/secretary/former/powell/remarks /35906.htm.

————. "Remarks to the Press in Kuwait." US Department of State, 29 July 2004. http://2001-2009.state.gov/secretary/former/powell/remarks/34794.htm.

————. "Remarks with Bulgarian Foreign Minister Solomon Passy after Their Meeting." US Department of State, 5 May 2004. http://2001-2009.state.gov /secretary/former/powell/remarks/32201.htm.

————. "Remarks with Bulgarian Foreign Minister Solomon Passy after Their Meeting." US Department of State, 22 July 2004. http://2001-2009.state.gov /secretary/former/powell/remarks/34612.htm.

————. "Remarks with Egyptian Foreign Minister Ahmed Aboul Gheit." US Department of State, 28 July 2004. http://2001-2009.state.gov/secretary/former /powell/remarks/34733.htm.

————. "Remarks with Foreign Minister Ismail of the Republic of Sudan." US Department of State, 29 June 2004. http://2001-2009.state.gov/secretary/former /powell/remarks/34034.htm.

————. "Remarks with Foreign Minister Mustafa Osman Ismail of the Republic of Sudan after Their Meetings at the Airport." US Department of State, 30 June 2004. http://2001-2009.state.gov/secretary/former/powell/remarks/34066.htm.

————. "Remarks with Georgian Prime Minister Zurab Zhvania after Their Meeting." US Department of State, 3 March 2004. http://2001-2009.state.gov/secretary /former/powell/remarks/31815.htm.

————. "Remarks with Serbian President Boris Tadic after Their Meeting." US Department of State, 20 July 2004. http://2001-2009.state.gov/secretary/former /powell/remarks/34519.htm.

————. "Remarks with UN Secretary General Kofi Annan after Meeting." US Department of State, 22 July 2004. http://2001-2009.state.gov/secretary/former /powell/remarks/34627.htm.

————. "Signing of the Naivasha Protocols." US Department of State, 26 May 2004. http://2001-2009.state.gov/secretary/former/powell/remarks/32867.htm.

Prosper, Pierre-Richard. "Ambassador-at-Large for War Crimes Testifies in Congress." US Department of State, 24 June 2004. http://allafrica.com/stories /200406250141.html.

Reagan, Ronald. "40th President of the United States, Remarks at the International Convention of B'nai B'rith." 6 September 1984. In *Public Papers of the Presidents of the United States: Ronald Reagan, 1987.* Washington, DC: GPO, 1994.

————. "Remarks at the National Legislative Conference of the Building and Construction Trades Department, AFL-CIO." American Presidency Project, 5 April 1982.

Reeves, Eric. "The Accelerating Catastrophe in Darfur (Sudan): Khartoum Fixes upon a Policy of War and Civilian Destruction." sudanreeves.org, 24 November 2003. www.sudanreeves.org/2004/12/17/the-accelerating-catastrophe-in -darfur-sudan-khartoum-fixes-upon-a-policy-of-war-and-civilian-destruction -november-24-2003/.

———. "All Quiet: America's Sudan Strategy Has Changed for the Worse." *New Republic Online*, 27 October 2005.

———. "The Beginning of the End for Sudan's Peace Process? Khartoum Engineers a Disastrous Suspension of the Naivasha Talks." *Sudan Tribune*, 22 January 2004. www.sudantribune.com/spip.php?article1555.

———. "Catastrophe in Darfur Exploding: UN Now Estimates That Millions Are Affected by War; Aerial Attacks on Civilians Accelerate Dramatically." sudanreeves.org, 27 January 2004. www.sudanreeves.org/2004/12/15/catastrophe-in -darfur-exploding-un-now-estimates-that-millions-are-affected-by-war-aerial -attacks-on-civilians-accelerate-dramatically-january-27-2004/.

———. "A Comprehensive Approach to Sudan" (interview). Voices on Genocide Prevention, 26 January 2006.

———. "Current Proposals for Responding to Genocide in Darfur: A Compendium and Critique of Suggestions from the International Community." *Sudan Tribune*, 23 September 2004. www.sudantribune.com/spip.php?article5621.

———. "Darfur and the Diplomatic Logic of Appeasement: Concluding Peace Talks at Naivasha Must Not, and Cannot, Entail Expediency." sudanreeves.org, 26 January 2004. www.sudanreeves.org/2004/12/15/darfur-and-the-diplomatic-logic -of-appeasementconcluding-peace-talks-at-naivasha-must-not-and-cannot -entail-expediency-january-26-2004/.

———. "Darfur 101." *New Republic Online*, 5 May 2006.

———. "'Ethnic Cleansing' in Darfur: Systematic, Ethnically-Based Denial of Humanitarian Aid Is No Context for a Sustainable Peace Agreement in Sudan." sudanreeves.org, 30 December 2003. www.sudanreeves.org/2004/12/17/ethnic -cleansing-in-darfur-systematic-ethnically-based-denial-of-humanitarian-aid-is -no-context-for-a-sustainable-peace-agreement-in-sudan-december-30-2003/.

———. "The Face of War in Darfur (Sudan): Many Tens of Thousands Flee Khartoum's Campaign of Aerial Bombardment, Militia Attacks." sudanreeves.org, 8 October 2003. www.sudanreeves.org/2004/12/17/the-face-of-war-in-darfur-sudan -many-tens-of-thousands-flee-khartoums-campaign-of-aerial-bombardment -militia-attacks-october-8-2003/.

———. "Failure to Mount a Humanitarian Intervention in Darfur: Historical Context for Dramatically Escalating Insecurity." sudanreeves.org, 29 November 2004. www.sudanreeves.org/2004/12/15/failure-to-mount-a-humanitarian-interven tion-in-darfur-historical-context-for-dramatically-escalating-insecurity-november -29-2004/.

———. "Genocide in Darfur: The End of Agnosticism." sudanreeves.org, 1 February 2004. www.sudanreeves.org/2004/12/15/genocide-in-darfur-the-end-of-agnosticism -february-1-2004/.

———. "Halting Genocide in Darfur, Preserving the North-South Peace Agreement: Both Require Removal of Khartoum's National Islamic Front from Power." sudanreeves.org, 9 August 2004. www.sudanreeves.org/2004/12/15/halting -genocide-in-darfur-preserving-the-north-south-peace-agreement-both-require -removal-of-khartoums-national-islamic-front-from-power-august-9-2004/.

———. "Human Destruction and Displacement in Darfur: War, Humanitarian Access, and 'Ethnic Cleansing.'" sudanreeves.org, 12 December 2003. www .sudanreeves.org/2004/12/17/human-destruction-and-displacement-in-darfur -war-humanitarian-access-and-ethnic-cleansing-december-12-2003/.

———. "Impending Failure in Abuja, UN Security Council Inaction, Humanitarian Deterioration: The Darfur Crisis out of Control." sudanreeves.org, 24 August 2004. www.sudanreeves.org/2004/12/15/impending-failure-in-abuja-un-security -council-inaction-humanitarian-deterioration-the-darfur-crisis-out-of-control -august-24-2004/.

———. "Kofi Annan Declares He Has Seen No Reports to Suggest 'Ethnic Cleansing' or Genocide." sudanreeves.org, 18 June 2004. www.sudanreeves.org/2004/12/15/kofi-annan-declares-he-has-seen-no-reports-to-suggest-ethnic-cleansing-or-genocide-june-18-2004/.

———. "New Attacks on Civilians Far to the North in Darfur; More Than 1,000 Human Beings Now Dying Weekly in Darfur: What Is the Threshold for an Emergency Humanitarian Intervention?" sudanreeves.org, 8 February 2004. www.sudanreeves.org/2004/12/15/new-attacks-on-civilians-far-to-the-north-in-darfur-more-than-1000-human-beings-now-dying-weekly-in-darfur-what-is-the-threshold-for-an-emergency-humanitarian-intervention-february-8-2004/.

———. "No Further Evasion of the Essential Question: What Will We Do in Darfur?" sudanreeves.org, 4 April 2004. www.sudanreeves.org/2004/12/15/no-further-evasion-of-the-essential-question-what-will-we-do-in-darfur-april-4-2004/.

———. "Secretary of State Colin Powell's Genocide Determination: What It Does, and Doesn't, Mean for Darfur." sudanreeves.org, 10 September 2004. www.sudanreeves.org/2004/12/15/secretary-of-state-colin-powells-genocide-determination-what-it-does-and-doesnt-mean-for-darfur-september-10-2004/.

———. "Sudan Peace Talks Face the Threat of a Month-Long Break: Darfur Will Pay the Terrible Price for Adjournment." sudanreeves.org, 21 January 2004. www.sudanreeves.org/2004/12/15/sudan-peace-talks-face-the-threat-of-a-month-long-break-darfur-will-pay-the-terrible-price-for-adjournment-january-21-2004/.

———. "US Congress Calls on Khartoum 'to Grant Full, Unconditional, and Immediate [Humanitarian] Access to Darfur,' Even as the Regime Deliberately Blocks US Aid Efforts and Officials: The Genocide Accelerates." sudanreeves.org, 19 May 2004. www.sudanreeves.org/2004/12/15/us-congress-calls-on-khartoum-to-grant-full-unconditional-and-immediate-humanitarian-access-to-darfur-even-as-the-regime-deliberately-blocks-us-aid-efforts-and-officials-the-genocide-accelerates-may-1/.

———. "Watching Genocide, Doing Nothing: The Final Betrayal of Darfur." *Dissent*, Fall 2006.

———. "Holding Khartoum accountable in Darfur." *Boston Globe*, 6 September 2007.

———. "As the International Community Postures, Sudan's Many Crises Deepen." *sudanreeves.com*, 14 February 2006. www.sudanreeves.org/2006/03/30/as-the-international-community-postures-sudans-many-crises-deepen-february-14-2006/.

Rice, Condoleezza. "Press Briefing by National Security Advisor, Dr. Condoleezza Rice on the G8 Summit." American Presidency Project, 7 June 2004.

Simon, Paul, and Jim Jeffords. "A Letter to President Clinton, Dated May 13, 1994." *Congressional Record* 140, no. 72 (June 1994). www.gpo.gov/fdsys/pkg/CREC-1994-06-10/html/CREC-1994-06-10-pt1-PgS35.htm.

Snyder, Charles. "Sudan: Peace Agreement around the Corner?" (Testimony before the Subcommittee on Africa of the House International Relations Committee). US Department of State, 11 March 2004. http://2001-2009.state.gov/p/af/rls/rm/30356.htm.

United Nations. *Charter of the United Nations and Statute of the International Court of Justice*. New York: United Nations Department of Public Information, 2003.

———. *The Convention on the Prevention and Punishment of the Crime of Genocide*. 1948. www.unhchr.ch/html/menu3/b/p_genoci.htm.

———. *General Assembly Resolution A/47/92*. 17 December 1992.

————. "International Criminal Court Prosecutor Presses for More Active Security Council Role in Supporting Arrest, Transfer of Indicted Fugitives." 20 June 2018. www.un.org/press/en/2018/sc13388.doc.htm.

————. "Myanmar Military Leaders Must Face Genocide Charges—UN Report." *UN News*, 27 August 2018. https://news.un.org/en/story/2018/08/1017802.

————. "Press Briefing on Humanitarian Crisis in Darfur, Sudan." 2 April 2004. www.un.org/News/briefings/docs/2004/egelandbrf.DOC.htm.

————. "Press Statement on Darfur, Sudan by Security Council President" (UN Document SC/8050 AFR/883). 2 April 2004.

————. "Report of the International Commission of Inquiry on Darfur to the United Nations Secretary-General." 25 January 2005.

————. "Security Council's 5040th Meeting" (UN Document S/PV.5040). 18 September 2004.

————. *Security Council Resolution 918.* 17 May 1994.

————. *Security Council Resolution 1547.* 11 June 2004.

————. *Security Council Resolution 1556.* 30 July 2004.

————. *Security Council Resolution 1564.* 18 September 2004.

————. *Security Council Resolution 1574.* 19 November 2004.

————. "Statement by the President of the Security Council." 25 May 2004.

————. "Sudan: More Pressure on Parties Urged in Prelude to Talks Resumption." UN Integrated Regional Information Networks (IRIN), 5 February 2004.

USAID. "Statement by Andrew S. Natsios USAID Administrator and Special Humanitarian Coordinator for Sudan." *ReliefWeb*, 3 February 2004.

USAID. "Statement of Roger Winter, USAID Assistant Administrator for the Democracy, Conflict and Humanitarian Assistance Bureau." 31 March 2004.

US Department of State. "Congress Set to Declare Darfur Region a Zone of Genocide." 13 July 2004.

————. "Daily Press Briefing by Deputy Spokesman Adam Ereli." 30 July 2004. http://2001-2009.state.gov/r/pa/prs/dpb/2004/34825.htm.

————. "Daily Press Briefing by Spokesman Richard Boucher." 24 June 2004. http://2001-2009.state.gov/r/pa/prs/dpb/2004/33891.htm.

————. "Daily Press Briefing—25 May 2004." http://2001-2009.state.gov/p/af/ci /su/prs/33040.htm.

————. "Documenting Atrocities in Darfur." 9 September 2004. http://2001-2009 .state.gov/g/drl/rls/36028.htm.

————. "G-8 Statement on Sudan." 11 June 2004. http://2001-2009.state.gov/r/pa /prs/ps/2004/33469.htm.

————. "Signing of the Darfur Humanitarian Cease-Fire" (press statement). 9 April 2004. http://2001-2009.state.gov/r/pa/prs/ps/2004/31271.htm.

————. "Signing of the Naivasha Protocols" (press briefing by Assistant Secretary Snyder). 27 May 2004. http://2001-2009.state.gov/r/pa/prs/dpb/2004/32817.htm.

————. "Sudan: Situation in Darfur" (press statement). 16 December 2003. http://2001-2009.state.gov/r/pa/prs/ps/2003/27323.htm.

US House of Representatives. "H.Con.Res.75. 'Expressing the Sense of Congress That the Atrocities Perpetrated by ISIL Against Religious and Ethnic Minorities in Iraq and Syria Include War Crimes, Crimes Against Humanity, and Genocide, 14 March 2016.'" available: www.congress.gov/bill/114th-congress/house-concurrent -resolution/75.

————. "H.Con.Res.403. 'Condemning the Government of the Republic of the Sudan for Its Attacks against Innocent Civilians in the Impoverished Darfur Region of Western Sudan.'" 17 May 2004. http://beta.congress.gov//bill/108th -congress/house-concurrent-resolution/403/.

————. "House of Representatives Resolution H. Con. Res. 467: 'Declaring Genocide in Darfur, Sudan.'" 22 July 2004.

Washington Post. "Horror in Rwanda, Shame in the U.N." 3 May 1994.
———. "US Shift on Darfur Policy." 27 December 2004.
White House. "G-8 Statement on Sudan." American Presidency Project, 10 June 2004.
———. "Press Gaggle by Scott McClellan." American Presidency Project, 16 July 2004.
———. "Statement by the Press Secretary: President Directs Secretary Powell to Travel to Sudan." American Presidency Project, 29 June 2004.
———. "Statement of Administration Policy: H.R. 4613—Department of Defense Appropriations Bill, FY 2005." American Presidency Project, 22 June 2004.
———. "Text of U.S.-EU Declaration on Sudan." American Presidency Project, 26 June 2004.
Winter, Roger. "Sudan: Statement of Roger Winter, Assistant Administrator USAID, Before the Committee on Foreign Relations Subcommittee on Africa." USAID, 15 June 2004. http://allafrica.com/stories/200406160588.html.

SECONDARY SOURCES

Abd-al-Wahab, Najib al-Khayr. "Sudan Prefers AU Mediation in Darfur Crisis, Says US Stance Isolated" (interview). *Global Newswire—Asia Africa Intelligence Wire*, 12 September 2004.
Agence France-Presse. "West Sudan's Darfur Conflict 'World's Greatest Humanitarian Crisis.'" *Sudan Tribune*, 19 March 2004. www.sudantribune.com/spip.php ?article2161.
Albright, Madeleine K., and William S. Cohen. *Preventing Genocide: A Blueprint for U.S. Policymakers.* Washington, DC: US Holocaust Memorial Museum, 2008.
Almond, Gabriel A. *The American People and Foreign Policy.* New York: Harcourt Brace, 1950.
American Progress Action Fund. 2005. www.americanprogressaction.org/issues /general/news/2005/03/09/1405/be-a-witness/.
Amnesty International. *Sudan: Looming Crisis in Darfur.* London: Amnesty International, 2003.
Annan, Kofi. "Action Plan to Prevent Genocide. Speech Delivered to the UN Human Rights Commission, 7 April 2004." UN press release, SG/SM/9197 AFR/893 HR/CN/1077.
Aronoff, Yael S. "An Apology Is Not Enough: What Will Happen in the Next Case of Genocide?" *Washington Post*, 9 April 1998, A25.
Art, Robert J., and Patrick M. Cronin. *The United States and Coercive Diplomacy.* Washington, DC: US Institute for Peace Press, 2003.
Ayoob, Mohammed. "Third World Perspectives on Humanitarian Interventions and International Administration." *Global Governance* 10 (2004): 99–118.
Bachman, Jeffrey S. *The United States and Genocide: (Re)Defining the Relationship.* New York: Routledge, 2018.
Barker, Alex. "Bush Faces Pressures to Call Sudan 'Genocide.'" *Financial Times*, 14 July 2004.
Bartoli, Andrea, and Tetsushi Ogata. "Supporting Regional Approaches to Genocide Prevention: The International Conference on the Great Lakes Region (ICGLR)." Paper presented at the annual meeting of the Genocide Prevention Advisory Network, 2010. www.gpanet.org/content/supporting-regional-approaches-genocide -prevention-international-conference-great-lakes-regi.
Bauer, Yehuda. "Remembrance and Beyond." Keynote address at the United Nations Holocaust Memorial Day, 27 January 2006.
BBC News. "Mass Rape Atrocity in West Sudan." 19 March 2004. http://news.bbc.co .uk/2/hi/africa/3549325.stm.

————. "'Never Again': John Danforth Interview Transcript." 3 July 2005. http://news.bbc.co.uk/1/hi/programmes/panorama/4647211.stm.

Beaumont, Peter. "US 'Hyping' Darfur Genocide Fear." *Observer*, 21 October 2004.

Bellamy, Alex J. "Responsibility to Protect or Trojan Horse? The Crisis in Darfur and Humanitarian Intervention after Iraq." *Ethics and International Affairs* 19, no. 2 (2005): 31–54.

————. "Whither the Responsibility to Protect: Humanitarian Intervention and the 2005 World Summit." *Ethics and International Affairs* 20, no. 2 (2006): 144–160.

Bellamy, Alex J., and Paul D. Williams. "The UN Security Council and the Question of Humanitarian Intervention in Darfur." *Journal of Military Ethics* 5, no. 2 (2006): 144–160.

Lance W. Bennett. "Toward a Theory of Press-State Relations in the United States." *Journal of Communication* 40, no. 2 (1990): 103–125

Birney, Mayling, Ian Shapiro, and Michael J. Graetz. "The Political Uses of Public Opinion. Lessons from the Estate Tax Repeal." Unpublished paper, 2007.

Blaney, Harry C., III. "Speaking Out: The Lessons of Darfur." *Foreign Service Journal* 81, no. 12 (December 2004): 8.

Bloom, Mia M. "Comparative Review Essay of Stuart J. Kaufman, Modern Hatreds: The Symbolic Politics of Ethnic War (Cornell University Press, 2001) and Kenneth J. Campbell, Genocide and the Global Village (NY: Palgrave, 2001)." *Nationalism and Ethnic Politics* 8, no. 3 (Summer 2003): 116–118.

Bloom, Paul. *Against Empathy: The Case for Rational Compassion.* London: Bodley Head, 2017.

Blum, Rony, Gregory H. Stanton, Shira Sagi, and Elihu D. Richter. "'Ethnic Cleansing' Bleaches the Atrocities of Genocide." *European Journal of Public Health* 18, no. 2 (2008): 204–209.

Bogert, Carroll. "Another Africa Calamity—Will Media Slumber On?" *Los Angeles Times*, 28 April 2004.

Bosco, David. "Crime of Crimes." *Washington Post*, 6 March 2005.

Brand, Henry W. *What America Owes the World: The Struggle for the Soul of Foreign Policy.* Cambridge: Cambridge University Press, 1998.

Brody, Richard A. *Assessing the President: The Media, Elite Opinion and Public Support.* Stanford, CA: Stanford University Press, 1991.

Brunnée, Jutta, and Stephen J. Toope. *Legitimacy and Legality in International Law: An Interactional Account.* Cambridge: Cambridge University Press, 2010.

Buchanan, Allen. "The Internal Legitimacy of Humanitarian Intervention." *Journal of Political Philosophy* 7, no. 1 (1999): 71–87.

Burbach, David T. "Presidential Approval and the Use of Force." Defense and Arms Control Studies working paper, May 1994.

Campbell, Kenneth J. *Genocide and the Global Village.* New York: Palgrave, 2001.

Caplan, Gerald. "From Rwanda to Darfur: Lessons Learned?" *Pambazuka News: Weekly Forum for Social Justice in Africa*, 12 January 2006. www.pambazuka.org/en/category/features/31248.

Cheadle, Don, and John Prendergast. *"Not on Our Watch": The Mission to End Genocide in Darfur and Beyond.* New York: Hyperion, 2007.

Chicago Council on Foreign Relations. *Global Views 2004: American Public Opinion and Foreign Policy.* Chicago: Chicago Council on Foreign Relations, 2004.

Chicago Council on Global Affairs. *Global Views Poll 2006.* Chicago: Chicago Council on Foreign Relations, 2006.

Chicago Council on Global Affairs and WorldPublicOpinion.org. "Publics around the World Say UN Has Responsibility to Protect Against Genocide." 2007. http://thechicagocouncil.org.

Chin, Sally. "No Power to Protect: The African Union Mission in Darfur" (interview). Voices on Genocide Prevention, 5 January 2006.

Chomsky, Noam. *The New Military Humanism: Lessons from Kosovo*. London: Pluto Press, 1999.

Christopher, Warren. "Human Rights: Cambodia." *Department of State Bulletin*, February 1978, 32.

Clark, David. "Iraq Has Wrecked Our Case for Humanitarian Wars: The US Neocons Have Broken the Kosovo Liberal Intervention Consensus." *Guardian*, 12 August 2003.

Clark, Ian. *International Legitimacy and World Society*. Oxford: Oxford University Press, 2007.

———. *Legitimacy in International Society*. Oxford: Oxford University Press, 2005.

Clough, Michael. "Darfur: Whose Responsibility to Protect." New York: Human Rights Watch, 2005.

———. "It's Hell in Darfur, But Is It Genocide? The Sudanese Government Has Targeted Villagers, but Not a Whole Race." *Los Angeles Times*, 14 May 2006.

Cohen, Bernard. *The Public's Impact on Foreign Policy*. Boston: Little, Brown, 1973.

Cohen, Herman. "Getting Rwanda Wrong." *Washington Post*, 3 June 1994.

Converse, Philip E. "The Nature of Belief Systems in Mass Publics." In *Ideology and Discontent*, edited by David Apter. New York: Free Press, 1964.

Daly, Martin W. *Darfur's Sorrow: A History of Destruction and Genocide*. Oxford: Oxford University Press, 2007.

Davidson, Andrew, Kas Roussy, Mark Gollom, and Jessica Wong. "Bush, Clinton Get Standing Ovation after Toronto 'Conversation.'" *CBC News*, 29 May 2009. www.cbc.ca/news/canada/toronto/story/2009/05/29/clinton-bush-conversation -toronto.html.

Deng, Francis M. "Specific Groups and Individuals: Mass Exoduses and Displaced Persons." Report of the Representative of the Secretary-General on Internally Displaced Persons, United Nations Economic and Social Council (E/CN.4/2005/8), 27 September 2004.

de Saussure, Ferdinand. *Writings in General Linguistics*. Oxford: Oxford University Press, 2006.

de Waal, Alex. "Sudan: The Turbulent State." In *War in Darfur and the Search for Peace*, edited by Alex De-Waal, 1–39. Cambridge, MA: Global Equity Initiative, Harvard University, 2007.

———. "What Does Adding the 'Genocide' Label to the Darfur Crisis Really Mean?" *Index on Censorship*, 2 February 2005.

DeYoung, Karen. "Falling on His Sword." *Washington Post*, 1 October 2006.

DiPrizio, Robert C. *Armed Humanitarians: U.S. Interventions from Northern Iraq to Kosovo*. Baltimore: Johns Hopkins University Press, 2002.

Edelman, Murray. *Political Language: Words That Succeed and Policies That Fail*. New York: Academic Press, 1977.

Egeland, Jan. "The World" (interview). *BBC/Public Radio International*, 18 December 2003.

Entman, Robert M. "Framing: Toward Clarification of a Fractured Paradigm." *Journal of Communication* 43, no. 4 (1993): 51–58.

———. *Projections of Power: Framing News, Public Opinion, and U.S. Foreign Policy*. Chicago: University of Chicago Press, 2004.

Evans, Gareth. "Genocide or Crime? Actions Speak Louder Than Words in Darfur." *European Voice*, 18 February 2005.

Everts, Philip. "When the Going Gets Rough: Does the Public Support the Use of Military Force?" *World Affairs* 162, no. 3 (Winter 2000): 91–107.

Feierstein, Daniel. "Getting Things into Perspective (from a Symposium on the Albright-Cohen Report)." *Genocide Studies and Prevention* 4, no. 2 (2009): 155–160.

————. "Human Rights? What a Good Idea! From Universal Jurisdiction to Preventive Criminology." Paper presented at the annual conference of the International Association of Genocide Scholars, University of Queensland, July 2017.

Fessenden, Helen. "Lawmakers Seek Viable Solution to Sudan's Humanitarian Crisis." *CQ Weekly* 62 (3 July 2004): 1638–1639.

Finkel, James P. "Atrocity Prevention at the Crossroads: Assessing the President's Atrocity Prevention Board after Two Years." Center for the Prevention of Genocide Series of Occasional Papers no. 2, September 2014.

————. "Global Approaches to Atrocity Prevention: Introduction to the Special Issue." *Genocide Studies and Prevention* 11, no. 3 (2018): 3–5.

————. "Moving Beyond the Crossroads: Strengthening the Atrocity Prevention Board." *Genocide Studies and Prevention* 9, no. 2 (2015): 138–149.

Flint, Julie. "Peace in South Sudan Hinges on End to War in Darfur." *Daily Star*, 19 February 2004. www.dailystar.com.lb/News/Middle-East/Feb/19/Peace-in-south -Sudan-hinges-on-end-to-war-in-Darfur.ashx#axzz2DwAbeASc.

Flint, Julie, and Alex de Waal. *Darfur: A Short History of a Long War.* New York: Zed Books, 2006.

Fowler, Jerry. "A New Chapter of Irony: The Legal Definition of Genocide and the Implications of Powell's Determination." In *Genocide in Darfur: Investigating the Atrocities in the Sudan,* edited by Samuel Totten and Eric Markusen, 127–140. New York: Routledge, 2006.

————. "Voices on Genocide Prevention." US Holocaust Memorial Museum, 6 November 2006. http://blogs.ushmm.org/index.php/COC2/C19/P60/.

Franck, Thomas M. *The Power of Legitimacy among Nations.* New York: Oxford University Press, 1990.

Fulbright, J. William. *The Arrogance of Power.* New York: Random House, 1966.

Fulwood, Sam, III. "Clinton Steps Up His Support for Military Action in Bosnia." *Los Angeles Times,* 6 August 1992. http://articles.latimes.com/1992-08-06/news /mn-5351_1_military-action.

Gedda, George. "Sudan Is Removed from a US Terror List." *Boston Globe,* 19 May 2004. www.boston.com/news/world/africa/articles/2004/05/19/sudan_is _removed_from_a_us_terror_list/?camp=pm.

Gelb, Leslie H., and Justine A. Rosenthal. "The Rise of Ethics in Foreign Policy." *Foreign Affairs* 82, no. 3 (2003): 2–7.

Global Policy Forum. "US Interventions: US Military and Clandestine Operations in Foreign Countries—1798–Present." 2005. www.globalpolicy.org/empire/history /interventions.htm.

Gordon, Michael. "A State Dept. Aide on Bosnia Resigns on Partition Issue." *New York Times,* 5 August 1993, A1, A11.

Graber, Doris A. *Processing the News: How People Tame the Information Tide.* 2nd ed. New York: Longman, 1988.

Grono, Nick, and John Prendergast. "To Halt Sudan's Atrocities, Follow the Money." *International Herald Tribune,* 22 August 2006.

Guarino, Kia. "American Presidents and Humanitarian Crises: The Rhetorical Marginalization of Genocide in Cambodia, Bosnia and Rwanda." Honors thesis, Boston College, December 2008.

Gutman, Roy. "American Public Opinion, the Media and Genocide Prevention." In "Genocide Prevention, Morality, and the National Interest," by Jerry Fowler, Samantha Power, David Scheffer, Holly Burkhalter, Scott Feil, Roy Gutman, Allen Hertzke, Steven Kull, and Aryeh Neier. *Journal of Human Rights* 1, no. 4 (2002): 429–467.

Haass, Richard N. *The Opportunity: America's Moment to Alter History's Course.* New York: Public Affairs, 2005.

Haeri, Medina. "Saving Darfur: Does Advocacy Help or Hinder Conflict Resolution?" *Praxis: The Fletcher Journal of Human Security*, no. 23 (2008): 33–46.

Hamilton, Rebecca. *Fighting for Darfur: Public Action and the Struggle to Stop Genocide*. Basingstoke: Palgrave Macmillan, 2011.

Hamilton, Rebecca, and Chad Hazlett. "'Not on Our Watch': The Emergence of the American Movement for Darfur." In *War in Darfur and the Search for Peace*, edited by Alex De-Waal, 337–366. Cambridge, MA: Global Equity Initiative, Harvard University, 2007.

Hansen, Lene. *Security as Practice: Discourse Analysis and the Bosnian War*. London: Routledge, 2006.

Harff, Barbara. "Genocides and Politicides Events 1955–2002." Genocide Prevention Advisory Network, 2009. www.gpanet.org/content/genocides-and-politicides-events-1955-2002.

Harff, Barbara, and Ted R. Gurr. "Toward Empirical Theory of Genocides and Politicides." *International Studies Quarterly* 37, no. 3 (1988): 359–371.

Heinze, Eric A. "The Rhetoric of Genocide in U.S. Foreign Policy: Rwanda and Darfur Compared." *Political Science Quarterly* 122, no. 3 (2007): 359–383.

Helms, Jesse. "American Sovereignty and the UN." *National Interest*, 1 December 2000.

Henry, Jehanne. "US Considers Lifting Sudan's 'Terror State' Designation: Move Ignores Sudan's Abuses Against Its Own People." Human Rights Watch, 7 November 2018. www.hrw.org/news/2018/11/07/us-considers-lifting-sudans-terror-state-designation.

Hintjens, H. "Review of Kenneth J. Campbell, Genocide and the Global Village (NY: Palgrave, 2001)." *African Affairs* 102, no. 406 (2003): 162–164.

Hinton, Alexander Laban, Thomas La Pointe, and Douglas Irvin-Erickson. "Introduction." In *Hidden Genocides: Power, Knowledge, Memory*, edited by Alexander Laban Hinton, Thomas La Pointe, and Douglas Irvin-Erickson, 1–18. New Brunswick, NJ: Rutgers University Press, 2013.

Hodgson, Godfrey. *The Myth of American Exceptionalism*. New Haven, CT: Yale University Press, 2009.

Hoffmann, Stanley. "American Exceptionalism: The New Version." In *American Exceptionalism and Human Rights*, edited by Michael Ignatieff, 225–241. Princeton, NJ: Princeton University Press, 2005.

Holbrooke, Richard. "How Did 'Never Again' Become Just Words?" *Washington Post*, 4 April 2004.

Holsti, Kalevi J. *International Politics: A Framework for Analysis*. 5th ed. Englewood Cliffs, NJ: Prentice Hall, 1988.

Holsti, Ole R. "Foreword." In *The Impact of Public Opinion on U.S. Foreign Policy since Vietnam: Constraining the Colossus*, by Richard Sobel, vii–x. Oxford: Oxford University Press, 2001.

———. *Public Opinion and American Foreign Policy*. Ann Arbor: University of Michigan Press, 1996.

Human Rights Watch. "Darfur Destroyed: Ethnic Cleansing by Government and Militia Forces in Western Sudan." 6 May 2004.

———. "Sudan: Massive Atrocities in Darfur." 3 April 2004.

———. "Too Little, Too Late: Sudanese and International Response 2004." http://hrw.org/reports/2004/sudan0504/8.htm.

———. "UN: Darfur Resolution a Historic Failure." 2004.

Hunt, Michael. *Ideology and US Foreign Policy*. New Haven, CT: Yale University Press, 1987.

Huntington, Samuel P. "American Ideals versus American Institutions." *Political Science Quarterly* 97, no. 1 (1982): 1–37.

————. *American Politics: The Promise of Disharmony.* Cambridge, MA: Harvard University Press, 1981.

Independent International Commission on Kosovo. *The Kosovo Report.* Oxford: Oxford University Press, 2000.

International Court of Justice (ICJ). *Case Concerning the Application of the Convention on the Prevention and Punishment of the Crime of Genocide (Bosnia and Herzegovina vs. Serbia and Montenegro),* 26 February 2007.

International Crisis Group. "ICG Africa Report N°80: Sudan: Now or Never in Darfur." 23 May 2004.

International Crisis Group and Zogbi International. "Africa Briefing No. 26: Do Americans Care about Darfur?" 1 June 2005.

International Development Committee, British House of Commons. "Darfur, Sudan: The Responsibility to Protect, Fifth Report of Session 2004–2005." 2005.

Iyengar, Shanto, and Jennifer McGrady. *Media Politics: A Citizen's Guide.* New York: Norton, 2007.

Jablonsky, David. "Army Transformation: A Tale of Two Doctrines." In *Transforming Defense,* edited by Conrad C. Crane, 45–88. Carlisle, PA: Strategic Studies Institute, December 2001.

Jacobs, Lawrence R., and Benjamin I. Page. "Who Influences U.S. Foreign Policy?" *American Political Science Review* 99, no. 1 (2005): 107–123.

Jakobsen, Peter Viggo. "Focus on the CNN Effect Misses the Point: The Real Media Impact on Conflict Management Is Invisible and Indirect." *Journal of Peace Research* 37, no. 2 (2000): 131–143.

Jehl, Douglas. "Officials Told to Avoid Calling Rwanda Killings 'Genocide.'" *New York Times,* 10 June 1994.

Jentleson, Bruce W. "The Pretty Prudent Public: Post Post-Vietnam American Opinion and the Use of Military Force." *International Studies Quarterly* 36 (1992): 49–74.

Joffe, Josef. *Uberpower: The Imperial Temptation of America.* New York: Norton, 2006.

Jones, Adam. *Genocide: A Comprehensive Introduction.* 2nd ed. New York: Taylor & Francis, 2010.

Kahneman, Daniel, and Amos Tversky. "Choices, Values, and Frames." *American Psychologist* 39, no. 4 (1984): 341–350.

Kane, John. *Between Virtue and Power: The Persistent Moral Dilemma of US Foreign Policy.* New Haven, CT: Yale University Press, 2008.

Kapila, Mukesh. "Statement of UN Humanitarian Coordinator." UN Integrated Regional Information Networks, 22 March 2004.

Kasfir, Nelson. "Sudan's Darfur: Is It Genocide?" *Current History* 104, no. 682 (May 2005): 195–202.

Kennan, George F. *American Diplomacy, 1900–1950.* Chicago: University of Chicago Press, 1950.

Key, Valdimer Orlando, Jr. *Public Opinion and American Democracy.* New York: Knopf, 1961.

Kingibe, Baba G. "African Union Briefing" (interview). Voices on Genocide Prevention, 9 March 2006.

Kissinger, Henry A. *American Foreign Policy.* 3rd ed. New York: Norton, 1977.

Klare, Michael T. "The Clinton Doctrine." *Nation,* 1 April 1999.

Knecht, Thomas. "Public Opinion and Foreign Policy: The Stages of Presidential Decision Making." *International Studies Quarterly* 50 (2006): 705–727.

Kohut, Andrew. "Post–Cold War Attitudes toward the Use of Force." In *The Use of Force after the Cold War,* edited by H. W. Brands, Darren J. Pierson, and Reynolds S. Kiefer, 165–177. College Station: Texas A&M University Press, 2003.

Kohut, Andrew, and Robert C. Toth. "Arms and the People." *Foreign Affairs* 73, no. 6 (1994): 47–61.

Kollman, Ken. *Outside Lobbying: Public Opinion and Interest Group Strategies.* Princeton, NJ: Princeton University Press, 1998.

Kostas, Stephen A. "Making the Determination of Genocide in Darfur." In *Genocide in Darfur: Investigating the Atrocities in the Sudan,* edited by Samuel Totten and Eric Markusen, 111–126. New York: Routledge, 2006.

Krauss, Clifford. "U.S. Backs Away from Charge of Atrocities in Bosnia Camps." *New York Times,* 5 August 1992. www.nytimes.com/1992/08/05/world/us-backs-away -from-charge-of-atrocities-in-bosnia-camps.html?pagewanted=all&src=pm.

Kristof, Nicholas D. "A Wimp on Genocide." *New York Times,* 18 September 2005.

Kull, Steven. "American Public Opinion, the Media, and Genocide Prevention." In "Genocide Prevention, Morality, and the National Interest," by Jerry Fowler, Samantha Power, David Scheffer, Holly Burkhalter, Scott Feil, Roy Gutman, Allen Hertzke, Steven Kull, and Aryeh Neier. *Journal of Human Rights* 1, no. 4 (2002): 429–467.

Kull, Steven, and Mac I. Destler. *Misreading the Public: The Myth of a New Isolationism.* Washington, DC: Brookings Institution, 1999.

Kull, Steven, et al. "Americans on the Crisis in Sudan." PIPA/Knowledge Networks Poll, 20 July 2004.

Kull, Steven, and Clay Ramsay. "Elite Misperceptions of U.S. Public Opinion and Foreign Policy." In *Decision Making in a Glass House: Mass Media, Public Opinion, and American and European Foreign Policy in the 21st Century,* edited by Brigitte L. Nacos, Robert Shapiro, and Pierangelo Isernia, 95–110. New York: Rowman & Littlefield, 2000.

———. "US Public Opinion on Intervention in Bosnia." In *International Public Opinion and the Bosnia Crisis,* edited by Richard Sobel and Eric Shiraev, 69–106. New York: Lexington Books, 2003.

Kuperman, Allan J. "How the Media Missed Rwanda Genocide." In *The Media and the Rwanda Genocide,* edited by Allan Thompson, 256–260. London: Pluto Press, 2007.

Kurth, James. "Humanitarian Intervention after Iraq: Legal Ideals vs. Military Realities." *Orbis* 50, no. 1 (Winter 2006): 87–101.

Kuypers, Jim A., Stephen D. Cooper, and Matthew T. Althouse. "The President and the Press: The Framing of George W. Bush's Speech to the United Nations on November 10, 2001." *American Communication Journal* 10, no. 3 (2008): 1–22.

Lake, Anthony, and Roger Morris. "Pentagon Papers (2): The Human Reality of Realpolitik." *Foreign Policy* 4 (1971): 157–162.

Larson, Eric V., and Bogdan Savych. *American Public Support for U.S. Military Operations from Mogadishu to Baghdad.* Santa Monica, CA: RAND, 2005.

LeBlanc, Lawrence J. *The United States and the Genocide Convention.* Durham, NC: Duke University Press, 1991.

Lemkin, Raphael. *Axis Rule in Occupied Europe. Laws of Occupation. Analysis of Government. Proposals for Redress.* Washington: Carnegie Endowment for International Peace, Division of International Law, 1944.

Lepard, Brian D. *Rethinking Humanitarian Intervention: A Fresh Legal Approach Based on Fundamental Ethical Principles in International Law and World Religions.* University Park: Pennsylvania State University Press, 2002.

Levinger, Matthew. "A Core National Security Interest: Framing Atrocities Prevention." *Politics and Governance* 3, no. 4 (2015): 26–43.

———. "Why the U.S. Government Failed to Anticipate the Rwandan Genocide of 1994: Lessons for Early Warning and Prevention." *Genocide Studies and Prevention* 9, no. 3 (2016): 33–58.

Lippmann, Walter. *Essays in the Public Philosophy*. Boston: Little, Brown, 1955.
———. *The Phantom Public*. New York: Harcourt, Brace, 1925.
———. *Public Opinion*. New York: Harcourt, Brace, 1922.
Livingston, Steven. "Clarifying the CNN Effect: An Examination of Media Effects According to Type of Military Intervention." Research Paper R-18, Joan Shorenstein Center on Media, Politics and Public Policy, Harvard University, John F. Kennedy School of Government, June 1997.
———. "Limited Vision: How Both the American Media and Government Failed Rwanda." In *The Media and the Rwanda Genocide*, edited by Allan Thompson, 188–197. London: Pluto Press, 2007.
Livingston, Steven, and David Stephen. "American Network Coverage of Rwanda in the Context of General Trends in International News." In *Early Warning and Early Response*, edited by Susanne Schmeidl and Howard Adelman. New York: Columbia International Affairs Online, 1998, 1–18.
Luban, David. "Calling Genocide by Its Rightful Name: Lemkin's Word, Darfur, and the UN Report." *Chicago Journal of International Law* 7, no. 1 (2006): 303–320.
Luck, Edward. *Mixed Messages: American Politics and International Organization, 1919–1999*. Washington, DC: Brookings Institution, 1999.
Lynch, Jake, and Annabel McGoldrick. *Peace Journalism*. Gloucestershire: Hawthorn Press, 2005.
MacDonald, G. Jeffrey. "In Sudan Crisis, a Duty to Intervene?" *Christian Science Monitor*, 21 July 2004. www.csmonitor.com/2004/0721/p15s01-lire.html.
MacKinnon, Michael G. "The United Nations Security Council." In *The International Politics of Mass Atrocities: The Case of Darfur*, edited by David R. Black and Paul D. Williams, 71–99. London: Routledge, 2010.
Mahbubani, Kishore. "The Permanent and Elected Council Members." In *The UN Security Council: From the Cold War to the 21st Century*, edited by David M. Malone, 253–366. Boulder, CO: Lynne Rienner, 2004.
———. "The UN Security Council: From the Cold War to the 21st Century." Transcript of presentation at the Carnegie Council on Ethics in International Affairs, 4 March 2004.
Mansbridge, Jane. "Rethinking Representation." *American Political Science Review* 97, no. 4 (November 2003): 515–528.
Marley, Tony. "The Triumph of Evil" (interview). *Frontline-PBS*, 26 January 1999.
Mayroz, Eyal. "Between Empathy and Fear: Recalibrating Incentives for Atrocity Prevention." In *"Last Lectures": The Prevention/Intervention of Genocide*, edited by Samuel Totten, 34–39. London: Routledge, 2018.
———. "'Ever Again?' The United States, Genocide Suppression, and the Crisis in Darfur." *Journal of Genocide Research* 10, no. 3 (2008): 359–388.
———. "Genocide: To Prevent and Punish 'Radical Evil.'" In *International Criminal Law in Context*, edited by Philipp Kastner, 71–90. Oxon: Routledge, 2018.
———. "The Legal Duty to 'Prevent': After the Onset of 'Genocide.'" *Journal of Genocide Research* 14, no. 1 (2012): 79–98.
McCombs, Maxwell. "The Agenda-Setting Role of the Mass Media in the Shaping of Public Opinion." Manuscript, University of Texas at Austin, 2003. www.infoamerica.org/documentos_pdf/mccombs01.pdf.
———. "Building Consensus: The News Media's Agenda-Setting Roles." *Political Communication* 14 (1997): 433–443. http://blog.roodo.com/research_information/7496232b.pdf.
McCormick, James M. *American Foreign Policy and American Values*. Itasca, IL: F. E. Peacock, 1985.
McCrisken, Trevor B. *American Exceptionalism and the Legacy of Vietnam: US Foreign Policy since 1974*. Basingstoke: Palgrave Macmillan, 2003.

McElroy, Robert W. *Morality and American Foreign Policy: The Role of Ethics in International Affairs.* Princeton, NJ: Princeton University Press, 1992.

McFarland, Sam, and Melissa Mathews. "Do Americans Care about Human Rights?" *Journal of Human Rights* 4 (2005): 305–319.

Melanson, Richard. *American Foreign Policy since the Vietnam War: The Search for Consensus from Richard Nixon to George W. Bush.* 4th ed. Armonk, NY: M.E. Sharpe, 2005.

Melvern, Linda. "Missing the Story: The Media and the Rwandan Genocide." In *The Media and the Rwanda Genocide,* edited by Allan Thompson, 198–210. London: Pluto Press, 2007.

———. "Rwanda and Darfur: The Media and the Security Council." *International Relations* 20, no. 1 (March 2006): 93–104.

Mendez, Juan E. "United Nations Report from the Special Advisor on Genocide Prevention" (interview). Voices on Genocide Prevention, 16 February 2006.

Mennecke, Martin. "What's in a Name? Reflections on Using, Not Using, and Overusing the 'G-Word.'" *Genocide Studies and Prevention* 2, no. 1 (2007): 57–71.

Jonathan Mermin. *Debating War and Peace: Media Coverage of US intervention in the Post-Vietnam Era.* Princeton, NJ: Princeton University Press, 1999.

Mills, Kurt. *International Responses to Mass Atrocities in Africa: Responsibility to Protect, Prosecute, and Palliate.* Philadelphia: University of Pennsylvania Press, 2015.

Minow, Martha. "Naming Horror: Legal and Political Words for Mass Atrocities." *Genocide Studies and Prevention* 2, no. 1 (2007): 37–42.

Mitchell, Amy, et al. "How Americans Get Their News." Pew Research Center, 7 July 2016.

Moeller, Susan D. *Compassion Fatigue: How the Media Sell Disease, Famine, War, and Death.* New York: Routledge, 1999.

Morgenthau, Hans J. "The Evil of Politics and the Ethics of Evil." *Ethics* 56, no. 1 (1945): 1–18.

———. *Politics among Nations: The Struggle for Power and Peace.* 5th ed. New York: Knopf, 1954.

Morrison, J. Stephen, and Chester A. Crocker. "Time to Focus on the Real Choices in Darfur." *Washington Post,* 7 November 2006.

Morse, David. "Appeasement Driven by Oil: The Bush Administration and Darfur." TomDispatch.com, 2006. www.tomdispatch.com/index.mhtml?pid=124232.

Moses, Dirk. "Why the Discipline of 'Genocide Studies' Has Trouble Explaining How Genocides End?" Social Science Research Council, December 2006. http://howgenocidesend.ssrc.org/Moses/.

Mueller, John. "Public Opinion as a Constraint on US Foreign Policy: Assessing the Perceived Value of American and Foreign Lives." Paper presented at the National Convention of the International Studies Association, Los Angeles, 14–18 March 2000.

Murphy, Deborah. "Narrating Darfur: Darfur in the U.S. Press, March–September 2004." In *War in Darfur and the Search for Peace,* edited by Alex De-Waal, 314–336. Cambridge, MA: Global Equity Initiative, Harvard University, 2007.

Natsios, Andrew S. "Illusions of Influence: The CNN Effect in Complex Emergencies." In *From Massacres to Genocide: The Media, Public Policy, and Humanitarian Crises,* edited by Robert I. Rotberg and Thomas G. Weiss, 149–168. Washington, DC: Brookings Institution, 1996.

———. *Sudan, South Sudan, and Darfur: What Everyone Needs to Know.* Oxford: Oxford University Press, 2012.

———. *U.S. Foreign Policy and the Four Horsemen of the Apocalypse: Humanitarian Relief in Complex Emergencies.* Westport, CT: Praeger, 1997.

Nebehay, Stephanie. "US likens West Sudan 'Ethnic Cleansing' to Rwanda." *Sudan Tribune,* 22 April 2004.

Nolan, Cathal J. "Introduction." In *Ethics and Statecraft: The Moral Dimension of International Affairs*, 2nd ed., edited by Cathal J. Nolan, 1–16. Westport, CT: Praeger, 2004.

———. "The United States, Moral Norms, and Governing Ideas in World Politics: A Review Essay." *Ethics and International Affairs* 7 (1993): 223–239.

Nye, Joseph S. "Redefining the National Interest." *Foreign Affairs* 78, no. 3 (1999): 22–35.

Oberschall, Anthony. "The Historical Roots of Public Opinion Research." In *The Sage Book of Public Opinion Research*, edited by Wolfgang Donsbach and Michael W. Traugott, 83–92. Thousand Oaks, CA: Sage, 2008.

Osborn, Andrew, and Paul Brown. "Dutch Cabinet Resigns over Srebrenica Massacre." *Guardian*, 17 April 2002.

Oskamp, Stuart. *Attitudes and Opinions*. Englewood Cliffs, NJ: Prentice Hall, 1977.

Page, Benjamin I., with Marshall M. Bouton. *The Foreign Policy Disconnect: What Americans Want from Our Leaders but Don't Get*. Chicago: University of Chicago Press, 2006.

Page, Benjamin I., and Robert Y. Shapiro. *The Rational Public: Fifty Years of Trends in Americans' Policy Preferences*. Chicago: University of Chicago Press, 1992.

Patterson, Thomas E. "The News as a Reflection of Public Opinion." In *The Sage Book of Public Opinion Research*, edited by Wolfgang Donsbach and Michael W. Traugott, 34–40. Thousand Oaks, CA: Sage, 2008.

Piiparinen, Touko. "Reconsidering the Silence over the Ultimate Crime: A Functional Shift in Crisis Management from the Rwandan Genocide to Darfur." *Journal of Genocide Research* 9, no. 1 (March 2007): 71–91.

Pomakoy, Keith. *Helping Humanity: American Policy and Genocide Rescue*. Lanham, MD: Lexington Books, 2011.

Power, Samantha. "Bystanders to Genocide." *Atlantic Monthly*, September 2001, 1–24.

———. "Dying in Darfur: Can the Ethnic Cleansing in Sudan Be Stopped?" *New Yorker*, 23 August 2004.

———. "It's Not Enough to Call It Genocide." *Time*, 4 September 2004.

———. "Never Again: The World's Most Unfulfilled Promise." *Frontline Online*, 1998. www.pbs.org/wgbh/pages/frontline/shows/karadzic/genocide/neveragain.html.

———. *"A Problem from Hell": America and the Age of Genocide*. London: Flamingo, 2003.

———. "Raising the Cost of Genocide." *Dissent* 49, no. 2 (Spring 2002): 85–95.

Powlick, Philip J. "The Sources of Public Opinion for American Foreign Policy Officials." *International Study Quarterly* 39, no. 4 (1995): 427–452.

Prendergast, John. "Civilian Protection, Accountability and Root Causes in Darfur" (interview). Voices on Genocide Prevention, 23 March 2006.

———. "So How Come We Haven't Stopped It?" *Washington Post*, 19 November 2006.

Program on International Policy Attitudes. "The Darfur Crisis: African and American Public Opinion." June 2005.

Prunier, Gerard. *Darfur: The Ambiguous Genocide*. Ithaca, NY: Cornell University Press, 2005.

Reus-Smit, Christian. "The Politics of International Law." In *The Politics of International Law*, edited by Christian Reus-Smit, 14–44. Cambridge: Cambridge University Press, 2004.

Ricchiardi, Sherry. "Déjà Vu." *American Journalism Review*, February/March 2005. www.ajr.org/article.asp?id=3813.

Rice, Susan E., Anthony Lake, and Donald M. Payne. "We Saved Europeans. Why Not Africans?" *Washington Post*, 2 October 2006.

Rice, Susan E., and Gayle E. Smith. "The Darfur Catastrophe." *Washington Post*, 30 May 2004.

Rieff, David. "Moral Blindness: The Case Against Troops for Darfur." *New Republic* 234, no. 21/22 (2006): 13–16.

Robinson, Piers. *The CNN Effect: The Myth of News, Foreign Policy and Intervention.* London: Routledge, 2002.

———. "The CNN Effect Revisited." *Critical Studies in Media Communication* 22, no. 4 (2005): 344–349.

Ronayne, Peter. *Never Again? The United States and the Prevention and Punishment of Genocide since the Holocaust.* Lanham, MD: Rowman & Littlefield, 2001.

Rosenau, James N. *Public Opinion and Foreign Policy.* New York: Random House, 1961.

Rosenthal, Joel H. "The United States: The Moral Nation?" (Lecture 6). Carnegie Council for Ethics in International Affairs, 2001. www.cceia.org/education/002 /course_on_ethics_and_international_affairs/723.html.

———. "What Constitutes an Ethical Approach to International Affairs?" (Lecture 1). Carnegie Council for Ethics in International Affairs, 2001. www.cceia.org/education /002/course_on_ethics_and_international_affairs/718.html.

Rummel, Rudolph J. *Death by Government.* New Brunswick, NJ: Transaction, 1994.

———. *Statistics of Democide: Genocide and Mass Murder since 1990.* Münster: Lit Verlag, 1998.

Schabas, William A. "Genocide, Crimes against Humanity, and Darfur: The Commission of Inquiry's Findings on Genocide." *Cardozo Law Review* 27, no. 2 (2006): 1703–1721.

———. "Genocide and the International Court of Justice: Finally, a Duty to Prevent the Crime of Crimes." *Genocide Studies and Prevention: An International Journal* 2, no. 2 (2007): 99–122.

———. "What is Genocide? What are the Gaps in the Convention? How to Prevent Genocide?" *Politorbis* 47, no. 2 (2009): 33–46.

Scharf, Michael P. "International Law in Crisis: A Qualitative Empirical Contribution to the Compliance Debate." *Cardozo Law Review* 31 (2009–2010): 45–97.

Scharf, Michael P., and Colin T. McLaughlin. "On Terrorism and Whistleblowing." *Case Western Reserve Journal of International Law* 38, nos. 3–4 (2006–2007): 567–580.

Scharf, Michael P., and Paul R. Williams. *Shaping Foreign Policy in Times of Crisis: The Role of International Law and the State Department Legal Adviser.* Cambridge: Cambridge University Press, 2010.

Scheffer, David. "Atrocity Crimes: Framing the Responsibility to Protect." *Case Western Reserve Journal of International Law* 40, nos. 1–2 (2008): 111–136.

———. "Foreign Press Center Briefing." Federal News Service, 5 April 1999.

———. "Genocide and Atrocity Crimes." *Genocide Studies and Prevention* 1, no. 3 (2006): 229–250.

Schwarz, Norbert, and Gerd Bohner. "The Construction of Attitudes." In *Blackwell Handbook of Social Psychology: Intraindividual Processes*, edited by Abraham Tesser and Norbert Schwarz, 436–457. Oxford: Blackwell, 2001.

Semelin, Jacques. "An International but Especially an American Event." *Genocide Studies and Prevention* 4, no. 2 (2009): 161–166.

Seybolt, Taylor B. "The Darfur Atrocities Documentation Project: A Precedent for the Future? A Perspective from Washington D.C." In *Genocide in Darfur: Investigating the Atrocities in the Sudan*, edited by Samuel Totten and Eric Markusen, 163–170. New York: Routledge, 2006.

———. *Humanitarian Military Intervention: The Conditions for Success and Failure.* Oxford: Oxford University Press, 2007.

Shattuck, John. "Human Rights and Humanitarian Crises: Policy-Making and the Media." In *From Massacres to Genocide: The Media, Public Policy, and Humanitarian Crises*, edited by Robert I. Rotberg and Thomas G. Weiss, 169–178. Washington, DC: Brookings Institution, 1996.

Slovic, Paul. "'If I Look at the Mass I Will Never Act': Psychic Numbing and Genocide." *Judgment and Decision Making* 2, no. 2 (2007): 79–95.

Slovic, Paul, and Daniel Västfjäll. "The More Who Die, the Less We Care: Psychic Numbing and Genocide." In *Behavioural Public Policy*, edited by Adam Oliver, 100–101. Cambridge: Cambridge University Press, 2013.

Smith, Karen E. *Genocide and the Europeans.* Cambridge: Cambridge University Press, 2010.

Smith, Michael J., S. Neil MacFarlane, and Thomas Weiss. "Political Interest and Humanitarian Action." *Security Studies* 10, no. 1 (2000): 112–142.

Snow, Donald M. *United States Foreign Policy: Politics beyond the Water's Edge.* 3rd ed. Boston: Thomson Wadsworth, 2005.

Soroka, Stuart N. "Media, Public Opinion, and Foreign Policy." *Press/Politics* 8, no. 1 (2003): 27–48.

Stanton, Gregory H. "Genocide Emergency: Darfur, Sudan." Genocide Watch, 2004. www.genocidewatch.org/genocide/12waystodenygenocide.html.

———. "Genocide, Politicides and Other Mass Murder since 1945." Genocide Watch. www.genocidewatch.org/aboutgenocide/genocidespoliticides.html.

Stedjan, Scott, and Colin Thomas-Jensen. "The United States." In *The International Politics of Mass Atrocities: The Case of Darfur*, edited by David R. Black and Paul D. Williams, 157–176. London: Routledge, 2010.

Steele, Jonathan. "Darfur Wasn't Genocide and Sudan Is Not a Terrorist State." *Guardian*, 7 October 2005.

Sternberg, Dolf. "Legitimacy." In *International Encyclopaedia of the Social Sciences*, edited by D. Stills, 245. New York: Macmillan, 1968.

Straus, Scott. "'Atrocity Statistics' and Other Lessons from Darfur." In *Genocide in Darfur: Investigating the Atrocities in the Sudan*, edited by Samuel Totten and Eric Markusen, 189–198. New York: Routledge, 2006.

———. "Rwanda and Darfur: A Comparative Analysis." *Genocide Studies and Prevention* 1, no. 1 (2006): 41–56.

Strobel, Warren P. *Late-Breaking Foreign Policy: The News Media's Influence on Peace Operations.* Washington, DC: US Institute of Peace Press, 1997.

Teson, Ferdinand. *Humanitarian Intervention: An Inquiry into Law and Morality.* Dobbs Ferry, NY: Transnational, 1988.

Thakur, Ramesh. *The United Nations, Peace and Security: From Collective Security to the Responsibility to Protect.* Cambridge: Cambridge University Press, 2006.

———. "Western Medicine Is No Cure for Darfur's Ills." *Financial Review*, 31 August 2004.

Theriault, Henry C. "The Albright-Cohen Report: From Realpolitik Fantasy to Realist Ethics." *Genocide Studies and Prevention* 4, no. 2 (2009): 201–210.

Totten, Samuel. "The U.S. Investigation into the Darfur Crisis and Its Determination of Genocide: A Critical Analysis." In *Genocide in Darfur: Investigating the Atrocities in the Sudan*, edited by Samuel Totten and Eric Markusen, 199–222. New York: Routledge, 2006.

Totten, Samuel, and Eric Markusen, eds. *Genocide in Darfur: Investigating the Atrocities in the Sudan.* New York: Routledge, 2006.

———. "Research Note: The U.S. Government Darfur Genocide Investigation." *Journal of Genocide Research* 7, no. 2 (2005): 279–290.

Trout, Thomas B. "Legitimating Containment and Détente: A Comparative Analysis." Paper presented at the annual meeting of the Mid-West Political Science Association, Chicago, April 1979.

————. "Rhetoric Revisited: Political Legitimation and the Cold War." *International Studies Quarterly* 19, no. 3 (1975): 251–284.

Tubiana, Jérôme. "The Man Who Terrorized Darfur Is Leading Sudan's Supposed Transition." *Foreign Policy*, 14 May 2019. www.foreignpolicy.com/2019/05/14 /man-who-terrorized-darfur-is-leading-sudans-supposed-transition-hemeti-rsf -janjaweed-bashir-khartoum/.

Valentino, Benjamin A. "Still Standing By: Why America and the International Community Fail to Prevent Genocide and Mass Killing" (review essay). *Perspectives on Politics* 1 (2003): 565–578.

Vanayan, Cara. "Humanitarian Intervention and the Failure to Protect: Sham Compliance and the Limitations of the Norm Life Cycle Model." Master's thesis, University of Ottawa, 2008.

Van Dijk, Teun A. "Discourse and Manipulation." *Discourse & Society* 17, no. 3 (2006): 356–383.

Vehnämäki, Mika. "Darfur Scorched: Looming Genocide in Western Sudan." *Journal of Genocide Research* 8, no. 1 (March 2006): 51–82.

Vernon, Richard. "Humanitarian Intervention and the Internal Legitimacy Problem." *Journal of Global Ethics* 4, no. 1 (2008): 37–49.

Vollhardt, Johanna R. "The Role of Social Psychology in Preventing Group-Selective Mass Atrocities." In *Reconstructing Atrocity Prevention*, edited by Sheri P. Rosenberg, Tibi Galis, and Alex Zucker. Cambridge: Cambridge University Press, 2015, 95–124.

Wall, Melissa. "An Analysis of News Magazine Coverage of the Rwanda Crisis in the United States." In *The Media and the Rwandan Genocide*, edited by Allan Thompson, 261–277. London: Pluto Press, 2007.

Weiss, Thomas G. "Halting Genocide: Rhetoric versus Reality." *Genocide Studies and Prevention* 2, no. 1 (2007): 7–30.

Weiss, Thomas G., David P. Forsythe, Roger A. Coates, and Kelly K. Pease. *The United Nations and Changing World Politics*. 6th ed. Boulder, CO: Westview, 2010.

Wertheim, Stephen. "A Solution from Hell: The United States and the Rise of Humanitarian Interventionism, 1991–2003." *Journal of Genocide Research* 12, nos. 3–4 (2010): 154–167.

Western, Jon. "Sources of Humanitarian Intervention: Beliefs, Information, and Advocacy in U.S. Decisions on Somalia and Bosnia." In *The Domestic Sources of American Foreign Policy: Insights and Evidence*, 5th ed., edited by Eugene R. Wittkopf and James M. McCormick, 355–372. Lanham, MD: Rowman & Littlefield, 2008.

Wheeler, Gray C., and David W. Moore. "Clinton's Foreign Policy Ratings Plunge." *Gallup Poll Monthly*, October 1993, pp. 25–28.

Wheeler, Nicholas J. *Saving Strangers: Humanitarian Intervention in International Society*. Oxford: Oxford University Press, 2000.

Whelan, Daniel J. "Beyond the Black Heart: The United States and Human Rights." *Human Rights & Human Welfare* 3, no. 1 (2003): 25–56.

Whitcomb, Roger S. *The American Approach to Foreign Affairs: An Uncertain Tradition*. Westport, CT: Praeger, 1998.

Williams, Daniel. "A Third State Dept. Official Resigns over Balkan Policy." *Washington Post*, 24 August 1993.

Williams, Paul D., and Alex J. Bellamy. "The Responsibility to Protect and the Crisis in Darfur." *Security Dialogue* 36, no. 1 (March 2005): 27–47.

Williamson, Richard S. "National Voices—Stop the Genocide in Sudan." *Chicago Sun-Times*, 11 April 2004.

Wittkopf, Eugene. *Faces of Internationalism: Public Opinion and American Foreign Policy*. Durham, NC: Duke University Press, 1990.

Wittkopf, Eugene R., and Christopher M. Jones, with Charles W. Kegley Jr. *American Foreign Policy: Patterns and Processes*. 7th ed. Belmont, CA: Thomson, 2008.

Wolf, Frank. "Stop the Killing in Darfur." Remarks of Frank R. Wolf in the U.S. House of Representatives, 108th Cong., 2nd Sess. *Congressional Record* 150 (2 April 2004): E-518.

Woocher, Lawrence. "A Reflection from the United States: Advancing Genocide Prevention through a High-Level Task Force." *Politorbis* 47, no. 2 (2009): 135–148.

Wozniak, Antal. "Genocide in the News: Media Attention and Media Framing of the Darfur Conflict." Paper presented at the annual meeting of the International Communication Association, San Francisco, 2007.

Zagefka, Hanna, and Trevor James. "Psychology of Charitable Donations to Disaster Victims and Beyond." *Social Issues and Policy Review* 9, no. 1 (2015): 155–192.

Index

Page numbers in *italics* indicate figures.

accountability for inaction, 9, 25, 34, 130
action: constraints to US action on
  Darfur, 98–103; distinctiveness of
  genocide and, 127; fear of over-
  commitment to, 101–103; gap
  between ideals, institutional practices,
  and, 129; gap between rhetoric and,
  96–97, 123, 130–131; genocide-
  specific constraints on, 9; ineffective
  or insufficient, 180n14; options for,
  128–129; political will for, 117–118,
  131; unable versus unwilling to
  commit sufficient resources to,
  117–118, 128. *See also* factors in
  responses; humanitarian intervention;
  intervention policy; moral imperative
  to act; use of force
Afghanistan, impact of, 32, 107
African Union (AU): Observer Mission,
  92–93, 95, 100, 118, 120; support for
  Khartoum, 95, 100, 104
Alston, Philip, 101–102
American foreign policy: bureaucracy
  of, 18, 21–24, 28, 99; resentment
  toward, 17, 131. *See also* foreign
  policymaking
American Presidency Project, archives
  of, 38
"American values": as determinants of
  policy, 1, 16–18, 27, 51, 53; rebuke of,
  131. *See also* exceptionalism, American;
  moral imperative to act

Amnesty International, 77, 119
"Anfal" campaign, 7, 104
Annan, Kofi, 76, 80–81, 83, 127
apathy, 130
Arab League, 95, 100, 104
Armenian genocide, in discourse of
  presidents, 41
"atrocity crimes," 5, 128
atrocity prevention, 127, 129, 131–132,
  133, 134
Atrocity Prevention Board (APB), 133
attitudes of US public: effects of burden
  sharing on, 115; indicators of, 36, 58,
  67, 75, 107, 118, 122, 126; policy-
  maker perceptions of, in opinion-
  policy nexus, 32–35; public opinion
  as reflection of, 59–60
Ayoob, Mohammed, 15

Bashir, Omar al-, 133–134
Bellamy, Alex, 89, 94
Blaney, Harry, 108
Bogert, Carroll, 108
Bolton, John, 26
Bosco, David, 102
Bosnia: G. H. W. Bush and, 42–43;
  Clinton and, 43–44, 55–56, 103;
  debate over use of genocide term for,
  12; NATO and, 47, 69–71; polls
  conducted on, 60–61; public behavior
  and, 72; Rwanda compared to, 71–73;
  Sarajevo massacre in, 69; Scowcroft

207

About the Author

EYAL MAYROZ is a lecturer in the Department of Peace and Conflict Studies, University of Sydney, Australia. His research covers relationships between politics, ethics, and the law in the prevention of genocide, with a focus on influences of U.S. public opinion and the media on American foreign policy. He is a member of the Genocide Prevention Advisory Network, an international network of experts on the causes, consequences, and prevention of genocide and other mass atrocities. His most recent publications include "Genocide: To Prevent and Punish Radical Evil," in *International Criminal Law in Context*, ed. P. Kastner (2018); "Between Empathy and Fear: Recalibrating Incentives for Atrocity Prevention," in *Last Lectures on the Prevention and Intervention of Genocide*, ed. S. Totten (2018); and "The Distinctiveness of Genocide and Implications for Prevention: Destroying Groups versus Mass Killing of People," in *Teaching about Genocide*, ed. S. Totten (2018).